Low Pay,
High Profile

The Global Push for Fair Labor

Andrew Ross

THE NEW PRESS

NEW YORK
LONDON

Published in the United States by The New Press, New York, 2004
Distributed by W. W. Norton & Company, Inc., New York

LIBRARY OF CONGRESS CATALOGING-IN-PUBLICATION DATA
Ross, Andrew, 1956–
    Low pay, high profile: the global push for fair labor / Andrew Ross
       p. cm.
    Includes biographical references and index.
    ISBN 1-56584-893-4 (pbk.)—ISBN 1-56584-919-1 (hc.)
    1. Wages—Effect of international trade on. 2. Foreign trade and employment. 3.
    Sweatshops. 4. Labor movement. 5. Anti-globalization movement. 6. Wages—Effect of
    international trade on—United States. 7. Foreign trade and employment—United States. I.
    Title

    HD4909.R66 2004
    331.2'15—dc22   2003061554

The New Press was established in 1990 as a not-for-profit alternative to the large, commercial publishing houses currently dominating the book publishing industry. The New
Press operates in the public interest rather than for private gain, and is committed to
publishing, in innovative ways, works of educational, cultural, and community value
that are often deemed insufficiently profitable.

The New Press
38 Greene Street, 4th floor
New York, NY 10013
www.thenewpress.com

In the United Kingdom:
6 Salem Road
London W2 4BU

BOOK DESIGN BY LOVEDOG STUDIO

Printed in Canada

10 9 8 7 6 5 4 3 2 1

Contents

Low Pay, **High Profile**

The Global Push for Fair Labor

Confrontation in Berlin

(PHOTO BY JOSEPHINE MECKSEPER)

Introduction

JUST OFF THE SANTA MONICA FREEWAY, in downtown Los Angeles, is a garment factory that has attracted more than its share of attention in recent years. A banner, running the entire length of an old Southern Pacific rail depot, screams 165,000 square feet of T-shirt madness. Inside, all under the same roof, are the production, design, sales, and marketing departments of the American Apparel company. Every employee of the firm works on-site (no contract labor is used), and they all share the same elevator. More unusually, the lowliest of its thousand-plus employees earn about ten dollars an hour—higher than the city's living wage ($9.52), which is itself a slice above California's minimum wage ($6.75). To cap it all, the firm is a commercial success, grossing over $30 million in 2002 (with a profit of over $1 million) from its sale of T-shirts and underwear.

According to a consensus long held among business economists, industry spokespersons, and trade politicians, such a company should not exist, let alone enjoy a competitive position in today's clothing industry. The given wisdom is that garment manufacturing in the U.S. can only succeed in particular circumstances—either in high-fashion niche markets that require skilled craftsmanship close to home, or in the cutthroat sweatshop sector where wages rarely rise anywhere close to the level of the minimum wage. In theory, nothing else is supposed to be competitive with the low price of outsourcing overseas. Yet the product lines at American Apparel do not fall into either category. Their combed cotton T-shirts sell for three or four dollars—almost twice as much as the trade standard—and so they are a kind of fashion product, especially the baby-doll T's that established the firm's reputation through its Classic Girl line. Tightly woven with a thirty single-needle yarn instead of the more common eighteen, they are a cut above, but they are still commodity-branded items, and so they compete on price as well as quality.

As for the cost of labor, consider that Los Angeles has acquired a reputation as "the sweatshop capital of the world" with over 140,000 immigrant garment workers, almost all of them nonunionized, and most of them employed in substandard conditions, toiling from twelve to fifteen hours a day, at wages that annually average $7,200.[1] By contrast, a job at American Apparel, where management is employee-friendly, if shamelessly paternalistic, is a big step up. In some of the modular units, production workers can earn up to $18 an hour. The workplace is a clean and airy environment, and the workforce includes employees blacklisted elsewhere for their labor activism. American

American Apparel factory, downtown Los Angeles (Photo courtesy of American Apparel)

Apparel is decidedly not a sweatshop, in a city where only a third of the garment workplaces are in observance of federal and state laws.

More to the point, the company has eagerly advertised its products as sweat-free. During my visit to the factory in the winter of 2003, its founder, Dov Charnay, who is a turbocharged MTV version of the traditional Jewish garmento, described his firm as "a hyper capitalist-socialist business fusion," whose "goal is to make profits through innovation not exploitation." Somewhere along the way, he declared, with the kind of bravura last seen at the height of the dotcom boom, this "will become a business model that will make sweat-free production universally applicable." But Charnay himself is too much of a maverick to play by any universal rule book. "We are mind-fucks," he added, somewhat more obliquely, "for the unions and for the global sweatshop." Indeed, since the factory is not yet a union shop, it has attracted no end of suspicion from the L.A. labor movement, for whom American Apparel talks the talk but does not walk the walk. Has Charnay hijacked the rhetoric of the anti-sweatshop movement for his own ends? And if so, why does it matter, as long as his employees are satisfied, and as long as the firm publicly shows that there is an alternative to exploitation in the industry? After all, his own tireless efforts at self-promotion—he and his company have been profiled in *The New Yorker*, *Time*, *Los Angeles Times*, *Financial Times*, and on NBC and PBS—have generated priceless publicity for the cause.

In the early 1990s, in the fledgling days of the anti-sweatshop movement, it was virtually unthinkable that any company would use sweat-free advertising as positive publicity. At that time, a "Made in the USA" label still carried moral weight among some consumers, either for patriotic reasons or because it implied support for union-made products, though, in truth, the label could have been stitched on in any of the world's export-processing zones. As far as socially conscious publicity went, environmental advertising was generally perceived by marketers to be the only strategy that carried rewards for firms. There was no context whatsoever for a company to push its products as sweat-free. The message would have had little impact on public consciousness, and there was a strong disinclination within the industry as a whole to draw attention to labor matters. Today, as a result of the achievements of the anti-sweatshop movement, the situation has altered. The image of workers toiling in dismal safety conditions for below-poverty wages, subject to forced labor or debt bondage, holds a conspicuous place in the public imagination; sweatshops are a byword for the corporate greed that goes by the name of economic globalization; and the burden of proof, in matters of fair labor standards, increasingly lies with the manufacturer or retailer. The top multinational brands have gone to great lengths to respond to damning exposés of their subcontracting facilities. In a desperate effort to defend their tarnished names, the public relations, or corporate responsibility, department of every prominent name in clothing (in common with other global firms targeted by activists, such as Monsanto, Philip Morris, Pfizer, Disney, GE, Shell, Chevron, Wal-Mart, Taco Bell, Microsoft, ExxonMobil, Starbucks, and McDonald's) devotes more and more resources to profiling, if not overtly advertising, its brand as ethically sound.

As the corporate spin machine moves into high gear, it has been challenged everywhere, even in the courts. The extensive efforts on the part of Nike (the world's best-known sweatshop offender) to disavow its responsibility for substandard employee conditions ran into a major obstacle when, in May 2002, the California Supreme Court upheld the right of activist Marc Kasky to sue Nike for false advertising, asserting that the company misled the public when it denied, in ads, that its subcontractors mistreated workers in Southeast Asian factories. Nike's lawyers argued that the company's numerous statements about the treatment of its workers were contributions to the debate about economic globalization. The court ruled that these statements were "commercial speech," aimed primarily at selling merchandise, and were not entitled to First Amendment protection. At issue in *Nike v. Kasky* was how much constitutional protection should be afforded to company managers who respond to allegations about employee abuse and environmental spoliation with false claims. The legal issue was quickly labeled as "Nike's right to lie." When the Supreme Court took up the controversial case in April 2003, they were debating whether to redefine the free-speech rights afforded to corporations under the doctrine that corporate personhood is a legal category that warrants constitutional protection.

In effect, Kasky's suit had elevated a dispute over labor conditions in far-flung places into a test case that had an impact on every corporation in the land. It was another highly public illustration of the degree to which multinational corporations have been forced onto the defensive as a result of their subcontracting practices.[2]

By contrast, the conduct of a company like American Apparel illustrates the other, arguably more benign, side of the sweatshop movement's high profile. Charnay's company seized on the movement's public impact as a positive business opportunity. Nor was it alone. Sensing that there might, or even that there should, be an identifiable sweat-free market in the apparel industry, two other companies started up around the same time.

Less than two miles from American Apparel's factory is the production facility and offices of TeamX, a company structured as a cooperatively owned enterprise (jointly owned by management and employees, with no outside shareholders) after the model of the Mondragon worker cooperatives in Spain. TeamX, which produces the SweatX brand casual clothing, was launched in 2001 with venture capital from Hot Fudge, the social venture fund initiated by Ben Cohen, co-founder of Ben and Jerry's Ice Cream. Production workers, organized by the garment union UNITE, earn twice the U.S. minimum wage, and receive health benefits, pensions, sick days, and paid holidays. With only fifty worker-owners, the firm did a million dollars' worth of business in its first year, while collecting the apparel industry's Bobbin Award, and looks set to grow beyond the small plant in L.A. Headed up by Chris Mackin, with a Ph.D. from the Harvard School of Education, and with sixteen years of experience in management consulting in the field of employee ownership, TeamX is a textbook study in politically correct company formation. By contrast, Charnay's American Apparel is a freewheeling wager that socially conscious merchandising can add market value to a corporate product. With its union advantage, TeamX already produces for trade unions and nonprofits, and is beginning to collect socially conscious orders from universities and other institutional buyers. If it intends to grow, and meet larger orders, it will

Sweat-free label, TeamX
(Photo Courtesy of No Sweat Apparel)

have to outsource soon to other union shops, not only in North America but also in Central America, where it will put to the test the AFL-CIO's rhetoric about "cross-border solidarity."

In Cambridge, Massachusetts, a third company named Bienestar International began selling a No Sweat line of clothing in 2002, outsourcing from a string of factories worldwide, each with an independent trade union and a reputation for fair labor standards. Indeed, some of these sources, like the shops in Chittagong, Bangladesh, or the Mexmode factory in Atlixco, Mexico, have been the site of famous union victories. Unlike American Apparel, which trades on its being 100 percent U.S.-made, the activist founders of No Sweat (including Jeff Ballinger, who pioneered the exposés of Nike's Indonesian factories) acknowledge that workers in developing countries also need garment jobs, and that fair labor has to be encouraged *everywhere* for workers *anywhere* to benefit. The major debate within the sweatshop movement, they point out, is not about free trade vs. protectionism, but rather free trade vs. fair trade. All sources are openly advertised on their Web site, allowing them to self-advertise as "the world's first open source apparel manufacturer." Like TeamX, Bienestar is in business more to promote the cause than to amass profits, though both firms are mindful of the need to show that a sweat-free business model is feasible, and so they are set up to ensure access to capital from socially responsible mutual funds and union pension funds. However, for a company built on maxed-out credit cards and reliant on word-of-mouth publicity (www.nosweatapparel.com) to retail online, the going has been tough, especially since potential U.S. union customers have been nervous about their overseas sourcing. Nonetheless, their direct Web-retailing model produced sales in forty-nine states and twenty-two countries in its first year of operation.

In response to these other ventures, Charnay has pondered dropping the sweat-free claim from American Apparel's advertising. "We don't want folks to buy us out of charity," he explains. "It's like the chocolates from Israel which we Jews used to buy to support the kibbutzim," he adds. "We are Swiss chocolate, the best, and we don't want any 'sucker buys.' " Notwithstanding that commercial banks are unwilling to take risks with "uncompetitive" domestic manufacturing, he argues that it is all the more important for his firm to show that fair labor standards can be met in the U.S., even, and perhaps especially, without appeals to the socially conscientious consumer or investor. From the perspective of TeamX's Mackin, the notion of "dropping the anti-sweatshop brand is hugely premature. Branding is necessary," he insists, "branding is education, and we have only just begun to engage the enemy through education." In addition, as Mackin acknowledges, anti-sweatshop branding comes cheap. It hooks into already existing layers of public consciousness and spreads easily through media exposure, progressive political networks, and other alternative means of building recognition.

If these three companies are competitors to a degree, they are also acting on disparate principles that have been established in the course of the anti-sweatshop movement ("there is much more that unites us than divides us," as Mackin points out). The sweat-free branding excludes them, for the time being, from large retail store orders, because the presence of their products would imply that other products in the store were made in sweatshops. Consequently, they have barely made a dent on the overall clothing market. In many respects, as No Sweat's Ballinger points out, sweat-free business is starting out from the same point as natural foods; shunned initially by supermarket chains, until the combined economic heft of alternative health food stores, conjoined with growing consumer demand, forced organic produce into the mainstream markets. Just as important, however, the domestic sustainability of sweat-free firms is a counterbalance to the tendency of sweatshop activists to focus exclusively on brand-busting the big corporations for their substandard overseas operations. Critics of the movement allege that if

Twenty-first century Rosie the Riveter, No Sweat Apparel promotional
(PHOTO COURTESY OF NO SWEAT APPAREL)

activists cannot ensure that workers are treated well at home, they have no business making demands on reforming employment practices in developing countries. The domestic existence of model shops lends moral weight to the movement's efforts to establish standards aimed at eradicating the global sweatshop.[3]

In reality, it is impossible to separate the home front from what happens in offshore locations. The impact of economic globalization has meant that the lot of workers in L.A. is intimately connected to the fortunes of workers in China, Vietnam, El Salvador, and Turkey. It is no longer only high-paying union jobs in manufacturing that are affected by the offshore migration of factories. White-collar workers are now in the same boat, as skilled service sector jobs are increasingly transferred overseas. The low-wage sweatshop sectors in U.S. cities that try to compete with the price of offshore labor also now feel the impact of fluctuations in the wage floor on the other side of the world. Nor have investors been slow to play export zones off against each other. Since the Fox administration assumed the Mexican presidency in 2000, exports from the once-cheap *maquila* sector to the U.S. have decreased by 9.1 percent, with by far the greatest transfer of trade to China, now supplanting Mexico as the biggest exporter overall to the U.S. Despite its location on the border, the *maquila* can no longer command a competitive advantage in the U.S., the world's largest unified consumer market. Factory owners that want to stay in Mexico have begun the march south to Chiapas and other impoverished regions in southern Mexico, where the continent's newest export zones are being set up to exploit the misery of the indigenous poor. If the proposed Free Trade Area of the Americas comes into being, huge swathes of the hemisphere will be opened up to foreign investors seeking terms typically associated with the global sweatshop.

With the rapid expansion of the China trade (now claiming over half of the foreign direct investment in the world), Washington's most conspicuous geopolitical rival also now happens to be its biggest trading partner. The result is downright boggling to American politicians. One vivid example was the "Boxgate" speech on the U.S. economy that George W. Bush gave at a St. Louis shipping plant in January 2003. His backdrop was a banner—emblazoned with the logo "Strengthening America's Economy"—that had been designed to look like a stack of boxes stamped with the label "Made in the U.S.A." Next to the banner and stacked around the podium were real boxes stamped with "Made in China" labels that had been taped over by Bush handlers to preserve the PR illusion. A picture of the taped-over boxes was distributed by the Associated Press on wire services and was printed everywhere, to the discomfiture of the White House. The deception was widely interpreted as an allegory of the administration's penchant for duplicity. Not only was it an inadvertent reminder of economic policies that have papered over the largest trade deficit in history ($100 billion to China alone), but, to compound the insult, Dubya was using the occasion to make his phony pitch that more tax cuts for the rich would stimulate job creation.

Why should a slipup like this be a potential source of embarrassment to a U.S. president? Is the nation's dwindling manufacturing base really a matter for shame? For most politicians, job loss is a touchy subject, and it is easy to resort to the neoliberal platitude that free trade, like Bush's tax cuts, expands job creation in the export sector of the economy. In fact, the impact of free trade causes many more jobs to be lost in domestic industries that face import competition than are created in the export sector. In addition, these jobs tend to pay more than the ones in export, and much more than the poorer quality jobs in services that are created as a consequence of the trade deficit. After all, only a fraction of dislocated workers find new jobs that pay as well as the old ones. Just as in the developing world, the wages of unskilled U.S. workers tend to drop rapidly as a result of the introduction of export trade. In the face of the sobering statistics on trade-related layoffs, a speech about protecting American jobs might have been more appropriate for Bush's visit to St. Louis.

But American presidents got out of the protectionist business over a decade earlier when the Washington Consensus was adopted as official White House trade policy (though it is routinely violated to subsidize agriculture and steel, promote dumping, and guarantee drug patents). The result— the kind of free trade that openly sanctions offshore export zones in Big Emerging Markets—was promoted as a vehicle for fostering political freedoms and economic hope among the world's poor. Yet the conditions under which free trade is widely conducted are a savage indictment of policies, openly drafted and endorsed by the International Monetary Fund, the World Bank, and the World Trade Organization, that are designed to enrich the global elite of investors and corporate managers. In most cases, governments that solicit foreign direct investment must guarantee that wages will be kept down by ensuring that workers' rights are suppressed, that environmental and industrial safety regulations will be implemented only as a last resort, and that generous tax breaks and other concessions will quicken the flow of profit. Princely returns on investment are promised, and the rights to free speech, freedom of association, and collective bargaining go begging. The oversupply of export factories in the world's free-trade zones means that contractors and agents will accept orders with impossibly tight profit margins simply in hopes of establishing a more permanent arrangement with a big retailer. The wage floor slides under pressure from other regions with even lower labor costs, and the environmental impact on host communities can be catastrophic. As for ushering in political freedoms, the countries that have shown the highest export growth rates turn out to be among the most repressive. Free trade, on closer examination, looks much more like forced trade, and its conduct, in most countries, resembles the process that Marx described as primitive accumulation.

Workers, in the North as well as in the South, are unlikely ever to be beneficiaries of the free trader's race to the bottom unless they can organize on behalf of their interests, and do so in a framework of international cooperation. Ultimately, workers themselves make their own history—factory strikes and union campaigns in Nike's Indonesian backyard, for example, consistently raised wages in the course of the 1990s until the Asian financial collapse. But a good deal of the progress that has been made on this front is owed to the efforts of the anti-sweatshop movement. The oxygen of publicity provided by headline-seeking activists has made a high profile out of low pay. The public humiliation served upon the reputation of brand-name corporations has been a key weapon not only in highlighting the inequities of their subcontracting policies, but also in forcing their managers to acknowledge responsibility for what happens further down the contracting chain. The coalition of actors involved has been eclectic and enterprising. Trade unionists, scholars, students, people of faith, environmental and human rights activists, citizen groups, sympathetic politicians, and outraged consumers have all played a vital role. For college students in particular, this kind of turn toward labor has not been seen since the 1930s. Most of all, the sympathetic public response to these actions has proven that, contrary to conventional wisdom, ordinary citizens care in all sorts of ways about the conditions under which the daily objects they use are manufactured. Even Nike has acknowledged that its focus groups revealed that girls as young as twelve were deeply concerned about the labor issue.[4]

Model bra,
No Sweat Apparel promotional
(PHOTO COURTESY OF NO SWEAT APPAREL)

The critical point of view adopted throughout this book arises from my own experience as a scholar and activist within the movement. It is a book about fair labor, but it has been shaped by debates and issues that have consumed the attention and energies of a very particular corner of the labor movement. Sticking hard and fast to the doctrine of "Made in the U.S.A.," the American labor movement as a whole has not put the global sweatshop at the forefront of its concerns, even though corporate-led globalization has affected every industry and every union. The AFL-CIO is more and more willing to recognize the need for cross-border organizing, and for a strong stance on support for international collaboration. Even so, vestiges of its Cold War past (when it was a zealous anti-Communist agent for Washington all around the world) continue to bedevil its policy voice, undercutting any role it might play in supporting worker rights in nominally socialist countries like China. The decentralized solidarity networks and loose coalitions of NGOs and affinity groups that typify the anti-globalization movement (and which often include individual unions) have proven much more agile and effective than any institutional organization in pressing for change.

Because the anti-sweatshop campaigns have been focused on the garment industry, core details in several of the chapters (particularly those on the China trade, Made in Italy, and sports sponsorship and sportswear) are drawn from analysis of the needle trades. But I also look at other industries, most notably electronics assembly and microchip manufacture, which have played a frontline role in international development. The global map of high-tech production increasingly resembles the geographic spread of the garment trade, though its record of physical harm to employees and environmental devastation of host communities has not been subject to anything like the same scrutiny. The time is ripe for applying some of the lessons of sweatshop activism to an industry that wantonly deals in some of the world's most dangerous chemicals and which relies, for its profits, on the unsullied mystique of brand names.

Nor are these lessons irrelevant to the value-adding landscape of mental labor, often touted as a substitute, in the industrialized countries, for the lost empire of manufacturing. The struggle for fair labor is not solely a geographically distant matter, played out only in the poorest corners of the world, or among the lowest-paid domestic workers. It also applies to the degradation of domestic white-collar professions as the casualization of work in the domestic economy continues apace. Accordingly, my last chapter is devoted to the sacrificial labor traditions of artists and educators, once marginal to the productive economy, but now more routine and standard in the information-rich workplaces of the new knowledge industries. Just as the subcontracting system of the nineteenth-century garment industry has become a ubiquitous component of the global assembly line, so too older mentalities of work like the bohemian autonomy of the unattached artist and the disinterested dedication of the self-exploiting academic are now models for the flexible postindustrial employee.

Each of the chapters contains its own advocacy, which need not be rehearsed here. They are driven by partisan inquiry into the cruelty and indignity of modern workplaces, but they are also informed by the evidence that critique and action have brought results. Global elites who gather annually behind heavy security in places like Davos are no longer confident that they have a free hand in drafting the rules of the global economy. The patterns of trade and investment liberalization that they covet are everywhere met with resourceful resisters who use the Internet to circumvent the pro-capitalist media, who organize and educate each other across national borders, and who are piecing together progressive, humane versions of globalization.[5] If the tide is to turn in our direction, the next decade of opposition and proposition will have to be even more inventive than the last. If another world is indeed possible, it will require a spirited two-way traffic between intellectual activism and protest strategies.

For the movement activist, fair trade and fair labor are key slogans, to which are often attached an inventory of policy demands, economic principles, and codes of conduct. But they cannot be pursued as isolated, technical goals. After all, this is what corporate elites do when they "externalize" the cost of the impact of their trade on the environment, public health, and social quality of life of communities. The fight for fair labor must be approached as a pathway to the social and environmental well-being of an entire citizenry. The "social wage" that is its guiding goal must not only compensate workers for the full range of activities and burdens they undertake so that capital can reproduce. It must also be able to sustain a multisided modern life for the population to which they belong; and it must be adequate enough to protect the environments where they live.

In this endeavor, fairness (and fairness may only be a first step) is not an outcome with a settled nature or established coordinates. Nor is the travel plan so easy to interpret, at least not by the norms of approved politics. Apparent paradoxes must be embraced; freedom is fostered through regulation but not power, well-being through common knowledge but not mastery, and democracy through the kind of citizenship in which no one, and least of all the elected few, has the final say. For people who can thrive under these conditions, labor should no longer be an act of mere service; it might, instead, be the feat of creativity it aspires to be.

Jillian Johnson, Duke University, investigated Gap sweatshops in Central America

2,000 Gap factories in 50 countries. Do you know what goes on behind the label?

Deisy Hernandez, El Salvador, fired from a Gap plant for organizing a union

Armed guards intimidate workers at Gap clothing factories around the world

Billy Bragg, musician, fighting to end sweatshop labor worldwide

Typical home of Gap worker in Latin America. No electricity, no running water

Not for my generation!

 **Don't buy Gap this holiday season**
www.behindthelabel.org

Project of **UNITE!** and United Students Against Sweatshops

STOP
GAP
SWEATSHOPS

Anti-Gap campaign
(UNITE)

CHAPTER ONE

The Making of the Second Anti-Sweatshop Movement

THE LEGIONS OF PROTESTERS who have participated in the anti-globalization (or alternative globalization) movement are driven by many different issues: genetically modified foods, structural adjustment programs, undemocratic WTO decision-making, environmental spoliation, and enforced privatization, to name a few. Confronted with this sheer variety, some commentators have decried the absence of a unifying cause or overall political strategy. Others see the nurturing of a truly democratic spirit behind this "movement of movements"—a largely decentralized network of affinity groups and NGOs, each with its own history and priorities—and expect a long-term global constituency to emerge from its unpredictable harvest of energy and action. Indeed, the extraordinary worldwide protests against the war on Iraq, on February 15, 2003, were only possible because of activists' networked ability to share cross-border information and coordinate massive street actions, pioneered in each of the large anti-WTO demonstrations that have followed the Third Ministerial meetings in Seattle in 1999. Despite the common antimilitarist ground, the global protests against the Anglo-American war hosted the same miscellany of voices and causes as their fore-runners, foiling any single-minded efforts on the part of detractors to isolate and dismiss the motives of their participants.

Notwithstanding the assortment of causes, if we had to name one staple, enduring, target of activist attention in all quarters of the movement, it would be the global sweatshop. Indeed, the industrial sweatshop has become a byword for corporate-led globalization, even though its origins predate, by more than a century, the moment when production (as opposed, merely, to capital) became internationalized, and when offshore locations—with low-wage floors, minimal environmental and workplace safety regulation, and tax- and tariff-free incentives—became much cheaper and more serviceable than unionized sectors in the industrialized nations.

Jack Welch, former CEO of General Electric, among the world's largest multinational corporations, once described the optimum manufacturing model for his company: "Ideally, you'd have every plant you own on a barge." The barges, of course, would move periodically to an anchorage offshore whichever country or regional labor market was offering the best investment climate at any one time. Welch's barges are an investor's fantasy and a union organizer's nightmare. Two decades of trade and investment liberalization under the pressure of the West's leading neoliberal economic institutions have brought the barges that much closer to reality. The economic playing field governed by WTO rules is one in which corporations, not people, have global rights; in which the right to free trade takes precedence over every other human, civil, social, and environmental right. Yet the extensive damage wrought by free trade policies—economic stagnation, currency crises, stock market crashes, political collapses, environmental degradation, acute income polarization, and the worldwide shriveling of vital services in health and education—has taken its toll on the public credibility of the neoliberal cheerleaders. There is less and less faith in the Washington Consensus, an accord whereby U.S. financial elites promoted and managed free-trade policies around the world on behalf of the national capital pools of the G-8 industrial powers and the major banks. The anti-globalization movement that broke the surface of public awareness in Seattle and registered its presence at every world economic meeting since then has shaken the confidence of global elites in their ability to go on making decisions through institutions that are non-transparent and undemocratic. The legitimacy of their unilateral power has begun to unravel. September 11 provided an opportune moment to change the rules of a losing game, and switch public attention back to the demonology and nation-bashing that has attended the war on terrorism. The grisly spectacle of militarization came as a relief to many corporate CEOs, reeling from eight years of brand-busting and sweatshop exposés, not to mention the wave of Enronesque scandals that surfaced after the stock bubble burst in 2001.

One of the chief tributaries of anti-globalization action has been the anti-sweatshop movement itself, loosely but effectively coordinated among a network of groups: trade unionists, interfaith organizations, college and high school students, human rights groups, socially responsible investors, and small NGOs. In a relatively short space of time, this movement has raised public recognition of substandard workplace conditions to new heights. The result has surprised battle-weary activists, long resigned to seeing their causes treated with indifference. After all, most citizens of the North, however much they themselves are hurting, are not known for their discomfort at evidence that workers in poor countries are suffering too, and, more often than not, on their behalf. Most consumers don't want to know that the goods they are purchasing may have been made by workers with no rights, slaving through a ninety-hour workweek, in unsafe, unsanitary factories, with abusive supervisors. When they learn about these conditions, however, they generally want something done about them.

Brand-busting
(ANTI-AD BY *ADBUSTERS*)

As a result, activists have been successful not only in generating widespread outrage at the conditions they have exposed at home and abroad, but also in seeing follow-through on the part of a broad spectrum of institutions. Public attention was guaranteed early on in the 1990s by revelations about the likes of basketball prince Michael Jordan, who earned more ($20 million) in 1992 for endorsing

Nike's running shoes than Nike's entire 30,000-strong Indonesian work-force did for making them. Or Disney's CEO, Michael Eisner, who earned over $200 million from salary and stock options in 1993, which, at $97,600 per hour, amounted to 325,000 times the hourly wage of the Haitian workers who made *Pocahantas, Lion King,* and *Hunchback of Notre Dame* T-shirts and pajamas. Highly visible inequities on this scale opened the way for a decade of humiliating exposés, targeted at big-name retailers and manufacturers, whose household brand names have been tarnished by association with atrocity stories about their subcontractors' workplaces.

The follow-through, measured in institutional responses, has been swift, if not quite as far-reaching as some hoped for. The tug of war between corporations, activists, and government agencies has produced several outcomes: corporate codes of conduct, sweat-free city ordinances and schools, global monitoring groups like the Fair Labor Association and the Workers Rights Consortium, corporate-trade union-NGO alliances like the Ethical Trading Initiative, and, in some high-profile cases, the emergence of independent trade unions in export zone factories. Pressure to include fair labor standards in world trade agreements has been stepped up, generating a full-blown debate about the impact of these standards on the development opportunities of poor countries. Will these provisions hamper the ability of developing nations to compete for trade and investment, or are they the only guarantee that fair trade and fair labor standards will make headway throughout the global economy? Are core, or universal, labor standards the most equal way of reforming a chronically unequal system, or should labor standards be appropriate to the norms of local cultures? Are they too high a price that poor countries are asked to pay to appease the ethical conscience of activists in the affluent North, or are they justifiable costs to be borne by the transnational firms that exploit cheap labor pools wherever they can find them?

Whatever the outcome of this debate, which is by no means straightforward, the anti-sweatshop movement has already forged the first paths toward the establishment of ground rules for fair labor in the global economy. One hundred years earlier, the first crusade against sweatshops challenged corporations and trusts who exploited the creation of a national market to escape local and state regulations. National labor and safety standards, worker rights, and environmental protections were introduced as a result. This time around, the map is much larger, the potential to hide abuses in every corner of the globe is much greater, and so the tactics of activists have had to be more flexible, even experimental. This chapter reviews the ground conditions that gave rise to the movement, and analyzes some of its achievements.

The Garmento's Mixed Legacy

It is no coincidence that the most egregious examples of labor abuse are drawn from the garment and needle-trade industries, where the vast majority of workers are women, laboring for "women's wages," and often in conditions of indenture. The apparel industries are a showcase of horrors for the global economy, because they are in the vanguard, as always, of the newest efforts to accumulate capital and undermine labor power. Here, the gruesome face of neoliberal free trade is all too apparent as the corporate hunt for ever cheaper labor drives wages down in entire subcontinental regions where countries compete to attract foreign investment. While the greed of owners and investors is the primary cause of labor abuse, some part of the explanation for these conditions lies in the history and structure of the garment industry, the nature of its products, and the volatility of its markets.

Historically, apparel is where underdeveloped countries start their effort to industrialize. The barrier to entry is very low because apparel requires a minimum of capital investment and machinery, and the operations of sewing and assembly are labor-intensive. Indeed, not much has changed in the way of technology since the invention of the sewing machine. In the period of the European empires, primary commodities were shipped from the colonies, and goods manufactured in industrial centers like Manchester were exported back. Since the 1970s, a new international division of labor has allowed poor countries to enter the export market by competing at the low end of the production chain. Yet their participation in the global market and their capacity to attract capital are governed ultimately by the demands of those who control the retail markets in high-wage countries and who take the lion's share of the profit from the garment trade. Structurally, U.S. retail giants who command the world's largest internal market are in a position to call the shots globally. It is under their price pressure and concerns about their inventory risk that local contractors and suppliers are forced to pursue ever tighter profit margins in the enterprise zones and assembly platforms of the developing world.

Because the textile and apparel industries have seen some of the worst labor excesses, they have also been associated with historic victories for labor, and hold a prominent symbolic spot on the landscape of labor iconography; from the Luddite weavers' resistance to the introduction of power looms, to the mid–nineteenth-century protests of the "factory girls" in New England mills, the early twentieth-century garment workers' strikes against the sweating system, the unions' roles in forging pioneer labor-capital accords, and the recent rise to prominence of workers' struggles against the far-flung production empires of Nike, the Gap, and other leading brand names. In the public mind, the strongest association is with labor's successes in "eradicating" the sweatshop in the first two decades of the twentieth century. Of course, it never disappeared. Severely restricted in its zone of operations, the sweatshop dropped out of view, and lived on in the underground economy. Today, the repugnance attached to the term *sweatshop* commands a moral power, second only to slavery itself, to rouse public opinion into a collective spasm of abhorrence. For some, the public will to eliminate sweatshops from the labor landscape can designate a significant level of moral development on the part of a national community. It symbolizes a state of civilization that other nations cannot yet afford. Even in the U.S., which has routinely refused to ratify most of the labor standards proposed by the International Labor Organization (ILO), and where extensive commercial use is made of prison labor, the recognition of core labor rights and safe and sanitary workplaces is understood as a requisite of membership in the premier circle of civilized nations.

This claim to moral superiority on the part of developed nations is one of the reasons why the much-hyped "return of the sweatshop" to the North has provoked such revulsion in these countries. Few aspects of the corporate rollback of the postwar social contract have been greeted with the public outcry that followed revelations that sweatshops are thriving at the heart of most major North American cities, and that items of clothing on sale at family brand stores like J.C. Penney, Sears, Wal-Mart, and Kmart were made by young immigrant mothers and their teenage daughters toiling in inhuman conditions only a matter of miles away from the point of purchase. These disclosures summon up the misery and filth of turn-of-the-century workplaces—tenements, lofts, attics, stables—plagued by chronic health problems (tuberculosis, the scourge and signature sickness of the sweatshop, has also made a return of late), and home to the ruthless exploitation of greenhorn immigrants. They recall Jacob Riis's harrowing accounts of conditions in New York's Lower East Side tenements in *How the Other Half Lives*, the social photography of Lewis Hine's labor documentaries, Henry Mayhew's profiles of the rag trade in London's East End, or Friedrich Engels's descriptions of the hovels inhabited by Manchester's mill workers.[1]

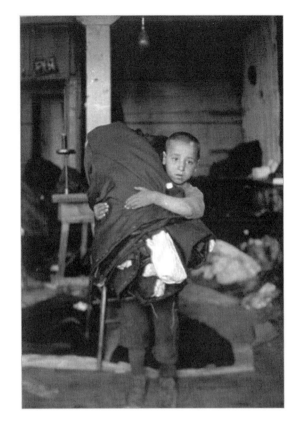

Boy carries work home from a New York City sweatshop, 1912
(PHOTO BY LEWIS HINE, COURTESY OF THE GEORGE EASTMAN HOUSE)

The dingy Victorian archetypes notwithstanding, sweatshops today come in all shapes and sizes. In Central America, they are brand new, brightly lit factories, policed by armed guards patrolling a barbed-wire free trade zone. In Los Angeles, they are in ranch-style suburban compounds and dwellings. A 1994 General Accounting Office (GAO) report estimated that over a third of New York's 6,500 garment shops are sweated, as are 4,500 of L.A.'s 5,000 shops, 400 out of 500 in Miami, and many others in Portland, New Orleans, Chicago, San Antonio, and Philadelphia. In the L.A. basin, $1 an hour is not an uncommon wage in Orange County's Little Saigon, while the New York City wage floor hovers around $2 an hour in Sunset Park's Chinatown. Government deregulation, a weakened labor movement, import competition, the contracting system, and the increased availability of immigrant workers with few other work options have all combined to create and sustain these conditions.

Much of U.S. production is concentrated in fashion-forward women's wear, subject to seasonal volatility and therefore requiring fast turnaround, yet, more and more, basic and sportswear lines are becoming fashion-conscious and time-sensitive. There are now as many as five or six industry seasons instead of two, and so products are kept on retail shelves for less and less time. Lean retailing means smaller and smaller quantities are ordered, and more often by the week instead of by the season.[2] One of the results of the accelerated fashion changes and reduced lead time is that domestic manufacturers are increasingly encouraged to compete, at the low end, with offshore producers. The typical immigrant firm can maintain a competitive advantage through its proximity to market and its production of short runs, though to do so, it usually has to run a shop that falls short of state and federal safety or labor standards. Retailers' need for timely replenishment of stock and cheap delivery from suppliers allows domestic or Mexican/Caribbean producers the slim margin they need to compete with overseas suppliers.

The GAO defines a sweatshop as a workplace "that violates more than one federal or state labor law governing minimum wage and overtime, child labor, industrial homework, occupational safety and health, workers compensation, or industry registration." Holding to this definition, however, means that we are more or less obliged to accept the existence of labor conditions that cover the legal standards, but only barely. Sweatshops are seen to be morally and politically apart from the lawful low-wage sector, which is condoned as a result.[3] The fact is that most low-wage jobs, even those that meet minimum wage requirements and safety criteria, fail to provide an adequate standard of living for their wage earners, let alone their families. In most respects, it is the systematic depression of wages, rather than conscious attempts to evade labor laws, that is the structural problem. Installing proper fire exits may turn a sweatshop into a legal workplace, but it remains a low-wage atrocity. All the more reason to define and perceive the "sweatshop" as a general description of all exploitative labor conditions, rather than as a subpar outfit, as defined by existing laws in whatever country the owner chooses to operate. Edna Bonacich and Richard Appelbaum argue for a broadening of "the definition of sweatshops to include factories that fail to pay a 'living wage,' meaning a wage that enables a family to support itself at a socially defined, decent standard of living. We include in the concept of a living wage the idea that people should be able to afford decent housing, given the local housing market, and that a family should be covered by health insurance."[4] Generally speaking, a living wage is from 50–100 percent above the local minimum wage.

In the nineteenth century, the term *sweating* referred to the system of subcontract, which, in contrast to the integrated and supervised factory system, consisted of the farming out of work by competing manufacturers to competing contractors. The small contractors "sweated" as much labor as they could out of immigrant workers. Sweating was indigenous to garment production because of its division of labor, separating the craft processes of design, marking and cutting, from the labor-intensive sewing and finishing, and organized around a three-tier system of small producers—the inside shop, the contractor, and the home. In this industry on wheels, neither the jobber nor the manufacturer nor the contractor were responsible for one other's conduct; each could blame the others for flagrant abuses of the system. To set up in the fly-by-night world of runaway shops required little more investment than you needed to rent a hole in the wall and a few sewing machines, and to have ready access to the immigrant labor pool.[5] The sweatshop's low-tech mode of production and the cutter's artisanal loft coexisted with semiautomated workplaces that would industrialize, with union guidance, into economies of scale under the pull of the Fordist factory ethic.[6]

Today's U.S. garment industry shows many similarities, with its preindustrial low-wage sector once again flourishing in proximity to postindustrial, high-tech workplaces, often on the same city block. The sewing machine's foot pedal is still in business, no longer competing with steampower but with the central processing unit of the computer, and the system of subcontracting is alive and well, ever driving wages and profit margins down. In 2000, the Bureau of Labor Statistics showed that full-time apparel workers in the *legal* sector earn among the lowest average annual wage among U.S. industries, at $16,675, only slightly better than sales-counter clerks, who made $16,059, nursery workers, at $15,667, and the fast food industry's burger flippers, who earned $13,350 on average. Ethnic entrepreneurship is as crucial as ever. Asian and Latino immigrants, often undocumented, are denied access to the mainstream labor economy through racial labor segmentation, and are thereby forced into ethnic work enclaves where labor laws are routinely neglected.[7] Where patterns of family labor are relevant, the obligations of youth to the immigrant culture of apprenticeship and to patriarchal cohesion add greatly to the degree of exploitation.[8] Women still make up the majority of sweated labor, their sewing skills traditionally undervalued, and their homework sustaining the most underground sector of the industry.

But there are just as many differences. Decades of industrial regulation have left a raft of labor laws on the books, even if they are patchily enforced. The rise and erosion of union power has left an uncertain legacy, especially among new immigrants drawn from countries with the modern equivalent of the Russian Pale's "Czarist repression," but for whom the labor movement is no longer perceived as a viable vehicle for socialism. The apparel industry is now global in scope, with dozens of countries producing for a small number of importing nations. The runaway shops are no longer in Trenton, New Jersey, or Scranton, Pennsylvania, or in antiunion states in the South. They are in the *maquiladoras* of the Caribbean basin, and their equivalent in Indonesia, Vietnam, China, and Thailand, often in live-in labor compounds that make the company towns of yore look like Pleasantville. Forced labor and debt bondage are common arrangements in the international supply chain.

The balance of industrial power within textile and apparel has shifted decisively toward the giant, vertically integrated retailers: Wal-Mart, Sears, Macy's, Federated Department Stores, May Department Stores, Kmart, Dayton Hudson, Allied Department Stores, J.C. Penney, and the Gap. They increasingly produce their own private brand labels in many of the sourcing countries, bypassing the manufacturer, the union shop, and the domestic worker. The big players are no longer industrial patriarchs, accountable to workers' communities through coreligionist ethics or ethnic ties, as in New

York City's once predominantly Jewish garment industry. For the most part, they are anonymous corporate executives, solely accountable to their boards and stockholders. By the 1990s, subcontracting was no longer the trademark of the garment industry only; it had become a standard principle of all post-Fordist production, used in auto parts, building maintenance, data processing, electronic assembly, public sector work, and every other industry restructuring itself away from central economies of scale and mass production. Disdained by early twentieth-century apostles of scientific management as a preindustrial relic, apparel's subcontracting system has come to be seen as a pioneer of the just-in-time flexible production that is geared to increasingly specialized, or niche markets.[9]

Last but not least, the global reach of fashion (turnover not dictated by the durability of garments) is no longer confined to elite women's wear worn in metropolitan centers of the developed countries. Stylistic variation of product is ubiquitous across the entire spectrum of casual wear, and popular fashion is now a mainstay of mall and High Street retailing, both at the high-end and discount end. The international consumer now wants the latest fashion posthaste, necessitating flexibility and turnaround at levels that disrupt all stable norms of industrial competition. Clothing style exerts an often pervasive influence on the consumer patterns and social outlook of men and boys, in addition to women and girls, in ever greater numbers all around the world. Indeed, the globalization of the youth fashion revolution has increasingly defined the terms on which the industry has had to respond through restructuring, adjustment, and rationalization. The worst manifestations of the global sweatshop are all the more tragic when adolescents in poor countries are toiling to meet the style demands of their age peers in the North who are fortunate enough to have disposable income.

Politics of Trade

Globalization's race toward the bottom of the wage floor is often cited as the cause of labor's malaise in apparel, but it also poses a challenge for the survival and rekindling of the labor movement in an industry that has benefited from an unusual degree of domestic protections. That story dates to the very beginning of the Industrial Revolution, when the British government imposed high tariffs on Bengali textiles (for centuries previously, the leader in international trade) in order to protect its own rising industries in Lancashire and the West of Scotland. In time and largely in response to British exports, the U.S. initiated its own protectionist tradition through import substitution and developed an effective system of tariffs and embargoes in the course of the nineteenth century. American manufacturers—in cahoots with European producers with whom it has shared a "gentleman's agreement" to waive all import duties—exercised enough political clout to exempt the textile and apparel trade from many of the key rules of the General Agreement on Trade and Tariffs (GATT). This arrangement clearly violated the GATT's founding principle that all countries must treat goods from all other countries on equal grounds.

From its 1947 inception to the Uruguay Round in 1994, the GATT's rules for reciprocal trade and against discrimination (most-favored-nation treatment), tariff protectionism, and quantitative restrictions on imports were all relaxed for textile and apparel. A series of international accords culminating in the 1973 Multi-Fiber Arrangement (MFA) sought to manage the trade flow from developing countries to Western markets through an elaborate system of bilateral agreements regarding import tariffs, quotas, and trade routes. This protectionist agreement was promoted in order to give developed countries time to adjust to the massive increase in exports from the South. Yet the competitive challenge of Asian producers, combined with the relentless push for trade liberalization on the part of Washington elites, led to the replacement, in 1995, of the MFA with the Agreement on Textiles and Clothing (just as the GATT had been replaced a year earlier by the World Trade Agreement). These agreements put an end to the tangle of trade restrictions and quotas that had protected industries in the North for so long. The result was a clear indication that the balance of power had shifted away from domestic producers and unions to the coalition of U.S. retailers and select multinational producers who stood to profit most from trade liberalization.

Even so, U.S. textile and clothing industry chiefs have lobbied hard—

mostly against the China trade—to force Washington to further stave off the consequences of the phasing out of the MFA, scheduled to take effect on January 1, 2005, when the final 49 percent of trade will be quota-free.[10] At that point, it is estimated that China will take control of 65–75 percent of the U.S. market, and its share of the global garment market will jump to 44 percent. With its vast post-WTO army of unemployed, its labor costs will undercut all other producers in the region, and eradicate many of the trade advantages enjoyed by NAFTA countries. The post-MFA free-trade order is otherwise likely to intensify patterns established over the last thirty years. Vertically integrated transnationals will encounter minimal regulatory obstacles in their exploitation of geography and labor. In each of the world's spheres of influence—Asian, European, and American—the domestic cores will hold on to the value-adding jobs in design and marketing, while steadily outsourcing manufacturing and assembly to the respective discount-labor regions. Thus, firms and suppliers from Hong Kong, South Korea, Singapore, and Taiwan will intensify their assembly operations in the least developed Asian countries—Vietnam, Bangladesh, Sri Lanka, Indonesia, and mainland China. For the Western European industries, the sewing will occur in Northern Africa, and increasingly in Eastern Europe. Indeed, sub-Saharan African countries may well play host to the next major round of expansion into hitherto unexploited labor markets. In addition, their place on the geopolitical map positions them ideally as a counter to the economic might of China—a reminder that the textile and apparel trade has never been divorced from politics.

Conceived as a way of reconstructing European industry after the war, the GATT was designed to replace national protectionism and autarchy by international reciprocity among the industrial powers. Increasingly, it fell under the influence of Cold War geopolitics. For example, the efforts of successive U.S. presidents (exercising, since 1934, their exclusive authority to set tariffs) to contain communism in Asia made direct use of reciprocal trade agreements to prevent the dominoes falling, one after another. The reconstruction of Japan's textile industry was the first step, opening a door to encouraging low-wage export production to the U.S. After the "loss of China" and North Korea, and in the face of Communist insurgencies all over East Asia, U.S. aid flowed to South Korea, Taiwan, Hong Kong, Malaysia, the Philippines, Indonesia, Singapore, and Thailand, each of which developed export-processing zones. In addition to the aid, access to the U.S. market through reduced tariffs was honed as an important tool of regional foreign policy.[11]

Obviously, this policy posed a threat to domestic producers, even those, like the textile industry, which had relocated to right-to-work states in the South to break the back of unions. Even so, concern about the loss of domestic jobs took second place in Congress to concern about Communist takeovers abroad. The perceived need to support economic development in target countries through access to the U.S. market generally prevailed. To mitigate the impact, quotas for East Asian imports were introduced in the 1960s, under the Short-Term and Long-Term Arrangements, and then in the MFA accord itself. Apparel and textiles were also treated as special cases under GATT rules, to manage the trade flow and to allow for domestic adjustment. But, in practice, U.S. customs lacked the manpower, and the will, to police the flow of Asian imports, lured additionally by an overvalued dollar and the vulnerability of standardized mass-produced clothing lines. U.S. producers struggled to meet their first test of structural adjustment through investment in new technologies. Very soon, manufacturers were being advised to "automate, relocate, or evaporate."[12] By the late 1980s, apparel was 40 percent automated, compared to 6 percent in the early 1960s, with textile production running much higher. But because the physical limpness of fabric precluded the spread of automation to labor-intensive sectors, the push for increased productivity through mechanization was supplanted by the promise of cheap labor markets offshore. No apparel-assembling technology could prove more efficient than the labor offered by human hands. Ultimately, this was the key factor in the hemorrhaging of domestic jobs and the skyrocketing U.S. trade deficit in apparel. Between the signing of the MFA in 1973 and 1992, 750,000 jobs in apparel and textiles were lost in the U.S.[13]

Because of its proximity to the largest internal market, the situation in the Caribbean and Central America was even more complex, and no less tangled up in Washington's political anxiety about socialist aspirations in the region.

From 1963, manufacturers could take advantage of a special provision (item 807) in the U.S. Tariff Schedule, which allowed cut garments to be exported for assembly and reimported into the U.S. Duties were paid only on the value added to the garment through low-cost assembly. In conjunction with the creation of *maquiladora* free-trade zones as part of the Border Industrialization Program, offshore production skyrocketed. In 1983, the Reagan Administration expanded the pool of sourcing countries through the creation of the Caribbean Basin Initiative (CBI), extending special trade privileges to twenty-two Caribbean countries (later increased to twenty-seven, and enhanced under Clinton to embrace benefits similar to those afforded Mexico under NAFTA) that offered tariff-free access for many export products. The 807 provision (now classified under the international Harmonized Tariff Schedule as 9802) remained in effect, guaranteeing that fabric could be manufactured and cut in the U.S., but reducing tariffs to encourage low-cost offshore assembly.

Anticommunism drove the CBI as much as it had guided Washington's encouragement of export-led development in Asia. In association with the World Bank and the IMF's house philosophy of structural adjustment, Washington began to shift its Cold War policies in the region away from support for authoritarian regimes to the active imposition of private-sector development. Aggressive neoliberal penetration of state-sector economies, backed up by low-intensity military conflict, was adopted as the most efficient way of combating Caribbean socialism. In the wake of the land and labor reform movements of the seventies, which gave rise to the Sandinista revolution in Nicaragua, Manley's socialist government in Jamaica, the New Jewel Movement in Grenada, and rebel-peasant insurgencies in several other nations, President Reagan announced a "state of danger" in the nation's backyard and began to pour money into the region in order to secure its economic and political dependency upon U.S. needs and interests. The result was orchestrated adjustment, designed to orient each national economy toward Washington and away from regional alliances. Offshore facilities owned by U.S. firms multiplied in the export-processing zones set up by loans and grants from USAID and other government agencies. Preferred trading arrangements ensured that class alliances between foreign investors and local elites were preserved; in countries like Haiti, Guatemala, and El Salvador, the *maquilas* are partly owned and managed by ex-members of military juntas, while the lure of industrial employment takes peasant reformist pressure off traditional landholding elites.

So too the gender division of labor was consciously exploited to preserve power and maximize profit. As Cynthia Enloe points out, the hemispheric free-trade market built by CBI, NAFTA, and now President Bush's proposed thirty-two-nation Free Trade Area of the Americas, "stretching," in the words of his father (who envisioned it), "from Port Anchorage to Tierra del Fuego," has been built explicitly on low female wages, in the "unskilled" sectors of garment-making, food-processing, and electronics assembly. As women moved into the export zone industries (making up 90 percent of EPZ labor), traditionally male manufacturing sectors like sugar, oil, and bauxite, with double the going wages of women, went into decline. Undervalued female labor also undergirds the U.S. domestic workforce, especially in the immigrant economy that supports sweatshops, where it is clear that the high rate of female and immigrant employment accounts today, as ever, for the low wages in apparel. Women and children's labor are on the front line of the new industrial investment all over the world, just as it was in the mills of Manchester at the dawn of the Industrial Revolution.[14] Their entry into the industrial workforce allows them more freedom of movement in the public sphere, and the potential for an independent income. Yet the labor regime they enter can be as patriarchal and coercive as the familial one from which they are escaping.[15]

Whether driven by U.S. security policy or by the logic of neoliberal trade, the consequences of offshore production for the populations of Central America and the Caribbean have amounted to a disaster by several criteria: human rights, environmental, economic, and political. The CBI failed to deliver improved trade earnings, and with the exception of the export zones cranking out profit for their foreign owners to the tune of heavy subsidies from host governments, almost every region has been hit hard. Local economies produced less and less for local consumption, economic nationalism and political sovereignty were severely eroded, and any chance of sustainable development was stillborn. Structural adjustment created a legacy of undiversified economies acutely vulnerable to every mild recession in the U.S. The combination of capital repatriation and curtailment of public spending debilitated those few resources—education, health, and monetary assets—that have staved off hardship by investing in a socially viable future.[16]

By contrast, export promotion has yielded a bonanza, both for U.S. transnational firms and for Korean and Taiwanese suppliers outsourcing in the region in order to be closer to the U.S. market and to circumvent Asian import quotas. Wages as low as 12¢ an hour in Haitian or 31¢ in Honduran and Salvadoran *maquilas* can be freely maximized: import quotas are unlimited; and local regulations against child labor, subminimum wages, and union repression are routinely waived by governments so hungry for foreign investment they will pay the companies' telephone and utilities bills. Until the recent economic recession, apparel companies enjoyed among the largest profits of all U.S. manufacturing industries; their stock prices and their CEO compensation swelled. After two decades of neoliberalism, living standards are in decline all across Latin America, and those governments are looking to plot a course away from Washington. Yet the offshore apparel industry remains the most notorious illustration of a free-trade economy going about its ruthless business: twenty-hour workdays forced on workers to fill their quotas, widespread sexual harassment, coercive birth control, brutal suppression of labor organization, and starvation wages.

These conditions are the result of programs designed to make U.S. apparel companies super-profitable, and if they have succeeded in filling the pockets of corporate executives and stockholders they have done little to help North American workers, forced into a downward-wage spiral for jobs through competition with their *maquila* counterparts or with immigrant workers in the core centers. Pitting First World against Third World workers has been a highly serviceable corporate strategy. It drives wages down on both sides, and allows businesspeople to portray labor rights advocates as domestic protectionists bent on depriving *maquila* workers of their industrial wage ticket out of poverty. (The same arguments are now cropping up in Asia, where the

Chinese wage floor is undercutting the labor market in countries throughout the region.) Those displaced from their jobs have mostly experienced downward mobility.

But the high-reward strategy pursued by investors and owners, backed by favorable tariff regimes and spurred on by 400–500 percent retail markups, also carries some risks—poor quality control, inadequate managerial supervision, political instability. As we will see, none are greater than the potentially humiliating exposure of human rights violations in the factories of companies that cannot afford to have the names of their designers, endorsers, or merchandising labels publicly sullied.

Tactics and Strategies

Indeed, it is the counterstrategy of public exposure that has fired the energies of labor and human rights activists over the last decade. In an economy that prizes brand-building above all else, the marketing integrity of the brand name is sacrosanct.[17] Media interest has been kindled by the spectacle of blue-chip names in retail and design scrambling to generate PR that showcases their efforts at corporate accountability. In the wake of the publicity scandals, companies have been pressured to implement codes of conduct and facilitate monitoring of labor conditions in their contractors' plants. Why has this strategy been necessary and why has it worked? First of all, the labor-capital accords of joint liability that used to govern the garment industry have eroded as the manufacturers lost their commanding position in the chain of production. Greater concentration and integration has afforded giant retailers the paramount power to exert downward price pressure, to circumvent manufacturers by designing and contracting their own private labels, and since retail jobs are not threatened by offshore production, to deflect union pressure. As Charles Bremer, director of international trade for the American Textile Manufacturing Institute, put it, "You don't tell Wal-Mart your price. Wal-Mart tells you."[18] By 1996, the four largest retailers in the U.S. commanded two-thirds of the market value of apparel sales.[19] Their chief point of vulnerability is their brand name, susceptible to bad publicity and to consumer boycotts. Equally, the weak link in the global chain of design, subcontracting, and merchandising is the willingness of First World consumers to pay huge markup prices. In the 1980s, Nike was able to move its factories from South Korea and Taiwan to Indonesia, China, Thailand, and Vietnam to exploit lower wages, but the comparative advantage means nothing if consumers are not willing to pay $125 for a shoe assembled for seventy or eighty cents. If consumer abhorrence for sweatshops has a decisive impact on sales patterns, all is lost.

Accordingly, the leading edge of activism shifted away from labeling ("Made in the USA" labels don't tell us very much anymore, and are often sewn on in Asia or Central America), toward the high-end publicity strategy of targeting the image of large, well-known companies. The groundwork for this tactic was established through the research on Indonesian export-sector factories undertaken by Jeff Ballinger when he was a textile union organizer, in the late 1980s, at the Asian-American Free Labor Institute. His extensive survey showed a majority of export producers paying well below the minimum wage (their workers earned under 14¢ per hour), with Nike's subcontractors among the very worst offenders. Phil Knight's company had just begun to enjoy its mercurial rise to the merchandising forefront of popular culture. With its celebrity endorsers, and hotshot "Just Do It" advertising campaign, targeting Nike was a perfect publicity vehicle for exposing the inequities of offshore export production. Ballinger's famous annotated blowup of the pay stub of one of Nike's Indonesian employees ("The New Free-Trade Heel") appeared in *Harper's* in 1992, and Press for Change, his one-man NGO, became the company's perennial gadfly, helping to establish Nike as the number-one villain in activists' demonization of corporate-led globalization.[20]

While media-driven targeting pays large dividends, its shortcomings are legion. In some export sectors, the worst offenders are producers for local markets who do not have a brand name that is globally recognizable. So too a high-profile fight with a brand name runs the risk of being declared passé once the villain is perceived to have changed its policies. Thus, both Nike and the Gap have benefited greatly from the public perception that they have

reformed their ways. In a thoughtful article on the anti-sweatshop movement's use of media-driven politics, B.J. Bullert distinguishes between public
relations activists—who "adopt" causes and frame them in terms of "heroes
and villains" to fit with media templates—and long-term activists, like
Ballinger, whose enduring focus on the unspectacular lot of workers cannot
be so easily served up for public consumption. Both are needed, she concludes, though the difference between them illustrates the gulf between
those for whom the movement is a potent weapon
in the anticorporate crusade and those for whom
the daily survival of workers is everything.[21]

In the contribution of a group like the National
Labor Committee (NLC), we can see a healthy
fusion of these tendencies. As with Ballinger's
work, the NLC's Charles Kernaghan and Barbara
Briggs have produced invaluable research on workers' conditions in the field, but they have also succeeded most effectively in capturing the public's
attention through media-driven campaigns.
Founded by three union presidents in 1980 to
combat the assassination of Central American
union organizers, the NLC helped organized labor
in the region survive Reagan's war, and then began
to concentrate its efforts on publicizing the ravages
of the *maquila* system.[22] Its 1992 report, *Paying to
Lose Our Jobs* (based on an undercover operation in
which NLC members posed as a small apparel
company looking for an offshore opening), documented the promotional activities and the economic support (to the tune of $1 billion) offered by
U.S. government agencies to induce American corporations into *maquila* production.[23] The report
was released amid widespread anxiety about a new
round of domestic job losses, and its profiling on

Campaign literature,
National Labor committee
(POSTCARD)

CBS's *60 Minutes,* followed by two *Nightline* programs, broke the news that U.S. taxpayers were funding, often through illegal channels, the transfer overseas of their jobs. Legislation was immediately passed to outlaw USAID funding of EPZs, and while the funding continued, the NLC's model of seeking high-level publicity for its exposés was established.

Increasingly, the NLC turned to specific corporate targets, linking their household names and labels to detailed accounts of *maquila* work atrocities. The Gap, a hugely profitable nonunion company with a progressive, hip streetwear image, was the object of a highly successful NLC campaign in 1995, aimed at national media coverage. Two fired *maquiladora* workers were featured on a national speaking tour: Judith Viera from the infamous El Mandarin plant in El Salvador producing for the Gap, as well as for Liz Claiborne, Eddie Bauer, J. Crew, and J.C. Penney, and Claudia Molina, from Global Fashions in Honduras. Top newspaper columnists (most notably, Bob Herbert at the *New York Times*) were attracted to the story, and a coalition of activists, from universities, unions, human rights and consumer organizations, and interfaith groups, were mobilized to pressure the Gap to remedy its labor abuses. Despite threats like the one issued by the owner of the San Marcos Free Trade Zone, former Salvadoran army colonel Mario Guerrero, that "blood will flow," union organizers were promised reinstatement, and the coalition prevailed. The agreement reached with the Gap was unprecedented, and sent a chill throughout the industry's corporate offices. Under the agreement, codes of conduct would be translated into Spanish and posted inside every factory, and independent monitors would be allowed to conduct regular inspections of labor and safety conditions. Like Nike's move, five years later, to disclose some of its factory locations—a concession to the dogged efforts of student activists—the Gap's decision was far from voluntary, and was achieved only through intense scrutiny and pressure.

In the summer of 1996, the NLC hit the publicity jackpot when, following Charlie Kernaghan's testimony at a congressional hearing, TV celebrity Kathie Lee Gifford's Wal-Mart clothing line was linked to child labor and human rights abuses, first in Honduras, and then by UNITE (Union of Needletrades, Industrial, and Textile Employees—the merger union of

ILGWU and ACTWU) workers to wage violations in a New York City sweat-shop. Gifford's saccharine TV personality, and her precious association with children's charities, were a perfect foil for revelations about the child labor behind her label. Gifford was spun-dried by a media maelstrom until the story was stage-managed by New York's most highly paid publicist, Howard Rubinstein. Each step of her painful public progress was obsessively documented and dissected in the national press and TV as it segued from fierce denial and resentment toward her accusers to slapstick self-vindication (when she started endorsing, for Kraft at the age of seventeen, she "didn't think she had to go check out the cows") to humanitarian sympathy with sweatshop workers and righteous anger at their bosses. The instant butt of jokes, and cartoons featuring "Sweatshops of the Rich and Famous," it took Gifford only three weeks to ascend to the saintly rank of labor crusader. Vowing to "shine a light on the cockroaches," she provided a photo opportunity for Governor George Pataki's signing of a Retailers Responsibility Bill to outlaw sweated products in New York, testified in further congressional hearings, and costarred in Labor Secretary Robert Reich's fashion industry summit conference in Washington in July 1996. Her decision to mandate independent monitoring for her line obliged Wal-Mart, the world's biggest retailer, and seller of the Kathie Lee line, to announce new codes of conduct for all its contractors.

At a time when celebrities are lining up to sponsor products, and when endorsements are the bread and butter of the sportswear business, Gifford's invitation to other celebrity endorsers to clean up their contracts opened a new window of vulnerability within the industry. Michael Jordan, at the top of the heap, shrugged off challenges from reporters as Nike, with 37 percent of the $6.86 billion sneaker market, faced a barrage of media criticism over its decision to manufacture in Suharto's Indonesia. Jordan's hard-boiled nonchalance was unavailable to Kathie Lee Gifford, whose public persona is based on a profile of emotional caring, empathizing, and full disclosure of her personal life. Nor did much dirt stick to the cartoon celebrities of Disney, target of the NLC's other summer campaign in Haiti, where Disney's fantasy world is embellished by Mickey Mouse and Pocahantas clothing sewn for starvation wages. Disney and other companies who use Haitian factories, like Sara Lee (owner of Hanes, L'Eggs, Bali, Playtex, and Champion) make donations to nonprofit causes to launder their public image, while employing workers who often toil for fifty straight hours and can still barely feed their families at the end of the week. The NLC's study of Disney operations in Haiti, and its subsequent reports on China and Bangladesh, helped to substantiate the argument that the doubling of workers' wages in these overseas apparel locations would have a negligible impact (2–3 percent) on the retail price of the clothing they help to produce. Three subsequent surveys of U.S. consumers showed that a large majority (up to 78 percent) of polled consumers declared they would be willing to pay up to 15–25 percent more for no-sweat clothing.[24]

Author in mouse's clothing, Annual Holiday Season of Conscience March, National Labor Committee
(PHOTO COURTESY OF THE NLC)

Several other important organizations took their place alongside the NLC in the struggle against sweatshops: Global Exchange, Sweatshop Watch, the Clean Clothes Campaign, Maquila Solidarity Network, Coalition for Justice in the Maquiladoras, Asian Law Caucus, Bangor Clean Clothes Campaign, People of Faith Network, the International Labor Rights Fund, Campaign for Labor Rights, STITCH, CISPES, Vietnam Labor Watch, Child Labor Coalition, Human Rights Watch, New York State Labor-Religion Coalition, Veritè, U.S./Guatemala Labor Education Project, and Press for Change. Grassroots workers groups, formed by laid-off or threatened employees, like Fuerza Unita (San Antonio), La Mujer Obrera (El Paso), the Thai and Latino Workers Organizing Committee (Los Angeles), and the Chinese Staff and Workers Association (New York City), waged their own campaigns through community-based workers centers in ways that have raised the local visibility of the issues.[25]

Two traditional institutions in this field also played their role: the U.S. Department of Labor, and the garment union, UNITE. While the Clinton Administration power-steered the passage of NAFTA over and against the opposition of organized labor, its Secretary of Labor, Robert Reich, was a compensatory voice in his attempts to curtail domestic sweatshop practices, the first incumbent in fifty years to do so. After a decade of nonenforcement of most labor legislation, Reich revived the Hot Goods provision of the Fair Labor Standards Act, and began to prosecute companies in violation of this law against the interstate transport of sweated goods. With only 800 federal inspectors to cover the industry's 22,000 cutting and sewing jobs, *in addition* to the nation's other six million workplaces, enforcement in the fly-by-night sector was futile in practice, and so the DOL resorted to the new action-oriented strategy of naming names.

In August 1995, a raid on the El Monte compound in southern California uncovered seventy-two undocumented Thai workers behind barbed-wire fences, locked up around the clock to produce garments for the likes of Montgomery Ward, and for sale at Nordstrom, Sears, Macy's, and Filenes. These conditions were legally recognized as peonage, and afforded the DOL the public momentum to mount what would become its own NO SWEAT campaign. After El Monte, Reich announced a "white list" of companies making honest attempts to rid their labor of sweated processes. Those excluded would be publicly shamed, and would have to submit detailed proof that they were shunning hot goods for their names to appear on this Fashion Trendsetters list. A quarterly Garment Enforcement Report commenced publication of the names of offenders prosecuted for back pay. Reich's strategy was a step in the right direction, but in the absence of any real political will to enforce regulations, it lacked teeth. Names on the DOL list barely grew from the initial thirty-six in December 1995, and a place on the list hardly guaranteed continued good conduct from any of the companies, as Guess workers' exposé of the firm's homework production in August 1996 made all too clear. When Alexis Herman took over the office from Reich in 1997, the campaign tailed off. The DOL has made little headway since, despite a slight increase in its staff of labor inspectors.[26] The Bush Administration put Elaine Chao, an antilabor secretary of labor in office, and the result has been a hands-off policy.

In response to the DOL list, the powerful National Retail Federation established its own Retail Honor Roll for companies in compliance with labor laws, and launched a publicity war with the DOL, calling on Reich to "stop wasting millions of taxpayer dollars on counterproductive media witch hunts and devote his energies to enforcing the law."[27] It was clear which strategy the retailers preferred. By July 1996, the big retailers had been sufficiently embarrassed by the Kathie Lee Gifford–Wal-Mart scandal for many to participate in discussions about an industry-wide effort at compliance and regulation, convened at Reich's fashion summit conference at Washington's Marymount University. On hand to showcase their own codes of conduct were most favored companies, like Levi Strauss (whose 1991 Global Sourcing and Operating Guidelines was a pioneer code of corporate standards), Nordstrom, Nicole Miller, Guess (the target of the homework exposé just one month later), Liz Claiborne, Patagonia, and Kmart—"we are in a learning process"—while the NRF's president, Tracey Mullin, defensively pointed a finger at immigration politics and organized crime. Union representatives and journalists told harrowing tales about child and bonded labor in factories where management by terror is enforced. Industry associations and the Compliance Alliance all agreed that sweatshops were bad for business. The few celebrity endorsers who attended—Gifford, Richard Simmons, Cheryl Tiegs—were greeted like social martyrs: "If you have a terrible outrage like El Monte or what Kathie Lee has gone through. . . ."

In April 1997, a presidential task force—the Apparel Industry Partnership (AIP)—reached an agreement on workplace codes of conduct. This group, which had first convened at the White House in August 1996, included UNITE, the National Consumers League, the Retail, Wholesale, and Department Store Union, the Interfaith Center on Corporate Responsibility, and Lawyers Committee for Human Rights, and also had industry representatives from Liz Claiborne, Nike, Reebok, Phillips-Van Heusen, Patagonia, and L.L. Bean. Agreements on health and safety, forced labor, child labor (banning employment under fifteen years, except in certain countries) and anti-harassment and nondiscriminatory practices had been reached early on. Accords were eventually reached on limited protections of the right to freedom of association and collective bargaining. Less satisfactory was the task force's acceptance of a sixty-hour workweek as the industry norm— forty-eight plus twelve hours overtime. Its recommendation of a sixty-hour maximum, which could, however, be exceeded "in extraordinary business circumstances" (i.e., any rush order), and its commitment to a cap on "mandatory" overtime, were both loose and imprecise gestures in an industry where employers and managers already find it all too easy to declare that workers are putting in "voluntary" overtime, or are working under "extraordinary" circumstances. In addition the agreements required only that workers are paid "at a rate at least equal to their regular hourly compensation" for overtime.

Predictably, the biggest split among the task force participants had been over wages and the issue of independent monitoring. The labor and human rights groups had pushed for a "basic-needs" standard for a "living wage," rather than the legal minimum wage, which in most offshore countries is purposely set well below subsistence level in the hope of attracting foreign investment. The task force accords did little to discourage the maintenance of these minimum wage levels, incapable of sustaining a healthy, dignified life for most workers. In rejecting the pressure for a livable wage, the industry representatives also pushed for a system of "external monitoring" (as opposed to "independent monitoring") that would allow them to use large auditing companies like Ernst & Young and PriceWaterhouseCoopers to assess and adjudicate local and international standards that might apply to any area of compliance with the codes. Transnational corporate auditors would thus be playing the role hitherto pioneered by local NGOs familiar with the social and cultural conditions of peoples' working lives. While the task force's accords advised the external monitors to consult with those institutions that are likely to have the trust of workers and knowledge of local conditions, they did not oblige companies to establish independent monitoring relationships with the labor, human rights, and religious groups in the region. Nor, since the agreements are voluntary, did they carry the threat of penalties for companies that violate the provisions of the code. The large loopholes in the agreements meant that the AIP had failed to propose meaningful standards or codes that can be effectively implemented. Elaine Bernard, director of Harvard's Trade Union Studies Program, suggested that the agreements merely gave the "good housekeeping seal of approval to a 'kinder, gentler,' sweatshop." The result was an impasse that led to the withdrawal of the labor and interfaith groups from the partnership.

The AIP's monitoring arm, the Fair Labor Association (FLA), was set up without their participation and immediately garnered the reputation of being a corporate front. Because the board operates by a supermajority vote, the companies that have a seat can effectively exercise veto power on all resolutions. They do not have to disclose their factory locations, nor are they obliged to employ independent monitors. While the FLA has played a significant role (sometimes in conjunction with the activist-initiated Workers Rights Consortium) in pressuring and brokering agreements between owners and workers, and while it has introduced reforms in response to pressure from United Students Against Sweatshops (USAS), its monitoring continues to be done primarily by for-profit auditors accustomed to serving the apparel industry. It took until May 2003 for the organization to make public any of its monitoring reports, and the locations of factories under investigation are still not readily available.

The conception of the FLA was effectively brokered by the legal aces of companies like Nike, desperate for the PR cover it provides. Nike would go further and outsource its PR to an NGO, the Global Alliance for Workers and Communities, which shills in the field of corporate responsibility. By the summer of 2000, Phil Knight was standing shamelessly by the side of Secretary-General Kofi Annan at the launch of the UN's Global Compact, in the forefront of the fifty founding companies who had pledged to observe labor rights and environmental standards in their global business practices.[28] Yet a 2001 report by the international human rights organization Global Exchange shows that workers making Nike products are still forced to work excessive hours, are not paid enough to meet the most basic needs of their children, and are subject to harassment, dismissal, and violent intimidation if they try to form unions or tell journalists about labor abuses in their factories.[29] In striking contrast were the efforts of Levi Strauss to abide by its pioneering code of conduct. An early leader in the corporate responsibility movement, the company actually pulled out of China in 1993, owing to concerns that human rights violations would tarnish its virtuous reputation. Five years later, with sales in steep decline, it had softened its code, and reversed its policy amid a tumult of hand-wringing about how to balance ethical integrity and commercial success. Twenty-two domestic factories were shuttered, 13,000 workers lost their jobs, and an opportunity to set a golden standard in the global economy was lost.[30] Nike's shoddy tactics and Levi Strauss's moral agonizing both illustrate, in quite disparate ways, the dangers involved in persuading corporations to self-regulate. Indeed, the move for companies to introduce codes of conduct and assume responsibility for ensuring the monitoring of their suppliers may be leading toward what Neil Kearney, (General Secretary of the International Textile, Garment and Leather Workers' Federation) has described as "the privatization of the implementation of labor law." As more and more NGOs are involved in the process of monitoring, they may become a "permanent obstacle to trade union organizATION." Monitoring, in Kearney's view, will become "the new solidarismo" and the "new yellow unionism."[31]

Students and Labor

That corporations need such organizations is testimony to the heat they are feeling from grassroots activists. Arguably the most pressure in recent years has come from the student organization USAS, which, since its founding in the summer of 1998, has run a brilliant and mercurial campaign against corporate abuse from the ethical stronghold of college campuses. The campaign involved the integrity of some of the more prominent U.S. varsity names in a $2.5 billion sector of the garment industry, and it was based on the premise that universities need to safeguard these names as assiduously (and often for much the same revenue-minded reasons) as corporations protect their commercial brands. College licensing contracts were perceived to be a strategic pressure point in the larger anti-sweat movement, and students at several key schools, beginning in January 1999 at Duke University, petitioned their college presidents to establish codes of conduct governing the labor conditions under which licensed articles, bearing the college name, are manufactured.

In the winter of 1998–99, the Collegiate Licensing Company (CLC), which brokered licensing agreements with colleges, asked college administrators to review and sign its own code of conduct, loosely based on the set of regulatory provisions drawn up by the AIP. The CLC code lacked provisions on transparency and living wage, and therefore ran into student opposition for many of the same reasons as the AIP had with labor and interfaith groups. USAS had formed earlier that year, and its first sparks lit a prairie fire of activism that spread throughout its network of college chapters. The national mobilization of students eventually resulted in campaigns, sit-ins, and occupations at almost 200 campuses, amid a blaze of media coverage. For the first time since the 1930s, students appeared to be turning in large numbers toward the cause of labor.[32]

At many of their campuses, students secured agreements about codes of conduct that were then undercut when administrators flocked to join the FLA.

In response, USAS initiated a second round of campus campaigns in a bid to persuade college presidents to join the Workers Rights Consortium (WRC), a new organization, free of corporate influence, that was formed in April 2000. Conceived as an alternative to the FLA, the WRC sponsors independent monitoring and verification of workers' complaints by local human rights groups. The intent is to introduce bottom-up monitoring, where workers themselves feel they have taken the initiative, rather than the top-down approach of the FLA, whose monitors initiate the process and verify a set of standards established independently of workers' needs. Ultimately, the aim is to establish a relationship where factory workers are able to use activists and outside sources as allies and tactical tools, and thereby avoid the situation whereby Northern activists are in a position to tell workers what they should want.

Another important core component of the WRC approach is its insistence that licensees agree to full public disclosure of all of their factory locations. Companies had initially resisted this principle, on the basis that locations were a "trade secret"—a spurious argument, given that the same factory often supplies several rival companies. The agreement on disclosure introduced a crucial measure of transparency into the working policies of licensees, while infuriating corporate managers with big college contracts. Less than a month after its founding, the WRC was handed a windfall of free publicity when Phil Knight, in a tantrum, canceled Nike contracts with WRC members, Brown University, and the University of Michigan, and withdrew a $30 million gift to his alma mater, the University of Oregon. To date, over 110 colleges have joined the WRC, and it has already successfully investigated, and partially resolved, workers' complaints in several key locations. Monitoring and close investigation of antiunion repression at Kukdong (Mex-Mode), a Mexican factory producing for Nike and Reebok, concluded in the summer of 2001 with the recognition of SITEMEX, an independent trade union. New Era, a factory in western New York state producing baseball caps for 400 colleges and universities, as well as for Major League Baseball, was also pressured by the WRC into union negotiations with workers. At PT Dada in Indonesia, which produces caps and stuffed toys for Adidas (bearing the logo of WRC-affiliated colleges), working conditions were radically improved along with union contracts.

USAS has also established close relationships with workers struggling to launch unionization campaigns in several export-processing zones. One of the longest-running relationships was with organizers who were fired in 1997 at BJ&B, a collegiate cap-making factory in Villa Altagracia, Dominican Republic, which supplies major brands like Reebok. In November 2002, the reinstated workers won a collective bargaining contract that made the union the largest independent free-trade-zone union in the country, and possibly the world.[33] Buoyed by victories at BJ&B and Kukdong, where USAS provided crucial support, pressure, and organizing aid, and building on their highly successful effort to win disclosure on factory locations, USAS is now campaigning to force companies to agree to full public disclosure of the wages of collegiate-apparel workers. The aim of this campaign is to open the way to establishing living-wage levels that are locally sustainable.

Even when USAS's highly publicized investigations often have little immediate material impact on the mass of workers' lives, they are important moves in the ongoing war of position with the major apparel companies. In establishing that unions can exist in EPZs, they may soon serve as models of the kind of international action that is needed to address labor standards. Supporting workers' own local efforts to organize and remedy their grievances—the WRC model—may well be perceived as preferable to issuing companies with a sweat-free bill of health, as in the FLA model that mandates top-down monitoring by the same consultancies that audit the company books.[34] Extensive media coverage of USAS activities has helped to expand public consciousness of the issues, and their campaigns have reaffirmed what is rapidly becoming common sense—no one, least of all college presidents, wants their company or institution associated with a brand sullied with the taint of sweatshops.

The student movement received considerable support, from an early point, from the labor movement. In part, this was an acknowledgment of the bilateral role that unions themselves were playing in an anti-sweatshop crusade that they once monopolized. Indeed, the bargaining power and political repute of the garment unions derived from their much-lionized success in eradicating the turn-of-the-century sweatshop and reforming "industrial conduct." The tragedy of the Triangle Shirtwaist Factory fire, which took the lives of 141 seamstresses in 1911, proved to be the milestone event that put the first anti-sweatshop movement over the top. After the strikes of the female shirtwaist makers (the famous "Uprising of the Twenty Thousand") in 1909, and the male cloak makers the following year, garment chieftains had met with labor leaders to sign the Protocols of Peace, the prototype of collective bargaining agreements, mediated by Progressive jurist Louis Brandeis. The first step on the road to the suppression of the sweatshop, the Protocols established the preferential union shop, a fifty-hour week, wages going to arbitration, and rules against the permanent replacement of strikers.[35] Organized labor learned that management would make big concessions in return for uninterrupted production, while the manufacturers found a way for labor to accept their coming creed of scientific management and industrial efficiency.

Thus were sown the seeds of labor-capital's social contract, conceived as the joint control of industrial democracy, governed by the modernist creed of productive efficiency, and committed to a more humane form of capitalism than that embodied by the sweatshop. In its Cold War heyday, organized labor's role in this contract was that of a powerful co-guarantor, blessed by a degree of government patronage unimaginable forty years before. The corporate breakup of that social contract, hastened on by the Reagan and Bush administrations' punitive war on the basic organizing rights of labor, hit the garment unions especially hard in an industry on the front line of job attrition. ILGWU membership decreased from 457,517 in 1969 (when 70–80 percent of New York City factories were union shops) to less than 200,000 by the time of its 1995 merger with the ACTWU. UNITE's entire membership now stands at less than 250,000. With a employment peak of 1.45 million in 1973, domestic apparel jobs had fallen to 846,000 by 1995 (which saw a year's decline of 10 percent in the first big wave of NAFTA losses) and 523,000 by April 2002 (according to the Bureau of Labor Statistics). With the loss of larger, centralized factories producing standardized clothing lines, the opportunities to increase union membership have clearly diminished, and are more and more concentrated in the informal sector that is notoriously difficult to organize.

For a while industry and union endeavors to retain jobs focused on high-tech, high-skill programs, where computer-assisted design, point-of-sale data, and quick-response technologies maximize flexibility, minimize inventory, rationalize consumer preference and demand, and strengthen the capacity to deliver fashion goods just in time. The emphasis was on craft, quality, and reliability that are unavailable offshore. In addition to this boost to flexibility and turnaround time, modular, team-based production systems with multi-tasking workers have made the domestic delivery of fashionwear more competitive than many forms of outsourcing. But escalating competition in casual and sportswear lines has also exacerbated the conditions under which domestic sweatshops proliferate. In anticipation of the devastating impact of the MFA phase-out in 2005, UNITE has turned its organizing efforts to the retail and distribution workforce of the big brands—as many as half a million domestic workers.

Nonetheless, UNITE's own anti-sweatshop campaign, in partnership with the National Consumers League, has been an important source of consumer information (reminding us, for example, that "the care tag tells you how to treat the garment but not how the worker who made it was treated"). Union and nonunion workers' active role in the exposure of illegal conditions has often been organized out of UNITE's Worker Centers in L.A., New York, and San Francisco. A leading participant in the southern California coalition that runs Sweatshop Watch, the union's connections in the industry have also been crucial to maintaining public pressure on converting retailers and man-ufacturers' public image concerns into effective action. Just as important, UNITE served as a crucible for the campus campaigns, supporting and par-ticipating in the work of USAS from its roots in intern research and at the AFL-CIO Union Summers in 1996 and 1997.

For unions, the challenge of offshore organizing is even greater, especially when the local Maquiladora Manufacturers' Association, or its regional equivalent, can always produce a "company union" representative to mouth the regional benefits of outsourcing when U.S. reporters come calling. In developing countries under repressive rule, activism that calls for unioniza-tion is often less effective than appeals to international human rights conventions, which tend to attract the global media. At the level of trade policy, countries like the U.S. can take the moral high ground in banning imports made with child labor, but they will not prefer nations that raise the level of other labor protections. Nor does the high ground yield justice when it only serves the morality of the affluent. Without making any alternative provision for its impact on overseas workers, the 1993 Child Labor Deterrence Act pushed tens of thousands of children out of the formal workplace in countries like Bangladesh, exposing them to much more hazardous and exploitative conditions in the informal economy.

More and more, unions like UNITE have looked for leverage to citizens campaigns, often tied to consumer boycotts that have proven effective in the case of South African oranges, infant formula, canned tuna fish, and the table grape campaign of the United Farm Workers. The sustained access to publicity can have a powerful effect in the streets, stores, and factories of the U.S., where 25 percent of the world's economic activity occurs. Yet the weapon of the consumer boycott is a controversial one for unionists who are more interested in improving work conditions than in chastising, or chasing away, companies. Like trade sanctions, boycotts can punish the most vulnerable workers, when plants shut down in communities that need jobs and wages. More effective, in theory, is UNITE's new strategy of putting public pressure on big brand names through coordinating campaigns by workers in several of the company's overseas factories. The prototype for this strategy was the 2003 campaign to organize workers, internationally, at H&M, the Swedish discount fashion brand.

Another weapon is the movement for socially responsible investment and trade. Boasting a diverse range of participating funds and organizations across the globe, and with a steadily increasing share of financial portfolios, its power to apply shareholder pressure on corporations is growing. It has the capacity to serve as a powerful supplement, if not an alternative, to the feeble system of corporate regulations currently recognized by international law.

However contentious, some boycotts have successfully taken their toll on the world of high fashion. PETA's (People for the Ethical Treatment of Animals) antifur campaigns had an immense impact for a while upon the furrier and animal-skin markets. So too groups whose image is distorted or ignored in fashion advertising often undertake a more diffuse form of boycott. The racially exclusive face of fashion and the preternaturally thin female body types favored in modeling have been heavily condemned for almost two decades now. African Americans, conscious of their consumer power, expect to see increased representation in advertising images from companies whose products they patronize. Sometimes, the response can be quite complicated. For example, in 1994, Timberland ran some outrightly racist ads as part of an attempt to dissociate its name from the inner-city hip-hop youth who had adopted the trademark boots and outerwear. The ads contrasted an "out there" of white nature lovers with the "out there" of freaky black club kids, making it quite clear which group Timberland favored. As it happens, this may have been a shrewd marketing move, designed to neutralize a boycott. Hip-hop youth made a public point of continuing to wear Timberland in the aim of embarrassing a company that did not (officially) want their custom. A subsequent move on the part of the same consumers to patronize the preppy clothing of Tommy Hilfiger, Nautica, Ralph Lauren, and Burberry proved that the game of tag that youth subcultures play with mainstream fashionwear is increasingly part of the business cycle. By 2001, Hilfiger's resentment at being dropped was cleanly matched by Burberry's concern about being adopted, around about the same time.

The vast sportswear profits generated by endorsers like Michael Jordan, Shaquille O'Neal, and Charles Barkley have helped to create high-profile employment for dark-skinned African American male models who look athletic and defiant. Such images, presented as the epitome of beauty, are a notable breakthrough in a history of public aesthetics that has either maligned or exploited the look and physique of black males. But controversy over these issues of representation are usually disconnected from the stories about garment industry sweatshops; as Jordan or others in his position can say, "that's not my department." This is a reminder that some groups have preestablished priorities, and that labor-oriented coalitions and boycotts will have to respect and negotiate these priorities while working on a broad multiracial front.

Another example surfaced in April 2002, when the Abercrombie & Fitch clothing company introduced a series of designer T-shirts featuring stereotypical cartoon images of Chinese faces with slanted eyes and "rice hats." One T-shirt design had a slogan that read WONG BROTHERS LAUNDRY SERVICE—TWO WONGS CAN MAKE IT WHITE, and another announced ABERCROMBIE & FITCH BUDDHA BASH—GET YOUR BUDDHA ON THE FLOOR. The clothing generated a firestorm of protest from Asian American groups over racist representation, while the company, known for its provocation marketing, harvested yet another round of bad-boy publicity. Notably absent from the protests, however, were references to the abhorrent labor conditions in Saipan factories where indentured workers from China and Thailand produce for Abercrombie & Fitch and a host of other brand names. In the western Pacific island of Saipan, U.S. labor laws do not apply, but producers can legally stitch on a "Made in the U.S.A." label.[36]

In the intimate environment of campus protests, the prioritization of issues can generate some friction. Thus, many chapters of USAS have found themselves in an uneasy relationship with antiracist student groups, who often resented the massive publicity that the predominantly white USAS chapters seemed to be able to generate on behalf of their concern for overseas workers of color. Conscious that USAS had garnered a reputation for evading domestic issues, and a capacity for dealing with race only at a distance, many activists sought to build better alliances without abandoning the focus on labor.[37] Some chapters, for example, expanded their activities to support labor struggles among campus workers—in janitorial and dining hall services—and in local campaigns for a living wage. Support for farmworker groups—and against sweatshops in the fields—stepped up, resulting in a campaign aimed at Taco Bell's exploitation of Immolakee tomato pickers in Florida. USAS has also launched a campaign in support of immigrant rights.

The Debate on Development

A similar caveat applies to the relationship between garment workers in the South and Northern anti-sweatshop activists. Critics of the sweatshop movement have preyed on activists' white guilt to suggest that the standards of affluent countries are being imposed on countries that can ill afford them. Suspicion of U.S. intervention, even in the form of well-intentioned activism, goes a long way in countries with a long history of reasons to mistrust American ideas about their development. Guilt-tripping young middle-class protesters is a well-rehearsed sport, yet no one in their right mind expects to see EPZ workers achieve Northern wage levels anytime soon. Even if the charge was justified, it is not at all clear who would enforce this imposition. There is little historical basis, at this point, for assuming that a centralized system of regulators will ever be in a position to dictate universal conduct throughout the global economy. Industrial elites and like-minded commentators from developing countries have also argued that the activists' cause is fundamentally protectionist. This charge is equally dubious, given that domestic protectionism, in textiles and apparel at least, has been a dead duck on the legislative front since the demise of the MFA. Besides, there is no real evidence that frontline activists are motivated by anything other than concern for economic fairness. It is true that activists will often exploit anxiety about loss of domestic jobs in order to publicize their cause, and that this is a strategy that may play into the hands of domestic unions seeking to slow the decline of manufacturing jobs. Yet it is increasingly recognized, even within trade unionist circles, that the interests of domestic workers are best served by pushing for labor-friendly growth in every country. In a global economy, there is no real alternative.[38]

With somewhat more rationale, anticolonial critics on the left have pointed out that the movement's portrayals of sweatshop workers as helpless victims of brutal labor conditions tends to reinforce degrading stereotypes of passive Third World women. The diverse experience, complex aspirations, and vivid personality of workers on "the supply side" of the picture are routinely reduced to one-dimensional roles in the often formulaic atrocity stories circulated by activists to generate publicity for campaigns.[39] Much remains to be done in fully incorporating into the movement voices and arguments from the South, and not just those who speak on behalf of workers. Heather White, director of Verite, the Massachusetts human rights monitoring group, points out that the place to begin is with basic worker literacy about the structure of wages, and then proceed to education in labor rights. Without this education, workers will "be overly dependent on outside auditors to initiate improvements.[40] So too activists need to emphasize provisions to educate workers, most often children, who are likely to be displaced from "improved" workplaces into the vastly inferior workplaces that far outnumber those in the export sector.[41]

Free-trade economists have gone much further in their criticism of the movement by arguing that developing countries will forfeit their capacity to compete for jobs and investment if they have to prematurely accept increased labor costs. Low-wage export sector jobs and the accompanying foreign investment, they argue, are needed in order to embark on the path toward development, and all countries pass through a low-wage phase on this path. All other considerations aside, the laws of the free market demand it. In the much-quoted words of Columbia economist Jeffrey Sachs, "my concern is not that there are too many sweatshops but that there are too few." Even Paul Krugman, an economist known for his liberal views, once defended the use of child labor as a comparative advantage that developing countries cannot afford to renounce.[42] The pro-sweatshop economists argue that, in time, as civil society develops in tandem with industrialization, wages will rise and labor standards will emerge organically and in conformity with market forces. The reduced price of imports will benefit domestic consumers just as the industrial wage of export-zone workers allows them to become consumers in the first place. Indeed, the neoliberal fantasy of free trade is one in which all trading partners experience some gain. Critical to this position is the argument, included in a letter circulated by free-trade economists to undermine the influence of USAS, that export sector workers are "generally paid no less than the prevailing market wage," and sometimes considerably more.[43]

Most of the free-trader arguments are based entirely on the narrow, formal assumptions that neoclassical economics prizes, or else they rest on norms of market criteria—like "the prevailing market wage" cited previously—that have already deteriorated rapidly under neoliberal penetration. No one can morally oppose the right of a poor country to attract investment on the basis of its cheap labor pool. It clearly is a comparative advantage to be able to produce a good more cheaply than elsewhere. But the conditions that are almost universally attached to investment in low-wage export production *are* morally unacceptable. In the semiautonomous EPZ enclaves, the state's environmental and safety regulations go unheeded, and governments have to guarantee to multinationals that wages will be kept low by suppressing workers' rights, such as free speech, the right to freedom of association, and the right to bargain collectively. Just to cite one example, the Bangladesh Export Processing Zone Authorization Act of 1980 explicitly exempted EPZs from all of the country's labor laws.[44] Nor is child labor a matter of meeting labor supply needs. The highest rates of child labor are in countries where adult unemployment is excessive.

Labor rights are not privileges that carry a price tag, and poverty does not preclude entitlement to them. There is no reason why core labor standards (recognized by the ILO) should be subject to a cost-benefits analysis. In any case, whatever increased costs are incurred from observing these rights should not be borne by host nations, but by the multinational firms that reap vast profits from the sweatshop system. Even if the costs were passed on to consumers (a more practical assumption), there is a reasonable expectation that they could be absorbed without much pain. In a comparative study of garment production in Mexico and the U.S., economists Robert Pollin, Justine Burns, and James Heintz estimate that 100 percent wage increases for workers at all points of the production chain would still only translate into a retail hike ranging from 2–6 percent, well below the premium of 15–25 percent that surveyed U.S. consumers are willing to pay.[45]

Nor will poverty pass from the face of the earth as a result of the free traders' beloved market forces. Without the right to bargain for themselves, workers seldom achieve wage increases, and, with capital flowing unrestricted, higher living standards simply will not materialize, let alone usher in a realm of general global prosperity. The record of free trade in countries hosting export industries with no links to the domestic economy is clear enough. Rising unemployment and falling wages are the result, in Central America and Asia alike, where the average apparel worker earns far below the estimated living wage. The NICs (Newly Industrializing Countries) of East Asia are often cited as examples of how export jobs in garments and electronic assembly triggered higher levels of development and living standards. Yet, as UNITE's Mark Levinson points out, the Asian tigers achieved economic growth through "trade protection, state controls on capital, and manipulated exchange rates."[46] They were also beneficiaries of Cold War funding, to some significant degree. The deregulated system that sustains today's global sweatshop in Asia and the Americas has no such aid or controls, and is primarily designed to ensure the free movement of capital after the model of Jack Welch's barges. That is why wage levels have dropped not only in the South but in the North as well, where the slippage of labor standards, by comparison, has been much greater. Far from lifting all boats, globalization, in the form of trade and investment liberalization, has generated a state of economic apartheid—bonanzas for those on the top end, and a dramatic rise in poverty for those on the lower rungs.

Until workers can self-organize and share in the wealth that they produce, activists in the North will have an important role to play. They are needed, first and foremost, to petition for all workers to enjoy a living wage according to local standards of subsistence. The more farsighted, and optimistic, speak of a comprehensive "social wage" that owners and investors owe to the communities where they locate factories. If these efforts are perceived to be insufficiently radical (cleaning up capitalism rather than rewriting the ground rules of society), as some critics on the left have claimed, these charges are hardly new to labor organizers, who have long placed their faith and energy in building power incrementally by distributing it downward. At the other end of the power spectrum, the goal is to win a voice at the table of the world economic community, where elites from government and industry, unencumbered by labor representatives, make the key decisions about capital regulation and allocation of the debt burden.[47] Until that kind of top-level participation is achieved, labor and environmental standards will only get lip service. Even so, the elite consensus has eroded more rapidly than anyone could have imagined. Every strategy, tactic, campaign, and media exposure contributes to the pressure at all points in the chain: from world trade policy to international human rights, workplace regulation, labor organizing, consumer education and politics, and institutional activism. Whether using the powerful public vehicle of moral abhorrence or the power of reason to argue for rights and justice, the accomplishments of the second anti-sweatshop movement, in less than a decade, have been immense. Public awareness has skyrocketed; corporations have scrambled for PR cover just as they have been forced into a concessionary stance; strategic legislation has been introduced; international coalitions have been formed; steps toward the establishment of a global monitoring structure have been taken; and a wide-ranging debate about the shape of world trade agreements has begun. While the anti-sweatshop movement appears to be aimed primarily at economic goals, its social and political character has lent it an epochal profile with few rivals.

Italia in style

CHAPTER TWO

Made in Italy: The Trouble with Craft Capitalism

IN THE SUMMER OF 2002, during a trip to London, I visited the Fila store in Covent Garden. I asked the shop assistant where the clothing on display was made, and he announced, with a hint of swagger, that everything was made in Italy. A brief but thorough investigation revealed that none of the items on the racks were made in Italy. All of the labels communicated either an Asian or Turkish place of manufacture or assembly. When I pointed this out to the assistant, he confessed that it did not surprise him. His manager, he said, insisted that employees stick to the script in responding to customer queries—a fact that, in turn, did not surprise me. After all, who would pass up the sales advantage that accompanies an association with Italian manufacture? Which discerning consumer could be oblivious to the Bel Paese guarantee of quality, craftsmanship, and innovative technique; the proposition of panache; or the sensible pricing? A "Made in Italy" label promised all three, and more besides. Indeed, by the turn of the century, the moniker bore a significance that was quite unique on the international landscape of commodity trade. No other country could add so much value to a range of products by the mere attachment of its name.

As it happens, "Made in Italy" was heading into its third lucrative decade of unparalleled success as a national trade brand with a distinct mercantile profile. I refer to it as a brand because the trademark, as it applies to products of the fashion, design, and furniture industries, was, in large part, the progeny of a promotional campaign, beginning in the early 1980s, undertaken by several trade organizations and institutions like Ente Moda Italiana, the Italian Trade Commission, and Sistema Moda Italiana. From the campaign's outset, the consistent mission has been to champion these industries in established export markets in Europe, North America, and Japan, and in emergent ones in East Asia and Latin America. The runaway success of the campaign revolved around building the visibility of designer brands in quality ready-to-wear or epicure markets that enjoyed newfound economies of scale and scope because they were able to achieve genuinely international dimensions. With mass manufacturing all but lost to the developing countries, the 1980s saw the designer brand emerge as the anchor of the value-adding economy that now supports the remnants of manufacturing in the West. Pioneering this path in the fashion world were Armani, Missoni, Valentino, Versace, Gigli, Ferre, Krizia, Gucci, and Fendi, followed later by Moschino, Dolce & Gabbana, and Prada. Among designers, the magic names included Gio Ponti, Ettore Sottsass, Bruno Munari, Vico Magistretti, Achille Castiglioni, Marco Zanuso, Enzo Mari, and Tobia Scarpa. Before long, any and every commodity in pursuit of added-value had to be linked to a name with cachet. Perhaps the most telling example of this strategy was Alessi, a tableware producer that managed to transform its everyday kitchen products into mass market cult-style items through association with celebrity architects and designers like Michael Graves, Hans Hollein, Aldo Rossi, Robert Venturi, and Phillipe Starck.

But it was quality ready-to-wear fashion that provided the leading face of the new national iconography. By the mid-1970s, the countercultural revolt against style conventions had all but demolished the structure of the traditional fashion system in countries around the world. The reconstruction of fashion (often described as a "restoration," and shamelessly trading on the rich visual repertoire of Italy's own Renaissance history) was undertaken by design houses willing to respond to the new informality and its loosened mores. Armani's destructured jacket, introduced in 1975, is often taken to be the milestone, since it spoke directly to the transformed gender roles of modern men and women, and was enough of a departure from bourgeois probity to pass muster with recovering bohemian rebels.[1] On the international image landscape, it helped to displace the bad-for-business publicity generated by Italy's domestic Marxist-Leninist revolutionaries—especially the violent factionalism waged by the Red Brigades. In the attention economy, the Armani suit siphoned off some of the seductive radical chic of the leather-jacket-and-gun, and rode the wave of an economic resurgence.

As part of the garment industry response to the latest economic demands of custom, just-in-time production, a new fashion system was established in the early 1980s in Milan, supplied by a network of regional producers. Milan's ascendancy as the ready-to-wear capital was based on industrial production of the designer's cut, as distinct from the traditional practice of the couture houses—which had involved spinning an off-the-rack line from an atelier out-cut. Production was organized around batch-runs for quick response (*pronta moda*) to customer taste. The result met the demands of the new export markets devoted to custom design products with a distinctive, or iconic, identity. Italian names quickly dominated the ranks of the export leaders and a cluster of homegrown industries took a fast ride on their coattails.

From that point onward, the mercantile image of "Made in Italy" would be built around products with a high aesthetic or creative content. As Mario Boselli, president of Pitti Immagine, a key agency for organizing and promoting textile and clothing fairs, noted in 1999, the "capacity to communicate meaning and identity is a powerful multiplier of the economic value that Italy continues to design and create."[2] The prosperity of this image-conscious economy was hitched to the international rise of the urban service professionals, or yuppies, whose lifestyle Zeitgeist was marked by the expression of idiosyncratic taste in furniture, clothing, food, and design. Essential to the national brand formula was the visibility and novelty of modern design set against the backdrop of a civilization rich in aesthetic heritage. Consequently, the objects associated with "Made in Italy" were not just leading export commodities, they were products of high culture, and were promoted as among the highest achievements of a nation with an unsurpassed record of artistic and epicurean glories. Naturally, non-Italian producers try to cash in wherever possible on the cachet of Italy. Today, for example, Hong Kong stores are full of Italian-sounding labels that you won't find in the land of Moschino and Valentino.

Though I have been focusing on the manufacture of the national brand, I do not, of course, mean to suggest that, prior to 1980, Italy had a negligible history of craft manufacture. Quite the contrary. Venerable handicraft and artisanal traditions abounded, as did longstanding regional expertise in a variety of industries: textile, clothing, ceramics, glass, knitwear, leather, furniture. Florentine linen, woolens from Biella, knitwear from Prato, ceramics from Sesto and Montelupo, shoes and leather from the Marches, and the silk industry of Como—all had been justly famous for their craft for centuries. Indeed, the new national brand leaned heavily on homage to craft antiquity, even as it drew on the mercurial reputation of the artisanal-industrial districts of the Third Italy that proved an endless source of fascination to economists in other G7 countries from the 1960s onward.

Nor was the idea of the national brand itself an entirely new concept in Italy. Mussolini had been there before with the trademark *Ideazione e Produzione Nazionale* ("Conceived and Made in Italy"), issued by his National Fashion Authority in 1935. Dressmakers had to observe national quotas; at least 50 percent of any collection had to bear the trademark or they would be fined. The Fascist version of *la linea italiana* drew entirely from homegrown styles (mostly based on regional peasant dress), materials, and methods of manufacture, and was ordained by Mussolini's autarkic policy of import substitution. The policy aimed at industrial and stylistic self-sufficiency, liberated from the orbit of Paris, and was directed chiefly at domestic markets.[3] The national brand proposition that emerged in the 1980s was assisted, though not directed or dictated, by government policies, and it was aimed primarily at export markets where it has proven powerful enough to sidestep the French influence, all but vanquishing Parisian competition in some quarters.

Nor, finally, do I mean to suggest that "Made in Italy" is merely a brand, enjoying an exclusively Platonic, or immaterial, life in the upper world of finance capital. The trade statistics that underpin it are real enough and they are very impressive. Taking advantage of a low exchange rate for the devalued lira, which made exports relatively cheap, volume in the garment and textiles trade tripled in the course of the 1980s. By 1999, fashion and design were a $22 billion export industry, boasting more than 70,000 companies, employing more than 700,000, and claiming world leadership in the ready-to-wear market. Wood furnishing, another number-one export, which experienced a similar boom, accounted for $8 billion in overseas sales, and employed another 400,000 in Italy.[4] Other products that make Italy a world trade leader include eyeglasses, ceramic tiles, kitchen products, lamps, and refrigerators. By far the most notable achievement, however, is that today Italy is the only significant exporter of homespun clothing among the advanced industrial countries, and that it sustains a large share of an industry that is otherwise almost wholly the preserve of low-wage, developing nations. All the more remarkable that it has done so under the rubric of small-scale craft, rather than mass production. No wonder that the Italian way has been heralded as the darling of postindustrial growth and development in the rich countries of the world.

Though the Italian manufacturing system is touted as the savior of craft manufacture, it has escaped close scrutiny because a large part of it is off-the-books. *Craft* is a key term in the promotional rhetoric of virtually every Italian manufacturer, because it evokes an unbroken tradition of making things by hand in artisanal workshops as old as the Renaissance. The elusive style—*la bella figura*—of the Italian product is supposed to derive from the knowledge passed down in these workshops. Some part of this reputation is sheer necromancy, conjured up to breathe value into the product's price. Traditionally, the mystique attached to craft was a result of the survivalist need of its practitioners to protect their knowledge of techniques and rules of the trade, inducting apprentices only under closely controlled conditions. This legacy is strong enough that, even today, craft skills are perceived to harbor some charismatically hidden element that cannot be duplicated by machines. Yet the modernized craft units of production that support "Made in Italy" bear little resemblance to the preindustrial workshop. In one respect, however, they have added a new "intangible" element to the traditional mysteries of craft. They thrive on an underground economy—by far the largest in the industrialized world—that must stay hidden from view, lest its substandard labor conditions corrode the aura of the product.

Whether it can be restored to former glories, or reinvent a new mode of production, craft is not a magic wand that spirits away habitual forms of labor exploitation. Yet the craft-conscious story of "Made in Italy" has encouraged us to imagine that it could do so. Which is why I began this chapter with my story about the Fila store. With the emergence of a vigilant anti-sweatshop movement in the last decade, the world's leading garment companies have been living dangerously. They are all too aware of the damage that headline-grabbing exposés of brutal labor conditions can do to their brands. Despite the tendency of anti-sweatshop activists to hold "Made in Italy" in relatively high esteem, Italian producers have hardly been immune, or blameless, and have lately been targeted by European watchdog groups like the Clean Clothes Campaign. Top-of the-line houses like Gucci (the savior, in 2000, of an industry in the doldrums) have taken a hit in recent years from revelations about its contractors' sweatshops in India, where child labor is rife, and where workers are often paid less than one cent per garment. Gucci's parent firm, PPR (which also owns Yves Saint Laurent), has a deplorable track

The mysteries of craft, artisanal shop, Florence
(PHOTO BY AUTHOR)

record for working conditions at its suppliers' factories in Bangkok (which the Thai Labour Campaign reports as some of the worst it has seen): in Bandung, Indonesia, where workers collapse on the job from exhaustion; in Romania, where fourteen-hour days, seven days a week are a common work schedule; or in Karachi, Pakistan, where its employee wages are far below the legal minimum.[5]

Child labor has also come under scrutiny in the Turkish contract shops of mid-market leader Benetton, best known for its carefully cultivated image as a socially concerned company, through its provocative ad campaigns and eco-conscious *Colors* magazine. Heralded as an innovator of just-in-time production, point-of-sale distribution feedback, and savvy "global village" marketing, Benetton has long attracted criticism for its use of as many as 600 nonunionized subcontractors, an increasing number of whom are located in the cheapest labor markets of the South. With only a fraction of its workers directly employed by the company, its supplier shops are purposely located in places like inland Sicily in order to draw recruits from the nation's poorest pockets of labor. Female employees at one such Sicilian supplier were told to schedule their marriages and pregnancies in shifts to ensure the continuity of production. Most recently, the Clean Clothes Campaign has collected a spate of complaints about conditions in Benetton suppliers in Egypt and Romania, where one woman, for example, reported that she "has to work an average of 240–260 hours a month to reach the target and receive her basic wage (which is not a living wage)."[6]

With this kind of evidence of the upward creep of labor exploitation into the mid-end and quality garment markets, no one can be surprised to discover that a sportswear house like Fila has joined its rivals like Nike and Adidas in taking advantage of the substandard wages of export zones in developing countries. Yet "Made in Italy" continues to enjoy a relatively benign reputation among anti-sweatshop activists in the U.S. for its association with humane labor conditions. Is this simply an outcome of effective marketing? Does it result from a need on the part of activists to be able to cite any kind of good news? Or is it an accurate reflection of some of the fundamental components of Italian manufacturing?

Ever Closer to Home

While the export zones of developing countries still provide the best bargains for cheap and easy production, sweatshops that employ Third World workers have moved much closer to home, and now account for a substantial portion of the garment production sector in Italy. Italy's large underground economy (*lavoro nero*) is mostly based on personal, familial, or community bonds that have been deeply rooted for generations. But it has been turbo-boosted in the last decade by undocumented immigration and by people-smuggling on the part of international gangster networks. Traditionally a labor donor to more industrialized countries, Italy, since the early 1980s, has been a receiver of migrant labor, and largely because of the ease of entry into its underground economy. With the addition of the new immigrant streams, the irregular economy now accounts for an estimated 27 percent of gross domestic product, putting Italy way out in front of other industrialized countries (the European average is 15 percent).[7]

At the tip of the iceberg are indentured Chinese migrants, forced to work in near-slavery in garment, textile, and leather factories for little or no pay in order to remit the smuggling debts owed to their traffickers. In 1999, a series of police raids, culminating in the much-publicized "Operation Sunrise," uncovered a network of Chinese and Italian gangsters that delivered Chinese workers into substandard labor conditions in towns and cities all across Italy. Aside from the mini-Chinatowns springing up in major cities, immigrants from the old Soviet bloc, Turkey, India, Southeast Asia, and the Balkans have joined hundreds of thousands of Africans escaping from destitution in the *lavoro nero* that supports "Made in Italy" more than ever today. Indeed, it is estimated that the business of human trafficking into Europe is now larger than the drug trade.[8] In addition, Italy has an estimated 300,000 child workers, many of them laboring in concentrated urban areas, like the myriad of family businesses operating on the densely packed slopes of Mount Vesuvius in Naples.[9] The demand for overnight turnaround, the intense pricing pressure, and the industry's traditional patterns of putting out make the garment contractor shops the first port of call for traffickers looking to place unskilled and semiskilled workers. A sweatshop subcontractor can supply items at a fraction of the operating and labor costs of a legal, taxpaying shop. The most vulnerable workers can toil for years in these mini-factories without making much of a dent on contract debts that can run as high as $25,000 for their passage to the promised land.

Who knows how much of Italy's impressive growth in fashion and design is dependent on the sweatshops of the underground economy? The true estimate is buried somewhere between the *sommerso statistico*—or lost information, which the state does not collect—and the *sommerso economico*—or submerged economy, which employers will not disclose. One result is not in doubt, however. The health of the nation's trade figures hangs in the balance. Without its sprawling off-the-books economy—involving multifarious forms of irregular, informal, and illegal work—the oft-proclaimed "miracles" of Italian manufacturing would look more like mirages. In addition, for every employer tax receipt that goes uncollected by the state, and is therefore unavailable for redistribution as public investment and social security, an equivalent profit margin flows unrecorded into the individual treasuries of the private sector. In this way, the underground economy serves as an efficient vehicle for channeling money from the public to the private sector. The geographical impact of this money traffic is equally regressive. Perpetuating long-standing patterns of regional exploitation, the redistributive flow of wealth is still from the South, with the largest share of irregular labor, through the subcontractor supply chain, to the North where the parent companies are concentrated. The new economy of urban sweatshops in the North is only just beginning to alter this deeply embedded model of regional underdevelopment. Lastly, and most lamentably, it is women and children who are at the short end of the stick of irregularization, since they end up doing the most unpleasant, and lowliest paid, tasks.

What is most important to grasp is that these violations of fair labor and taxation standards are not merely a problem of recent provenance. In other words, they are not an unfortunate blight visited upon Italy by foreigners, streaming into the country through its semi-porous borders. They are rooted in conditions and industrial patterns that are a crucial element of the account of "Made in Italy" that romanticizes small, craft-based firms competing against all the odds on the unforgiving field of hardscrabble capitalism. Most relevant in this regard is the storied career of the Third Italy, that wide band of industrial districts in the country's central and northeastern regions— Tuscany, Emilia-Romagna, the Veneto, and the Adriatic Marches—which earned so much praise from economists from the 1960s through the 1980s for the petty entrepreneurial pluck of its artisans. In their heyday, the small firms and industrial networks of these regional districts competed directly in international markets, proving to many admirers of human-scale capitalism that such a thing could still be done in a G7 country.

For example, the Tuscan regional center of Prato, one of the more celebrated of the industrial districts, commands up to 20 percent of world exports in woolen knitwear. In the 1950s, its large integrated textile mills were broken down and distributed into a network of smaller shops linked by autonomous federations. The Pratese experiments with "fantasy" yarn (*tessuti fantasia*), cottage industry, and computer-based flexibility were hailed as a competitive way

Two great cuisines meet,
Prato Chinatown
(PHOTO BY AUTHOR)

forward.[10] Today, the continued success of this regional economy, still growing at an annual rate of over 15 percent, rests on the enterprise of its hundreds of Chinese-owned factories and workshops. Since the late 1980s, over 20,000 of these immigrants have taken up residence there (one-tenth of the area's population), and Prato's Chinatown is now the third largest in Europe, next to Paris and Milan. Many of the textile shops operate legally, but as many as 40 percent are underground, and they serve as a magnet for forced labor. In a statement more likely to be heard from a Chamber of Commerce president,

Giovanni Cortese, general secretary of labor union CISL in Prato, remarked: "The mentality of the Chinese is not far from the mentality of an Italian." Elaborating on this observation, he added, "Our family-owned companies also work eleven hours a day when necessary."[11] Such comments are likely to be taken with a grain of salt if you are putting in a seventy-hour week just to make ends meet, or to make a dent in your trafficker's debt. To be sure, Prato's dual economy is exacerbated by the immigrant flow, but its combination of a legal, high-wage core and a periphery of low-wage, sweatshop suppliers is not a "Chinese" import. This kind of structure has a long history in the international garment industry, and, as we will see, some version of it was apparent even in the heyday of the so-called economic miracle that occurred in regional centers like Prato from the late 1960s to the 1980s.

Prato Chinatown (PHOTO BY AUTHOR)

The Third Italy was actually the second of Italy's postwar "economic miracles." The first had occurred in the Industrial Triangle of the North when migrant workers from the South made common cause with Northern artisans in the Americanized factories of Fiat and Pirelli. In the effort to bring it fully into the international capitalist system, and because it was a crucial arena of the Cold War, Italy received a higher percentage of Marshall Plan aid than almost any other European country, and by far the largest volume of anti-Communist propaganda.[12] The introduction of U.S.-style Fordism, combined with deflationary policies that depressed wages, helped to transform Italy's largely peasant economy into that of an industrial power in the space of less than three decades. Northern textile factories had survived the war almost intact, and many industrialists used the Marshall money to import modern plant machinery, while taking advantage of relatively cheap labor to create a sizeable export market.[13] Yet the industrial system also brought an instant labor movement, forged out of artisans and peasants' traditions of resistance, and its strength and power quickened in tandem with the rapid modernization. Faced with rising wages, and an increasingly militant trade union movement, the industrialists began to decentralize and disperse their operations into subcontracting in order to regroup and regain control over the factories. Following the logic of fragmentation of work away from the factory assembly line, giants like Fiat even ended up producing some car parts in the home, in more or less the conditions of the cottage industry that had prevailed earlier in the century.

Not all of this decentralization was regressive, however. What proved more competitive than the devolution of mass production was the flexible division of labor generated by the small firms just to the south, many of them started up by artisans who had been expelled from the large industrial plants for their radical politics or who had become disaffected with the de-skilling they had confronted in the factory system. Freed from the rigid hierarchies of the large firm, these small enterprises were able to innovate with their employees' skills, and they proved more agile in finding industrial solutions to the challenge of international competition. They specialized in every phase of production, and were linked within their own industrial district to a cooperative network of suppliers and final firms concentrated within the same sector (such as footwear, knitwear, ceramic tiles, or jewelry). The districts also received benevolent, though differing forms of, support from a broad range of institutions, including local governments—both Communist, in Red Zones like Tuscany and Emilia, and Catholic, in White Zones like the Veneto. For many of these districts the result was a horizontal integrated system, nimble enough to respond to the new demands for product diversification and customization.[14] Labor conditions seemed decent, blue-collar income was higher than the national average, and unemployment dramatically lower than in the rest of the country.

The Emilian model, as it was sometimes known (though regional variations were considerable), was trumpeted as the answer to the problems faced by industrial societies after the crisis of Fordism in the 1970s.[15] Indeed, it was viewed as the first significant alternative to the mass production systems arrayed (like great industrial armies) on both sides of the Cold War, and its success evoked a future that lay beyond the mutually assured destruction of the fully Taylorized superpowers.[16] The parochial spirit of the district system, in particular, was hailed as an indigenous alternative to the universalizing system of national Fordism. Though it had acquired a national flag, anthem, and government, Italy remained, after all, a digest of regions with identities that were much stronger than that of the centralized state. So too it was estimated that communities of trust, bound by deep-seated personal ties to the extended family structure, were more likely to support initiative and innovation than the often impersonal relationships of the factory floor. Along with its German counterpart, Baden-Wuerrtemberg, the regional system of the Third Italy became the acceptable face of advanced capitalism in its frantic quest for a post-Fordist success story. Compared to the economies of NICs like Singapore, Taiwan, and South Korea, which were being developed under the direct control of state managers, the growth of the Third Italy appeared to be self-directed, even though the districts received a good deal of material support from local government, credit cooperatives, trade associations, and development agencies. Long the poor country cousin of its Northern and Western European neighbors, Italy was now the talk of the town.

After decades of assembly-line alienation under Taylorist management regimes, nothing was more alluring to labor-watching liberals than the prospect of free artisans choosing their own destiny. Listen to Charles Sabel, probably the most influential of the regions' Anglophone boosters: "If you had thought so long about Rousseau's artisan clockmakers at Neuchâtel, or

Marx's idea of labor as joyful self-creative association, that you had begun to doubt their possibility, then you might, watching these craftsmen at work, forgive yourself the sudden conviction that something more utopian than the present factory system is practical after all."[17] Sabel's Emilian "small-is-beautiful" model was a wet dream of happy artisans who had survived the onslaught of mass industrialization and were now beating the giants at their own game.

For analysts like Sabel, the impressive economic performance of the Third Italy in the 1960s and 1970s suggested that the basic labor principle of the hierarchical factory system—the separation of the conception of tasks from their execution—had not proved sustainable in the long run. Adam Smith's law of increasing efficiency through an ever greater division of labor had been triumphantly overturned, and craft production had prevailed.[18] In the workshops of the Third Italy's Marshallian districts, conception and execution were being reintegrated in ways that proved more efficient and competitive in the global economy. Artisans with multiple skills, and with both theoretical and practical knowledge of their tools and materials, were making decisions and solving production problems as they went along. The result must surely be stimulating to the minds of workers, at least in contrast with assembly-line alienation on the job. In his most idyllic portraits, Sabel reached for the inevitable comparison with artists. The craftworker, he wrote, is like "a versatile musician who sight-reads difficult works but also, drawing on the same underlying faculties, improvises interpretations," while "the group of cooperating firms is analogous to an orchestra whose members follow a conductor's general interpretation, but would be insulted in their musicianship if instructed as to how to produce the required sounds."[19]

A closer look at the workshops told a different story. Even Sabel noted that while some were spotless, and employed skilled workers were earning more than the northern factory union wage, others resembled traditional runaway sweatshops, relying heavily on the extended family to absorb the sacrifice of long hours, reduced overheads, and cost reduction.[20] In fact, the new industrial system had been fashioned out of legacies of a proto-industrial landscape that had hosted artisanal workshop production alongside sharecropping and feudal indenture. Many of the Third Italy's districts displayed a dual labor market—a core of skilled, and primarily male, craftworkers, whose skills were upgraded as a result of the new flexible production system, and a periphery of unskilled domestic outworkers, primarily women, who performed repetitive tasks, usually fulfilling one small phase of production. One analyst suggests that 15 percent were core, parent firms, employing the skilled artisans, while all the rest were low-wage subcontractors, either in small shops or working out of homes.[21] Large firms that were organized, like the regions, for flexible specialization, displayed much the same pattern. For example, Benetton's small, internal labor force, responsible for controlling and coordinating production, was skilled and predominantly male, while its vast contractor network (Fiorenza Belussi calls it a "big moving assembly line," or "decentralized Fordism") offered repetitive work to unskilled women aged between seventeen and twenty-five years.[22] Historically, it should be noted that this pattern is fairly typical in the garment industry, with skilled cutters and pattern makers enjoying some measure of artisanal autonomy and compensation, and a sweating system that employed low-wage sewers and homeworkers in substandard conditions.

In Italy, however, this pattern was reinforced not only by the new demands for flexible specialization, but also by new labor regulations introduced in the early 1970s. Under intense pressure from the labor movement, especially after the mass strikes of the *autumno caldo* in 1969, the government passed the Labor Charter (*Statuto dei Lavoratori*) in 1970, which guaranteed organizing and bargaining rights along with unemployment benefits to industrial workers in large firms. Just as important, however, the legislation exempted "artisans firms" (defined as under fifteen workers) from bargaining, and from meeting many tax and welfare responsibilities. Because of its two-tier provisions, the legislation was simultaneously a landmark in labor regulation *and* deregulation. One hand institutionalized a benefit-rich primary labor market, while the other hand encouraged industrial deconcentration and the underground economy. Outworking was now even more advantageous to firms struggling to keep their payroll under the magic number, thereby avoiding the full cost of employers' contributions for worker comp packages. The result was a huge boost in self-employment and small firm formation, directly tied to the prospect of profiting from off-the-books enterprise. By 1984, it is estimated that 95 percent of all Italian firms declared annual incomes below the $75 thousand threshold that would have required them, under the terms of the *Statuto*, to open up their books to the tax authorities.[23]

Homeworkers were also subject to new legislation in 1973. Relatively unknown before industrial manufacturing took root in the Third Italy, homeworking had swelled precipitously, only to be submerged in the *lavoro nero*. The legislation was passed in an effort to integrate homeworkers into the regular workforce; it was an attempt to regulate, and normalize, wages and working conditions in the home. In return for tax and social welfare contributions, homeworkers were entitled to pensions, benefits, maternity leave, and children's allowances. In practice, however, many homeworkers responded to the law by registering as artisans in order to avoid making contributions, or else their contractors forced them to do so to avoid their own employer contributions.[24]

For "true" artisans, the quality of work life was not quite as idyllic as the armchair analysts had imagined. Michael Blim's 1990 ethnography of a shoewear district in the Marches showed that artisans actually had little margin for autonomy. Their piece rate was rigidly set by subcontractors, along with quotas and rates of production. The fragile, shifting landscape of firms, constantly starting up and going out of business, made the quest for contractual stability ceaseless and all-consuming. Contrary to the favored portrait of their work as multiskilled, and technologically sophisticated, Blim found their tasks were more often labor-intensive and low-tech. The venerable know-how, tools, and self-direction of the artisanal cobbler were barely in evidence. According to Augusto Prosperi, a factory foreman who figures in Blim's book, the cutting, stitching, and glueing of the traditional shoemaker had the simple nobility of a "poor person's craft." "Skill was a consequence of finesse rather than force; it took a sure hand rather than a sophisticated tool. It was matter of making things fit." With the new machinery, Prosperi reported that it is "possible to make a shoe without finesse, without the attention to detail that marked the work of the traditional cobbler. Nowadays skill is equated with speed and accuracy" and productivity is all-important in a just-in-time market. Like the older, experienced workers, who knew that "the days of the true shoemaker are over," Prosperi concluded: "The workers employed now don't know a thing about how to make a shoe. . . . They know one machine and one set of motions: take them off their machines to help out in another area, and they can't perform—they're lost."[25]

Workers like Prosperi were lamenting the loss of true craftsmanship at exactly the moment that Sabel and others were touting the resurgence of craft as an innovative force in the districts. Yet if price pressure and technological de-skilling were taking their toll on craft traditions, as Prosperi observed, by far the larger burden fell on the unskilled. As competition with cheaper labor sectors in the Mezzogiorno, Mauritius, Turkey, Tunisia, East Asia, and South Asia increased, by the late 1980s the continued growth of the Third Italy depended more and more on the women, children, and the elderly—the most vulnerable members of the labor force.[26] Many of these other countries relied heavily on homework and familial exploitation, but the majority produced on contract for parent firms in the West. Italian firms were more unique in selling directly to the market, and so the constraints took more complex forms. The underground economy would become even more important when developing countries like Brazil began to challenge Italy's dominance in the quality markets, and when large firms had sufficiently restructured themselves into leaner, and meaner, organizations.

The Branding Years

The "Made in Italy" campaign, when it got under way in the late 1970s and early 1980s, was a godsend to some firms and an ordeal to others. Attaching your firm or supplier network to a designer brand name soon became the ticket to survival, not only for the small artisanal enterprises, but also for the large northern fabric companies that sought out and backed the most promising new designers who had been working solo: GFT backed Armani, IT Holdings backed Versace and Ferre, HDP backed Valentino. Milan appointed itself as the epicenter of ready-to-wear. Couture houses flocked there (Krizia and Missoni, the knitwear kingpins, were the first, in the mid-1970s) from the old *alta moda* capital of Rome, and the postwar fashion center of Florence, established after Giovanni Giorgino's famous Sala Bianca shows in the early 1950s at the Palazzo Pitti. Along with the move in location and exhibition, family companies with an established name in accessories like Trussardi (glovemaking), Gucci (leather), Fendi (fur), and later, Prada (bags and shoes) seized the opportunity to expand into full lines of pret-a-porter, taking advantage of the new supplier networks. The elegance, quality fabric, and casual profile of the Milanese lines were in winning contrast to the histrionic couture of Paris, with its over-the-top, elitist connotations. For a generation of tastemakers emerging out of the counterculture, Milan's refined sportswear would win many of the battles for fashion-world dominance.

With the mercurial rise of Armani and others, a star system was put in place around Milan that generated demand for the entire, quality ready-to-wear industry. The added value generated internationally by "Made in Italy" trickled down, in principle, to every provincial supplier. Lesser brands sailed along in the slipstream of the luminaries. While entrepreneurs from the provinces have always looked to hitch themselves to brand names, the need became more and more paramount. Many local networks sought to launch their own brands, even though they lacked the capital resources required to sustain the brand name on a global basis. From the mid-1980s, selling was more and more media-driven by the communicability and visibility of the design, and had less to do with the materiality of the product. Eventually, the 1990s saw a rash of mergers and takeovers as firms scrambled to acquire the capital to feed their brands. This occurred not only at the top, where the big-name houses went public and multinational, but all the way down to the industrial districts, whose firms had only been able to compete internationally by pooling their needs through a sales and marketing consortium, or by using the collective resource of regional service centers. The pressure of commercial marketing on a global scale was especially acute for small craft firms operating on a limited local base.[27] Small was no longer so beautiful, and many of the integrated sectors that had proved so resilient within the Third Italy's craft districts lost their edge. Increased competition from low-wage countries meant that the districts had to concentrate exclusively on quality wear. More and more of these regions' final firms were forced to use foreign subcontractors.[28] In addition, at the national level, their competitive advantage was being challenged by the new sweatshops of the immigrant underground economy, mostly located in major urban centers.

Nor was it clear that the national brand was making the same impact on a new generation of fashion consumers as it had for their parents. The most visible example was the rise of Diesel, an Italian youth fashion company whose international marketing made reference to almost every culture except Italy's. The company's celebrated campaign ("Diesel For Successful Living") introduced provocation ads that fully exploited the irony and bad-taste chic of Generation X.[29] Diesel's marketing was the exact antithesis of a brand like Pellegrino, for example—"Whatever Language You Speak, Live in Italian"— that exhorted international consumers to purchase a taste of La Dolce Vita. In Diesel's world, identification with Italy was a liability, as was any association with the kind of good taste to which "Made in Italy" appealed in its evocation of craft and quality. In addition, since the company contracts out 100 percent of its production, Diesel has no stake at all in proclaiming any local or regional affiliation.

In that same arena where the coolhunters roam, "Made in Italy" faced a new kind of competition from Cool Britannia, the Blair government's brazen attempt to rebrand its national culture with a more dynamic, postmodern profile. Like the Italian effort, which the U.K. was updating, Cool Britannia was aimed at the export markets for British pop music, design, art, fashion, film, and other cultural products.[30] Yet, with the exception of youth training programs aimed at the creative industries, Cool Britannia was almost entirely a promotional crusade. There was little direct government support for the industries themselves, and since few of them sustained manufacturing jobs of any significant quantity, the brand was not connected to an industrial base, as was still the case in Italy. Young solo fashion designers, for example, were no longer heralded as heroic prototypes of the petty entrepreneur, as they had been in Margaret Thatcher's day. In hopes that they could be paragons of export marketing by proving to the rest of the world the sheer superiority of ultra-hip

British image-making, they were encouraged to compete for themselves on an international basis.[31] With little in the way of resources, this would be a hard sell against predatory titans of corporate fashion like Prada. The flaw in the ill-fated Cool Britannia policy was that it took too literally the alleged power of immaterial values—style, image-making, and design buzz—to lead and shape economic patterns. Appropriately, the idea of national rebranding had an export life of its own, as country after country followed the U.K. in attempts to engineer a modernized self-image for international consumption.

A better, though much less visible, counterexample to "Made in Italy"'s national brand and Diesel's transnational version would be the recent rise of an Asian design infrastructure in Manhattan's Little Italy. With Chinatown on its eastern border, this neighborhood had hosted a tug of war between the two ethnic zones for several decades. The new storefront Asian boutiques, which opened in the early 1990s amid delicatessens and restaurants that purvey Italian produce primarily for tourist consumption, were, in large part, an intergenerational phenomenon. For their craft know-how and industry contacts, many of the young entrepreneurs relied on their extended families who had worked in the low end of the garment industry for decades. Their social capital emerged directly, and organically, as Thuy Linh Tu has argued, from the sweat equity of their parents and grandparents in the rag trade. Yet they were also riding the buzz generated by "Asian chic," a surge of Western interest in all things Asian that had followed in the wake of economic boom in East Asia.[32] The ascendancy of Italian fashion occurred after generations of migrant seamstresses and sewers had contributed greatly to the economy of other countries—Italians, for example, formed the majority of the garment workforce in New York City by the 1930s. The rise of Chinese design may follow suit, but it is just as likely to be a transnational affair, drawing resources from Chinatowns in the world's major urban centers, as from any strategic attempt, however unlikely, to transform "Made in China" from a bargain-basement label into a brand that evokes virtuoso flair. "Made by Chinese" may be a more accurate description of the result.

Anti-immigrant
sentiment in Italy
(PHOTO BY AUTHOR)

Second Thoughts

As if oblivious to all these changes underfoot, the juggernaut of national image development—i.e., the promotion of "Made in Italy"—runs on, as vigorously as ever, barely deviating from its well-worn path. Aside from the coordinating agency of the Italian Trade Commission, primary among the promotional organizations is Sistema Moda Italia (the Italian Association of Textile, Apparel, and Related Industries), which is the world's largest grouping of clothing manufacturers, offering a broad spectrum of support and promotional services to its members: industrial and economic policy, international marketing and promotion, R&D, training, technological innovation, in addition to financial support and concessions. Among its agencies are Promozione Moda Italia, which organizes the major Milan shows, Ente Moda Italiana, which promotes Italian brands in centers like New York, Paris, Tokyo, Moscow, and Hong Kong; and EFIMA and Pitti Immagine, which organize the wool, textile, and clothing fairs that have been a distinctive feature of Italian industry since medieval times.

The most high-profile product of the promotional apparatus is the canon-making solo exhibition at a premier art museum, like the Armani show at the New York Guggenheim in 2001, or the Versace show at London's Victoria and Albert in 2002. These headlining events in the art world are the culmination of fifteen years of landmark shows and exhibitions devoted to the thematic product range of "Made in Italy" at sites like the Stazione Leopolda in Florence, the Milan Triennale, and key trade locations overseas. Lavish catalogs from these shows combine serious academic commentary with unashamed boosterism.[33] As Raffaello Napoleone, CEO of Pitti Imagine, puts it, the "cultural research" undertaken by his organization's Fashion Engineering Unit, is "in step" with the "work of marketing," and the combined aim is to "give a voice and visibility to that system of 'person-fashion-furnishings-home-food' in which Italy has thus far established its international leadership."[34]

Notwithstanding the far-flung geographical scope of the subcontractor chain, both inside and, increasingly, outside the nation, promoters of "Made in Italy" can be counted on to point to the self-contained nature of the system's production, marketing, and distribution arms. For example, Mario Boselli, president of Pitti Immagine, draws attention to the coordination of each of the system's "fundamental assets": "the completeness and unification of the entire integrated manufacturing sector, the organizational flexibility of the companies, the social and economic networks of communications and cooperation in the various industrial districts, the wealth of professional skills and abilities, the widespread entrepreneurial spirit, and the international mind-set of the businessmen." The industrial efficiency with which these, and other features, are orchestrated is in marked contrast to the disorganization that Boselli describes as "the historic shortcomings of Italian society."[35] Indeed, the capitalist dynamism of "Made in Italy" is consistently differentiated from the nation's other claims to fame: its sclerotic, corrupt bureaucracy, and the dysfunctionalism of its political system. Yet the two are hardly disconnected. From the point of view of industrialists, the good arm of the state provides infrastructural and policy support for promotion of their private enterprise, while the "bad," dysfunctional arm enables the underground economy that provides much of the cheap labor to industry.

One of the strongest promotional elements is the emphasis on the family basis for the building of industrial empires. Many of the most well-known companies in the "Made in Italy" system are not listed on any stock exchange, and are firmly within the control of family members. Family dynasties (Benetton, Zegna, Gucci, Prada, Ferragamo, Missoni, Busnelli, Maramotti) run in the Italian grain, whether they have an aristocratic lineage, along with a requisite palazzo—as in the case of the debonair Emilio Pucci, the Marchese of Barsento and 1960s progenitor of ready-to-wear—or whether they came up in the school of hard knocks. Even hotshot individualists depend on close kin (Gianni Versace and his sister Donatella are the best-known example) to cement the strong ideology of the family business in the national culture. Yet this tradition of family capitalism is not always so kind to its female members and youth. For every Italian family that is a glossy success story, there are a thousand others that provide a cost-efficient base for low-wage manufacture, exacting especially heavy tolls on women who do double duty in the labor force and in reproducing the household. Amid the faceless corporate bureaucracy of modern capitalism, the Italian family enterprise is a noble entity, but its sacrificial labor system is an ancient curse.

In the course of the rise of the Third Italy, for example, the region's women enjoyed significant gains, and exceeded the national average in their share of the entrepreneurial, or self-employed labor force. Yet, they continued to shoulder the household and child-care burden, even as the home became the locus of their participation in output. The economic and cultural cohesion of the extended family also meant that elderly relatives and children were easily available to play their role in production as cheap, surplus labor. With much of this economic activity off the books, the kin-based unit of family production afforded the region its comparative low-wage advantage within Europe for several decades.[36] With the development of the immigrant urban sweatshop, provincial familialism would come to compete with an even cheaper form of the family as a work group.

At the high end of the "Made in Italy" production chain, the focus on family carries some additional risk, especially in the area of public relations. Within the public corporation, it has become rote for faceless managers and executives to evade responsibility for labor exploitation further down the supplier chain. Leaders of family organizations are more likely to be held accountable. Indeed, part of the aura of the family company involves assuming quasi-feudal responsibility for the well-being of all of its "children." Exposure of abuse or corruption has a direct impact on the firm through the personality of the figurehead, as was the case in the charges of tax evasion brought upon both Versace and Armani. Yet this risk is still far outweighed by the benefits accrued from milking the cozy iconography of the close-knit, industrious Italian family. In popular and official culture, caring imagery of this kinship group is celebrated time and time again as a bulwark against the curses of modern capitalism; its cruel anonymity, soulless materialism, and corporate giantism. At a time when the repute of the public corporation has seldom been lower, family firms in a kin-based industry have a distinct ethical advantage.

Promotion of "Made in Italy" joins the idolatry of family with a heady reverence for craft. The result is a potent cocktail, guaranteeing immunity from moral prosecution. This poses an especial problem for those of us in the anti-sweatshop movement who, all too often, have taken the romance of this national brand on trust. When the conscientious consumer asks for advice on sweat-free shopping, most anti-sweatshop activists will recommend that any "Made in Italy" label is likely to be a safe bet. More than likely, this belief arises from the carefully nurtured image of craft production in an advanced industrial democracy. So desirable is this image that Nike recently tried to earn some labor points by touting that it had chosen Italy—"a vibrant democracy," in the words of its PR wing—as one of its production bases. But when we recommend "Made in Italy" labels, what does this advice indicate? Certainly that Italian workers are better paid than production workers in South China's low-wage factories. But does it also assume that their jobs are more *precious* than those of Chinese workers? Or even that the jobs of Chinese migrant workers in Italy are more precious than those of Chinese migrant workers in an offshore zone like Saipan?

If so, then it is time we weaned ourselves from such notions, and accepted the equal value of workers' interests everywhere. It may also be time to take a closer look at the realities of Italian craft production, as I have tried to do briefly in this chapter. Artisans are not always labor aristocrats, neither today nor in preindustrial times. Just because artisans are not factory wageworkers does not make them free, or any more capable of controlling their time and labor value. Yes, an artisan can be a skilled, apprenticed craftsman (especially if he is male) who is functionally flexible in the application of those skills. But (and especially if she is a woman) she is more likely to be an off-the-books homeworker who accepts job enlargement (as opposed to job enrichment) as a matter of familial sacrifice or self-exploitation.

Italian history is a rich case study of the vagaries attached to the concept of the artisan, because politics plays a visible and ever-changing role in appealing to the artisan's self-image and self-interest. For example, the artisan-firm category was introduced originally by the Fascists as a wedge with which to forge a bloc between big capital and the petite bourgeoisie. For the Christian Democrats who exempted these firms under the *Statuto dei Lavoratori*, promoting the artisan was an effective way of introducing labor deregulation and eroding union power. For the Communists who governed many of the artisan-heavy districts in the Third Italy, it was a way of winning the allegiance of the petite bourgeoisie and staving off a revival of the Fascist coalition.[37] The identity of the artisan could evoke a history of resistance to the Fascists and the factory bosses alike, or it could simply be the legal category under which a homeworker registers herself because her *impannatore* tells her to do so. For the industrialists who pitch their wares by mouthing the "mysteries of craft," all of this is grist for the mill, but these distinctions should speak volumes for those of us who care about the conditions of those who make our clothing.

Manchester United crest/trademark

CHAPTER THREE

Friedrich Engels Visits the Old Trafford Megastore

PARIS CATWALKS are no stranger to oddity, and the Adidas shoes designed by Yohji Yamamoto, introduced to the retail trade for the spring 2003 fashion season, were hardly outrageous by *fashionista* standards. The celebrated Japanese designer had built some elaborate upper shoe variations upon the traditional sneaker sole, and tweaked the famous three-stripe emblem in distinctive ways. Yet his collection, which also included apparel and accessories, was the most high-profile evidence to date that the fashion and sports industries had entered into serious wedlock. After twenty years of flirting, courting, and coupling, they were now joined at the seam. Adidas's Sports Style division, set up to be directed by Yohji, was being groomed as the company's number-one growth sector for the foreseeable future. Adidas was hardly alone among its competitors in athletic wear—Puma had struck a deal with Hamburg design firm Jil Sander, Mindy Grossman, a designer from Polo Ralph Lauren, had been recruited by Nike to pump new life into its apparel lines, and Keds had hired Todd Oldham to redesign its low-tech classics in a nostalgia bid. On the other side of the aisle, lines such as Prada Sport, Missoni Sport, Polo Sport, and DKNY Activewear were all launched with a similar goal in mind—to establish a stake in the high-design market that has sought to convert the legendary allegiances of sports fans into consumer brand loyalties.

The growing synergy of these two industries—trading on the underlying sympathy between fitness and beauty—was a logical outcome of corporate efforts to sustain brands in a global market by expanding their domains of influence. Higher-end profits were being mined by injecting some glamour into an active-wear market with a lower price ceiling. Designer lines reached beyond ready-to-wear to tap into the much broader market for casual apparel. These merchandizing moves were very much in step with the steady march of informality into all aspects of our lives. In addition, the fashion-sports nuptials benefited from breaking apart some of the gender profiles that have traditionally governed the fashion and sports worlds. In particular, the street fashion influence of iconic male athletes like Dennis Rodman and David Beckham—neither of them men's men in any traditional sense—was a cornerstone of this crossbreed consumerism.

One of the consequences of the new synergy was that sports apparel produced with low labor costs now had high-impact visibility. The payoff in profits was much higher, but so were the risks of exposure and public criticism that came with all this extra attention. It became more difficult to disregard the ways in which celebrity athletes and sweatshop workers were linked through the sponsorship webs that underpin and promote fashion consumer branding. To gauge how this world has come into being, we might take a closer look at the gentrification of soccer—the most global of all sports, and the one that has been speed-fueling the engine of international fashion branding.

Soccer's Global Village

Soccer has not commanded my own fealty since my late teens. Increasingly, however, I find myself slung, like a wayward satellite, into its dizzy orbit. Even so, to watch today's game is to experience a vastly changed sport. Above all, there's the awareness of being part of the global connection—nothing else comes close to the scale of the soccer audience—which makes strange bedfellows of real-time spectators and fans all around the world. This is true not just of the World Cup, which dwarfs the Olympics as a mass spectacle, but also of top club soccer. Games in England's Premier League, Italy's Serie A, and Spain's La Liga are watched every week in hundreds of countries. The grandiosity of this spectacle and its imperious reach has very little in common with how I now remember the parochial game of my Scottish youth. Supporting our local team then was a rigid act of masculine faith, and the aura of violence and clannish devotion that it fed upon was glamorous to my mind and repugnant to my senses. Or was it the other way around? Perhaps the whole point of fandom is to obliterate this distinction, and to suspend our disbelief in the power of devotional acts. Bound by solemn claims on territory and lore, the game extracted oaths from us that were as near to tribal as you can get in modern life. In retrospect, I can now see how those barely secular vows (in Scotland, they were often played out on a sectarian battlefield) proved to be the seedbeds later cultivated by the engineers of commercial brand loyalty.

Today's players of the top European clubs have brand recognition (a corporate concept more or less accepted by their board members) that equals the

Heavenly numbers, European flea market
(PHOTO BY AUTHOR)

reach of international pop stars and Hollywood celebrities. Their fame out-runs that of the titans of U.S. sports (still an international minority passion, in spite of the colossal marketing efforts of the NBA, MLB, and NFL) like Tiger Woods, Kobe Bryant, Alonzo Mourning, Grant Hill, Jerry Rice, and Allen Iverson or gilt-edged team brands like the Chicago Bulls or the Dallas Cowboys. The Brazilian hotshot Ronaldo was recently preferred over Michael Jordan for the position of goodwill ambassador for the U.N.'s development program because he was more globally recognizable, especially in developing countries. Jordan's number 23, once ubiquitous as a global icon, has been displaced, in recent years, by Manchester United or Real Madrid shirts, whether licensed or counterfeit, that are now worn by the proverbial rural villager in remote corners of the world. In fact, soccer icons, along with the apparel they promote, are the only serious global contenders to the dominance of U.S.-derived commercial brands.

As any soccer buff in the U.S. knows, the enjoyment of the game is spurned by the U.S. media sports complex to the same degree that it is embraced en masse by urban immigrants and suburban teenagers, especially girls. The reasons for this exclusion are multifarious, but, in large part, it is because the game's rules of play are not particularly friendly to North America's demanding advertising rhythms. Who could forget FIFA's attempt to appease TV entities in USA-1994 by considering the subdivision of the game into four commercial-friendly segments, in addition to widening the goals, and substituting kick-ins for throw-ins? But no one can be smug about this happenstance. U.S. sports may be a byword for overcommercialization, but they do not have a monopoly on athletic capitalism. In other parts of the world, the elite circuit of professional soccer has long been bought off, lock, stock, and barrel by media barons like Rupert Murdoch and Silvio Berlusconi and large TV groups (Eurosport, KirschSport, BskyB, Canal Plus, Telepiu, Via Digital) whose lavish purchase of exclusive broadcasting rights has pumped vast amounts of capital into the coffers of the top clubs.[1] In the 1990s, satellite TV became "both the paymaster and ringmaster" of soccer,[2] and its infusion of lucre hastened on the financialization of the game to the point where the directors of top clubs are often little more than ersatz CEOs, shopping for high-price talent, and hustling their brands to squeeze a little more value out of their market share or stock price. As the historian Asa Briggs commented over a decade ago, in anticipation of the coming of the global village to soccer, "there is a new world around the corner and it will not be run by villagers."[3]

Even where TV is not a big factor, in the not-so-premier leagues, the game is still firmly under the sway of the leading sporting brands—Adidas, Reebok, Nike, Puma, Mitre, Umbro, Kappa, Lotto. Some of these also happen to be among the world's largest apparel companies and mid-market fashion leaders, and thereby hangs a tale about the most rapid and ecumenical conversion in the history of clothing. How did sports apparel become a huge fashion market, and how were the passions incited by a game like soccer converted into a fail-safe recipe for captive consumerism?

A Sporting Challenge

With favorites like Argentina, France, Italy, England, and Spain sent packing one after another, the early rounds of the 2002 World Cup proved exciting beyond measure. But for those with attention to spare, the real underlying competition was Nike's renewed challenge to Adidas, which has traditionally been the tournament's alpha sponsor. Largely through its long-established relationship with FIFA, the world soccer federation, the German firm has managed to hold on to its share of half the world's sales in soccer goods. But Nike has come a long way—securing second place in market share—since it decided in 1994 to make a serious foray into the most popular sport of all. As in the 1998 tournament, where Adidas-France triumphed over Nike-Brazil, both firms tried to book their place in the final a long time before they faced off in 2002's Germany vs. Brazil. Each brand's respective TV campaign ads assured them a highly visible halftime presence at virtually every match, and provided an ongoing story for journalists who were sold on the angle of this "other World Cup" being waged between the two corporate giants.[4]

Where Adidas's cozy ties with FIFA brought it official sponsorship of the World Cup, Nike's use of guerrilla and "ambush marketing" (placing ads next to those of the official sponsors) obliged FIFA to label the company a "parasite." Given Nike's ceaseless pursuit of rebel status, this is exactly where it wanted to be. For the 2002 tournament, Adidas's three-stripe logo was carried by ten teams, seventy-three referees, 25,000 officials, and all the competition balls, but it was the contest with Nike over the leading players that drew the most attention. On Adidas's payroll were stars like David Beckham, Zinedine Zidane, Fabien Barthez, and Alessandro Del Piero, all of whom appeared in its TV ads about an incurable disease being analyzed by medical experts at the "Institute for the Study of Socceritis." The strange symptoms exhibited by the stars in the ads could be read as an underhanded comment on the mysterious seizure suffered by Ronaldo, just hours before the 1998 final in which he was allegedly forced to play in order to fulfill the team's contract with Nike.

In keeping with the U.S. multinational's maverick image, the 2002 Nike campaign ads were more aggressive, and almost as memorable as the company's airport series directed by Hong Kong action film guru John Woo for France-1998 (which shut down Rio's airport, during filming, for twelve hours). For 2002, twenty-four stars were signed up to play a three-a-side sudden-death tournament in a cage inside an abandoned tanker. In the final match, emceed by a sinister, unshaven Eric Cantona, Thierry Henry, Francesco Totti, and Hidetoshi Nakata shot it out with Luis Figo, Ronaldo, and Roberto Carlos. As if in direct response to the Adidas effort, the ads, directed by Terry Gilliam, featured "A Little Less Conversation (A Little More Action)," which rapidly became a chart-topper in Europe as the very first remix of an Elvis song. When Adidas-Germany succumbed to Nike-Brazil in the final, with Ronaldo taking the goal-scoring honors, Nike's revenge for the debacle of 1998 was complete.

Nike favors the stripped-down game of three-a-side portrayed in its ads because it highlights the elite, brandable players, and allows spectators and consumers to focus on the individual feats of single athletes rather than overall team play. Indeed, as part of its marketing efforts, the company sponsors mammoth three-side tournaments, called Scorpion KO, for teenagers in its Nike Soccer Parks all over the world. Who knows, the popularity of this format, much faster and more virtuoso, may, in time, come to challenge association soccer, or at least generate a breakaway game with a momentum, and a cash nexus unto itself. As it happens, the 2002 World Cup turned out to be a great tournament for team play, and very few of the celebrity players who were expected to shine were able to deliver the exalted feats of which epic marketing landmarks are made. With the exception of Ronaldo, none of the Nike supernovas really rose to the occasion. In fact, the top performing player was a goalkeeper, Germany's Oliver Kahn, which is not exactly what the PR mavens had hoped for. Only bonny Beckham, whose brand recognition in multiple industries (sports, fashion, pop, lifestyle) is in a class unto itself, generated the kind of media buzz that advertisers crave. That he did so simply because of his presence (in Japan especially, where his cult is red-hot) and not on account of his performance on the field, which was middling at best, was the supreme proof of a powerful brand, built to maintain its high market share even with an average product. Likewise, one year later, it was his potential as a commercial asset in the "emerging markets" of East Asia and North America rather than his athletic prowess that underpinned Real Madrid's well-publicized effort to recruit him away from United at the end of the 2003 season. As the English club's CEO Peter Kenyon put it: "We accept he is the most recognized footballer in the world, perhaps the most recognized person. So, yes, he is important to us. And that's the reason we're going to keep him."[5] Weeks later, Beckham had signed with the Madrid club, and the most important part of the contract obliged the player to sign over 50 percent of every personal sponsorship contract he signs while with Real. Shortly after, Real announced Beckham's inclusion on a preseason tour of Asia, where his idolatry provided vital market leverage for the club's brand. As for Adidas, the transfer was a wet dream, bringing the number-one player on its payroll into the fold of its number-one club team.

While Beckham's direct marketing potential has eluded Nike (aside from Adidas, he is contracted to Vodaphone, Pepsi, Brylcreem, Police, Marks & Spencer, and Castrol, among others), the boys from Beaverton tried to capture some share of his radiance when they bought the licensing contract for Manchester United in 2002. By winning the Manchester contract, in the biggest sports sponsorship deal in history, Nike made its most portentous bid to capture the one truly worldwide sports market it does not yet dominate. Phil Knight had forged his empire on the basis of the overseas appeal of American sports, or in global games with elite constituencies, like tennis and golf. When basketball's overseas penetration leveled off in 1994, the company's rate of growth could only be sustained by getting into the global soccer market. In 1997, its overall North American and Asian sales began to slump, and Nike reaffirmed its decision to hitch its corporate future to the soccer wagon. The sport's blend of fanatical clubbability and lifestyle expressionism, its relentless expansion into emerging markets (spearheaded by the revenue-crazed policies of FIFA), and its increasing gentrification, offered the most fertile ground for the kind of super-tribalism to which branding aspires. The company's late entry into the game was backed by massive outlays, which, in addition to the star recruits, resulted in the signing up of some of the world's leading national (Brazil, Italy, Holland, Nigeria) and club teams (Arsenal, Inter Milan).

Just before France-1998, Nike shelled out a reported $200 million to Brazil's national team as part of a sponsorship contract that allegedly skewed the results of the tournament's final.[6] The scandal generated by the contract—which, among other things, gave the company the right to organize five international games a year—led to a high-level congressional investigation in Brazil that ended with the prosecution of over thirty officials on corruption charges and for renouncing national sovereignty to Nike. When the hullabaloo died down, it was clear that the players and the Brazilian soccer federation had taken all the heat, not the company that bought them off. Nike's rebel profile—nurtured by fifteen years of ads that pushed the in-your-face attitude of renegades like Charles Barkley, Dennis Rodman, William Burroughs, Dennis Hopper, Spike Lee, John McEnroe, and Denis Leary—has allowed it to ride out scandals that would have left a taint on other brands. Indeed, its soccer profile may have only increased as a result of the public exposure generated by Brazil's travails. When the team rose to glory once again in 2002, the scandal was all but forgotten, and the solidity of the Nike-Brazil brand was intensified.

United We Stand

National teams only play occasionally, however, and the real lifeblood of the game is at the club level, where capital is concentrated in the national premier leagues of Europe. It was only a matter of time before Nike came knocking at Old Trafford's door, where Manchester United had fashioned itself as the top dog in the course of a decade when soccer's cachet soared along with the revenues of the elite clubs. After an initial bid, in 1996, to buy out licensing rights over the club's kit, Nike succeeded six years later. As part of the deal, which began in July 2002 just as the World Cup ended, the company paid almost half a million dollars to Manchester United plc for exclusive rights to sponsor the club's clothing, manufacture, and sell its merchandise—which covers the entire lifestyle spectrum, from bed linen to hard liquor and ketchup—in addition to operating its worldwide retail business, which accounts for a huge portion of the club's income. A wholly owned subsidiary was set up to run the licensing and retail operations, and Nike won majority control over its board. In effect, the company bought unfettered access to the world's most successful soccer megabrand. For United to fulfill the thirteen-year contract, the team must stay in the English Premiership, and, more significantly, achieve a European competition place every season. If revenues exceed a certain target, the club receives a half share of additional profits too. Needless to say, United also benefits greatly from its association with the biggest sports brand of all. In signing with Nike (it also enjoys a big sponsorship deal with Vodafone, garnering $50 million over four years), it sundered its long-standing relationship with Umbro, a Manchester clothing company. Though Umbro is no slouch in the global soccer market (it sponsors England's national side, along with top club teams like Chelsea and Celtic), the switch neatly illustrates the transition from local ties to multinational affiliations. By the mid-1990s, United had become a byword for trading a community-minded regional identity, so cherished by soccer purists, for the "imagined community" of its global faithful—imagined, in turn, by the club's directors as an "emerging market."

Second only to the Dallas Cowboys in the net worth of its franchise, United's runaway success in building value through global branding is without parallel in the sporting world. Executive decisions had openly driven the mercurial rise of "Gold Trafford." Beginning with the 1992 recruitment of Edward Freeman, a merchandizing wiz enlisted from London club Tottenham Hotspur, and continuing through the reign of Peter Kenyon, recruited from Umbro, the club's corporate policy was that "we must treat the fan as a customer."[7] As a result, it was decided to expand the club's revenue stream far beyond gate receipts. Within a few years of Freeman's arrival, revenue from Old Trafford ticket sales accounted for less than half of the plc's commercial income, even though the ground was one of the biggest in the U.K. The strategy of converting fans into customers was aimed at the 20 percent of all British fans who say they support Manchester, and at the estimated fifty-four million active fans worldwide. Indeed, United now has fan clubs in twenty-five nations, TV deals in 135, its own cable subscription channel (MUTV) and fashion label (muct), and a megastore (plus two other stores) at Old Trafford that is possibly Manchester's number-one visitor attraction. With its licensed merchandise and paraphernalia flying off the shelves all across Asia, the club's only major holdout market is the U.S.—a little problem that was supposed to be addressed by a joint-marketing deal with the New York Yankees, though little has come of it.

Old Trafford souvenirs, Manchester Airport

(PHOTO BY AUTHOR)

Is this commercial repute supported by the team's performance? In the 1990s, the club's record in winning league titles and championships in England and Europe was unmatched, and these were the years when soccer's status as an ultra-fashionable domain of pop culture soared. So too the club flew high in the mid- to late 1960s, and earned itself a place in the glamorous forefront of Britain's "swinging sixties." But the period in between was mostly fallow. Overall, Liverpool FC, its great northern rival, has arguably a greater record of achievement, while the contribution of its fans to the sport has been much greater. Fed by an oral culture rich in popular music-hall comedy, Liverpool fans more or less pioneered the rituals of crowd chanting during games in the 1960s, and, in the 1980s, they innovated the "casual" styles that vaulted soccer into the orbit of the fashion world. The Merseyside team has also retained the reputation of serving as a model of regional community, especially after the Hillsborough disaster of 1989 (when a crowd crush took ninety-six lives), and its managers and directors are ever wary of their accountability to fans. The reversal of fortunes between the two clubs in the last twelve years is mirrored in the rise of Manchester's urban fortunes and the continued stagnation of Liverpool's deindustrialized economy.[8]

By contrast, Manchester's charisma (and its attendant hubris) is largely the result of image-building and adroit manipulation of its history.[9] The loss of most of its promising postwar players in the 1958 Munich air crash is a foundational myth of sacrifice that can be built on, again and again, each time the team rises to the occasion. So too the respective personalities of its storied 1960s players—Bobby Charlton (the honest English yeoman), Denis Law (the devil-may-care Scot), and George Best (the rebellious Irish playboy)—were treated with an equally mythic varnish when the club experienced its phoenix rise to prominence. As a result, the visitor's tour of the museum inside the otherwise run-of-the-mill Old Trafford stadium is a sanctified affair. Pilgrims are shown how the club's crest (its logo) and its kit (regularly upgraded product) have changed over the years. Then they move on to the Roll of Honor, the Trophy Room, and the shrine to the Munich disaster, travel back in time to the club's working-class foundation as the "Newton Heath, Lancashire and Yorkshire Railway, Cricket and Football Club," and finally enter the Legends Corridor, dedicated to relics of the "greats," and the Legends Café to refuel for another bout of shopping in the megastore. The theology of Manchester United is sculpted and tended as carefully as any venerating cult. That this closely cultivated piety coexists with the club's long-standing reputation as "Moneybags United," its recent coziness with investment bankers, its adventures in stock-market flotation, and its triumphs in merchandizing, makes United an exemplary MBA case study.

As a publicly traded company since 1991, United's first responsibility is to its shareholders, and so its corporate exploits have not always endeared its management to home fans. Yet many of them hold stock in the plc, and they have learned to have their say when executive decision-making appears to favor the business of selling replica kits over the competition for glory on the field. This skepticism has served fans well in their protests against two, high-profile business names: Rupert Murdoch and Nike. The Nike deal got off to an especially bad start because it was announced to London stockbrokers and investment bankers before fans (the club's part-owners if they are shareholders) and Umbro (the former licensee) even got an inkling of the contract negotiations. Shareholders United (SU), a collective of stockholders ("who care more about their club than their dividends"), expressed their outrage to management at making a deal with the leading paymaster of global sweatshops. The club's customer charter, they pointed out, explicitly opposes the exploitation of child labor, and forbids United from doing business with suppliers that employ children, or indeed any workers under illegal conditions: "[Manchester United] will not knowingly buy goods from any supplier or manufacturer who does not comply fully with the labour, safety and other relevant laws of the country of manufacture . . . No orders will be placed from suppliers employing child labour under the age allowed in the country concerned."

SU evolved from a group called Shareholders Against Murdoch, which was founded in 1998 to fight the planned takeover of the club by Rupert Murdoch's satellite operator, BskyB. Its own parent was the Independent Manchester United Supporters Association, galvanized initially out of contempt for overzealous stewards telling fans they had to stay seated while watching matches. The anti-Murdoch campaign mobilized top lawyers, economists, journalists, and academics in publicizing the media baron's more unscrupulous deeds and protesting the growing influence of television over the game.[10] The result was so effective that the Blair government referred the case to the Monopolies and Mergers Commission, which blocked the bid on the grounds that the takeover was anti-competitive in the media market, and that it was contrary to the public interest and would "damage the quality of British soccer" by exacerbating the gap between rich and poor clubs.[11] En route to its victory, Shareholders Against Murdoch had waged "the most sophisticated soccer campaign that there has ever been," dealing a highly public rebuff to the power of United corporate board members who had approved the deal.[12]

The Murdoch campaign was the most highly visible attempt by fans to exercise some homegrown control over the wave of corporate money-spinning, and the TV revenue in particular, that had fueled the soccer industry during the 1990s boom. As soccer rose in the ranks of global industry, its corporate development followed the familiar template established by the globalization of the economy: vast rewards for the investor and celebrity professional class, and starvation wages for the apparel-producing sweatshop class; diversification of product and extensive subcontracting of labor and services; expansion into emergent regional markets around the world; the aggregation of corporate media power and private ownership; and the rise to primacy of branding. In fact, the globalization of sport as a whole, brokered by the regional development policies of powerful organizations like FIFA and the IOC, and culminating in the commercial cornucopias of the World Cup and Olympics, tells us virtually everything we need to know about the impact of modern capitalist economics.[13]

In this new business model for soccer, fans increasingly have complained about being sidelined, cast either as loyal consumers of replica kits and other merchandise, or as showbiz extras required to be colorful and vocal in their role in the lucrative spectacle of televised soccer. Their participation in fanzine culture and independent supporters associations offers a chance, however marginal, to take a more active role in shaping the destiny of a game with the deepest of working-class roots. Shareholder power is a step further, and rests on the claim that the game, and the club, rightfully "belongs to us." The immediate goal behind the creation of SU was to encourage and facilitate supporters to buy shares so that they could influence decision-making: its "long term aim is to deliver ownership of the club [through Manchester United PLC] to its loyal supporters."

When I first spoke to him in the fall of 2002, Oliver Houston, SU's press officer, was quick to declare that, far from being an anti-Nike group, the organization plays an important role in share-buying and dividend-sharing for its members. To a large degree, then, the members feel that their investments are affected by decisions that may compromise "the independence and integrity and reputation of the club." It is in this role as an interested party that the organization sees itself protecting the club from adverse business decisions. For example, Houston pointed out that "there is a get-out clause in the contract for Nike if United is relegated from the Premiership, but no get-out clause for the club if Nike is exposed for employing child labor." In addition, his members were all too aware that "Nike is renowned for interfering in soccer matters," most notably in the Brazil case, and so they feared the consequences for United. Their guardian-like concern for the club extends to dismay at the actions of its directors, who introduced the clauses in the customer charter not long before the Nike contract was announced. While there are 30,000 shareholders in the club, only 20 percent of the shares are owned by individuals, and perhaps only 1 percent or 2 percent in the hands of the small shareholders who are members of Shareholders United. Though its takeover move was thwarted, BskyB was, until recently, still the largest shareholder in the club, with 9.9 percent. Nonetheless, Houston insisted that his organization has a good deal of influence over larger institutional investors and fund managers, not to mention press relations that generate headlines.

Even so, the group's campaign against the Nike contract was hardly powerful enough to move United's directors to action. In fact, it took the best part of a year before the plc's director, Peter Kenyon, met with SU representatives at all. In the course of the meeting, in October 2002, Kenyon confirmed that there had been no second thoughts on the Nike deal. He also expressed the plc's opposition not only to putting a supporter's representative on the board, but also to scheduling the annual general meeting for a weekend date when small shareholders could attend. SU had put resolutions to that end on the agenda of the 2002 shareholders meeting, whose slogan turned out to be the ponderous but stunningly accurate: "Manchester United, not just a soccer club . . . but a global brand." At season's end, a proposed meeting between Nike representatives, plc directors, and SU remained unscheduled, and SU had not as yet been permitted to view the Nike contract. Jonathan Michie, the chair of SU, acknowledged that the organization's successes overall had been "pretty limited," beyond getting the directors to acknowledge its existence.

United had long been criticized for exploiting its fans by issuing new strips almost every year. The first Nike strip was introduced in the fall of 2002, only fifteen months after Umbro's last—a gold kit to celebrate the club's centenary year. Yet the Nike outfit quickly established itself as the bestselling kit so far, and in a year when record profits were posted by the club (profits, before player trading, for the six months until January 31, 2003, showed an increase of 32 percent). Largely as a result of its booming business in soccer (its soccer revenues rose 24 percent, to $450 million, in 2001), Nike returned to double-digit profit growth in fiscal 2002, with its net income rising 12 percent, to $663.3 million.[14] Counterfeits of the Nike strip were available in Bangkok months before the rollout, and were being worn around Old Trafford almost as quickly. Better quality fakes were soon being produced by the East End sweatshops used by the official retailers. Almost indistinguishable from the real thing, and selling for half the price, they attracted the attention of United's hit squads, and reminded fans of the club's outrageous markups. Earlier in the year, the Office of Fair Trading had taken legal action against United, Umbro, the FA, and several retailers for fixing the astronomical price of retail kits.[15]

By mid-season, the blue "away" shirt had sold out, and Nike chose not to run up more in order to create demand for the next kit. Even so, it was alleged that the company had not been happy with the first year of merchandising profits (and were blindsided by Beckham's departure). Reportedly, Nike's revenues were even less than the upfront annual licensing fee it paid United. The deal had resulted in further friction with SU when some overseas fans were "converted" from being members of official fan clubs into members of Nike's merchandising subsidiary. But by the end of the first season as Nike's brand bearer, the buzz generated by SU's campaign had dissipated, with little apparent impact on the consumption patterns of supporters, ever eager to fork over money to show their brand loyalty. Compared to the success of the campaign against the Murdoch takeover, and despite the fact that Nike was as much a villain in the public eye as Murdoch had been, the complaints against Nike's labor profile came nowhere near to catching the imagination of the club's most influential supporters, let alone its vast fan base.

What accounts for this disparity between the two initiatives? For one thing, the Nike contract had been a done deal, unlike the Murdoch bid, which required an all-important interval before approval. In addition, rumors in 2002–2003 about new takeover bids commanded greater attention, along with a campaign to rescue the game from the scheduling priorities of TV paymasters and restore it to its traditional three P.M. weekend slot.[16] Nike's PR machine, trumpeting its "continuous improvement" of labor conditions, had also helped to persuade some doubters. When all is said and done, concerns about the club's association with child labor had not amounted to much compared to the undeniable appeal of the combined superbrand of Nike and United. If nothing else, this was a reflection of the difficulty many supporters now had in distinguishing the club's success on the pitch from the plc's success. United not only regained the English Premiership title in 2003, but also finished the season with a bill of fiscal health that was streets ahead of other clubs in the league, many of whom were on the verge of bankruptcy. The disparity underlined the degree to which raw capital resources are able to buy the kind of success on the playing field that fans crave. Financial superiority clearly brings the trophies home. The same story applied to the other members of the European elite such as Real Madrid, Barcelona, Juventus, Bayern Munich, and A.C. Milan, who virtually dominated both their national leagues and the European Champions League. Unlike in the business world, where competition is aimed at burying rivals, every soccer team depends on the competitive survival of others. The professional sport now faces a parlous future as the gap between the tycoon clubs and the rest of the field widens yearly.

Brand Protectionism

Despite Nike's efforts, by any means necessary, to counter the damage caused by exposé after exposé, the swoosh is now indelibly associated with the image of children slaving around the clock for a pittance to produce shoes that can retail for $150. Because of its history and corporate strategies, Nike has been the textbook illustration of the logic of the multinational free-trade corporation—from its origins as a distributor of Japanese knockoffs of Adidas running shoes, to its career as a contractor in Korea and Taiwan, and then, when wages in these countries rose, its enthusiastic participation in the "race to the bottom" in countries under authoritarian rule like Indonesia, Vietnam, and China, where half a million of the company's workers earn a famously sub-minimum wage. Ever since the late 1980s, the company has been saddled with the taint of sweatshops and has spent large amounts of money in lavish PR moves to cleanse its brand.[17] Nonetheless, the bad publicity is likely to have played some role in the flagging sales (down 11 percent) of the mid-1990s, and provided some part of the impetus to penetrate the soccer market. But any illusions that the move to this new sport would give the company a clean slate were quickly dispelled.

Concern about the sweatshops behind "the beautiful game" had ignited earlier in the decade when the first exposés of child labor in Pakistan's soccer-ball export industry came to light. At that time, Adidas monopolized the trade. In the U.S., the issue exploded in 1996 when Nike, the first major American contractor, was caught red-handed by prize-winning journalist Sydney Schanberg, who posed as an exporter to write about the brutal conditions under which children labored to stitch thirty-five million soccer balls a year in the production center of Sialkot. In a widely cited *Life* magazine article, he described the arduous working day of Tariq, a twelve-year-old "who earns sixty cents a ball, and it takes most of a day to make one." A village factory foreman offered Schanberg 100 stitchers for the price of the debt incurred by their masters, who had bought many of them as children from their parents.

I tell Afral Butt I'll consider his offer of bonded workers, but first I need one of the Nike balls for my engineers to test. No problem, he says, selling me one for 200 rupees (roughly $6). That's what it cost to make a quality football ball in Pakistan, in labor and materials, with a profit thrown in—just $6. In the U.S., these balls sell for $30 to $50. More than half the nine million football balls imported into the U.S. each year come from Pakistan and all enter the country tariff-free. The words "Hand Made" are printed clearly on every ball. Not printed is any explanation of whose hands made them. For the rest of that day in Pakistan, I keep thinking: Someone actually offered to sell me 100 men and children for less than $200 apiece. In effect, I would have owned them.

The article was accompanied by stark illustrations, one of them a photograph of a three-year-old stitcher, whose hands were so tiny she could barely handle the scissors. Combining her labor with that of her mother and her three sisters earned the family 75¢ per day.[18]

With advance knowledge that its labor practices would be highlighted in the article, Nike launched the first of a long series of counterstrikes by announcing a plan with a subcontractor to centralize the stitching process

Nike shoe
breakdown
(ADBUSTERS)

and eliminate child labor from its village operations. The International Labor Organization (ILO) soon entered into an agreement with the Sialkot Chamber of Commerce and Industry and UNICEF to regulate the industry, with the goal of ending the use of village children. Along with Reebok, Adidas, Mitre, Wilson, Puma, and other leading brands, Nike signed on, consenting to disclose its stitching locations and submit them to routine inspections by a group of ILO-recruited monitors. FIFA gave the agreement its seal of approval, and formulated its own good code of conduct, based on the core conventions of the ILO (freedom of association and collective bargaining, no forced labor, no child labor, no discrimination in employment, no excessive hours and the right to one day off per week, and a wage sufficient to cover basic needs). To date, FIFA is the only major sports federation to address the issue of sweatshop labor in the sporting goods industry.

Monitoring of production facilities is notoriously difficult, however, and in June 2002, another flare-up forced FIFA to issue a denial that World Cup balls were being produced in South Asian sweatshops. Taking a leaf from Nike's book of nonaccountability, Keith Cooper, FIFA's communications director, told a news conference: "We are responsible for organizing the World Cup, we are not responsible for the labor conditions in factories." The soccer stars who command huge salaries and handsome sponsorship fees are also "not responsible." Like Nike's stable of U.S. icons—Michael Jordan, Bo Jackson, John McEnroe, Tiger Woods, Andre Agassi, Allen Iverson, Monica Seles, the Williams sisters—their deafening silence on the topic is the glue that keeps the entire celebrity/branding/sweatshop system of the sports goods industry from unraveling. In the run-up to the World Cup, exposés of labor violations behind the leading soccer brands continued to surface, most notably in China's Guangdong Province, far from the monitor's eye, where the Hong Kong Christian Industrial Committee found egregious conditions in factories producing for Adidas, Puma, Wilson, Umbro, and Diadora. While quality control for hand-sewn balls was very strict, passing through ten inspections before finishing, the corresponding regulation of conditions in the workplaces barely existed. Manufacturing processes unique to soccer ball production exposed workers to industrial and health hazards—heat poisoning

101

FRIEDRICH
ENGELS
VISITS THE OLD
TRAFFORD
MEGASTORE

and burning, chemical contamination—in addition to the usual sweatshop diet of underpayment, exhaustion from long hours, and restrictions on personal freedom.[19] In the wake of these and other reports, pressure on FIFA came through the Clean Clothes Campaign and the Global March Against Child Labor, which ran a highly visible campaign to remind the world soccer authority of its commitment to Fair Trade monitoring and regulation.[20]

Over time, the ILO/FIFA monitoring system has offered corporations a blessing unforeseen in the original agreement. They can act to protect their brand property by notifying the ILO monitors about counterfeit balls if they do so in the name of combating child labor. Soccer clubs have followed this example by alerting government watchdogs about sales of counterfeit replica kits. In the U.K., the Office for Fair Trading and the Ministry for Consumer Affairs work in conjunction with the World Trade Organization and Interpol to hunt down the pirate producers and rely on tips from the merchandising directors of soccer clubs to carry out their work. These agencies act in the name of three principles: to stem the loss of tax revenue to the black market, to combat the sweatshop labor exploited by counterfeiters, and to protect the intellectual property rights of companies and clubs. Since counterfeit items are invariably produced in an additional run at the factory that makes the official goods, the principle of protecting labor is a spurious one. By contrast, the cause of protecting the brand is a huge boon to producers and marketers of the replica kits that carry a retail markup comparable to that of a Nike sneaker. Several years ago, Doug Hall, the loose-lipped chairman of Newcastle United FC, got himself into hot water by boasting to a tabloid reporter: "We sell 600,000 shirts a year. Every shirt costs £50, but the shirts cost only £5 to make in Asia." His comment was condemned for its casual assumption that fans are easily bilked, not because it exposed the club's reliance on substandard Asian jobs for a large part of its income.

In this respect, Manchester United is, once again, in a league of its own. Now that the team officially has a brand mark instead of a club crest, "Manchester United" is trademarked, and can be legally protected against all efforts to use the name on nonofficial goods. The result is often a vicious circle. For example, the club's aggressive moves to build its brand in the Asian market has compromised its own extensive garment operations in the region. Increased demand for kits inevitably encouraged local pirates who are often the same contractors used by the club. (The labor record of Umbro, based in Manchester itself, is hardly a cut above that of Nike, its successor, since it also outsources almost all of its production to Asian subcontractors). United set up its own counterfeit detection unit, and its investigators cooperated with Thai police in hundreds of raids on Bangkok sweatshops, confiscating millions of dollars of goods. Again, the club's directors can seize the high ground by claiming that their war on counterfeiters is also a crusade against labor exploitation. In truth, the primary reason for the flourishing of black market production is that a considerable profit can still be made even after undercutting the jumbo markup that the plc imposes on the official replica kits.

103

FRIEDRICH
ENGELS
VISITS THE OLD
TRAFFORD
MEGASTORE

Trouble at the Mill

The association of the name of Manchester with prized garments is hardly new in Asia, nor is the business of speculating about the worth of Asian markets a recent matter in the northern English city that served as the home of the Industrial Revolution, and was itself the mother of all sweatshops in the nineteenth century. In fact, the repute and wavering fortunes of Manchester cotton have been linked with South Asia for hundreds of years, and this latest twist is an ironic consequence of that history. Any explanation of the rise of Manchester from obscurity to its zenith as the prime manufactory of British industry and commerce is incomplete without accounting for the eradication of the Bengali textile industry, along with the creation of a plantation system in India to maintain a cotton supply for the mills of England's "Cottonopolis" that would compete with the product of U.S. slave labor.

Indian handicraft manufacture had long dominated the international textile trade. Bengali muslins, in particular, were much prized among the Arabs, Greeks, and Romans of the ancient world. In medieval times, India's manufacturing skills bore comparison with, or surpassed, the European equivalents in textile, ironwork, shipbuilding, glass, and paper. By the seventeenth century, ginghams, chintzes, and calicos from Bengal were the height of fashion all over Europe, and, in due time, the commercial preeminence of these imports began to pose a threat to the livelihood of rising domestic industries at that time.[21] A moral panic ensued about the potential ruin of national economies. Wearers of Indian-made cloth were reviled, and physically assaulted, for being unpatriotic, and politicians were bombarded with appeals for protective legislation to promote their native, European industry. In spite of its passion for laissez-faire trade, the British government passed a 10 percent import duty on Indian imports in 1685, doubled the tariff five years later, and passed a law shortly thereafter, banning the wearing of silks and calicoes and imposing fines on offenders. Legislation in 1700 and 1720 went further, banning all imports of printed, painted, or dyed fabrics.

After the 1757 conquest of India, the East India Company concentrated on profit from the textile export trade by squeezing the local hand-loom weavers whom it had brought under rigid contractual control. The Company's lucrative trade from its handicraft product continued to thrive in the face of the competition offered by Lancashire's mechanization of spinning and dyeing. The cheapness of the Manchester factory product still could not compete in many markets with the superior quality of Bengali product, and so commercial war had to be waged through other means. In 1813, the East India Company's trading monopoly was ended, and the import duty was raised to 85 percent while British goods were taxed at only a fraction of that duty on entry into the subcontinent. In 1840, members of a select committee of the House of Commons heard a witness cite the opinion of J.F. Shore, a retired East India Company administrator: "This supersession of the native for British manufactures is often quoted as a splendid instance of the triumph of British skill. It is a much stronger instance of English tyranny, and how India has been impoverished by the most vexatious system of customs and duties imposed for the avowed object of favouring the mother country."[22] Such sentiments were often on the lips of those, like Shore, who had seen, firsthand, the devastating impact on Bengali industry.

The mills' supply of U.S. raw materials was hit hard in 1861–63 by the "cotton famine" generated by the Civil War, and Manchester merchants lobbied hard for the India Office to develop a sustainable crop as an alternative source of supply to Confederate cotton. The campaign pitted the rising power of the northern parvenu capitalists against the rule of aristocratic politicians like Lord Palmerston and Sir Charles Wood, the first secretary of state for India. The requests of the Manchester men went against the grain of laissez-faire policy, and foundered initially on the poor state of transport and communications in the Indian interior. Yet several factors conspired to break the deadlock. Free trade, it was conveniently decided, was not particularly applicable to Indian trade; the prospect of vast areas of "underdeveloped" agricultural land was too much of a revenue bonanza to ignore for long; and cotton cultivation, in particular, was perceived to be an effective way of settling the interior with Europeans. These arguments were made by the Empire's "friends of India" in the name of mutual benefit, to the industrialist and to the Indian peasant alike. In the same vein, scientific improvement of agriculture, and the introduction of freehold tenure, were pronounced to be the potential source of rich rewards for the *ryot*.[23] Just as Bengal had been bled dry by the East India Company (in 1835, the company's director reported that "the bones of the cotton-weavers are bleaching the plains of India"), the wealth of the subcontinent's labor would soon flow into the bank accounts of British planters, industrialists, speculators, and colonial officials as India became the "milch cow of the Empire."

From the late 1830s, duties on the import of raw cotton from India were abolished, and by the 1870s, Anglo-Indian trade had begun to resemble the classic colonial pattern. Bengali's export textile industry had been laid low by repressive taxation and legislation, and the indigenous cotton staples that supplied it for centuries were now replaced by low-grade high-yield seeds grown specifically for Lancashire machines. Textiles bearing the name of Manchester flooded the international markets once dominated by Bengali goods. Dacca, ironically known as the "Manchester of India," was long since decimated: it lost 70 percent of its population between 1800 and 1839. (In 1757, Robert Clive had described the textile capital as "extensive, populous and rich as the city of London.") Most of India's precolonial manufacturing industries had been purposely ruined, and de-urbanization had set in. British capital would now be invested in extractive industries and in a plantation

105

FRIEDRICH
ENGELS
VISITS THE OLD
TRAFFORD
MEGASTORE

economy (indigo and jute proved even more lucrative than cotton) that made India a massive exporter of raw materials and importer of manufactured goods from Britain. To ensure this arrangement, all native attempts at manufacture and processing of textiles had to be successfully suppressed.

The standard textbook account of the Industrial Revolution attributes Manchester's ascendancy to a series of famous inventions—steam power, the flying shuttle, the spinning jenny, the throstle, the water frame, Crompton's mule, and the power loom. In fact, technological innovation was not the unilateral cause for the region's emergent economic power. Manchester merchants and industrialists prospered at the direct expense of the Indian craftworkers whose manufacture could not be beaten by fair trade, and who had to be reduced to serfdom by colonial imposition so that British industry would have cheap, raw materials for its mills and new markets for its own export trade. As a result, the fate and fortunes of both regions were inextricably linked. It was fitting, then, that the Indian independence movement was launched with a boycott of Manchester imports, and that Gandhi's spinning wheel became the most powerful symbol of anti-colonial economic resistance.

In the half-century after Indian independence, the regional patterns of production and trade would be restructured. By the late 1960s, the burgeoning garment export trade in East Asia and South Asia once again posed a threat to domestic industries in the developed countries. Domestic protection, while it was promoted, was no longer viable, however, not when multi-national companies could have favorable access to cheaper labor overseas, and thereby compete in the lucrative export market to the West. As mills in the North closed shop, the global sweatshop came into being, and quickly concentrated itself on the low-wage floors of Asia. When Manchester's name finally reappeared on goods, it was no longer to designate the place of manufacture. It was as a logo, in the form of United's soccer crest, that the name sustained its newfound fame, with Manchester claiming the lion's share of the profit, just as it had once been. However much transformed, the ties with Asia appeared to be as strong as ever.

107

FRIEDRICH
ENGELS
VISITS THE OLD
TRAFFORD
MEGASTORE

In their heyday, Manchester's merchants profited, at a distance, from the destitution of Bengal's hand-loom weavers and the enslavement of Africans who supplied King Cotton from the American South. But they had to physically share their city with the working men and women who formed the world's first industrial proletariat. Marx and Engels largely formed their picture of industrial labor from the appalling working and living conditions of these mill workers. "In a word," Engels wrote in his famous account, *Conditions of the Working Classes in England*, "the workers' dwellings of Manchester are dirty, miserable, and wholly lacking in comforts. In such houses, only inhuman, degraded, and unhealthy creatures would feel at home."[24]

In Engels's case, his knowledge came from close observation of Manchester's streets and factories, where he had been sent to work as a manager at his father's own mill in Salford. In his report, Engels noted that the typical bourgeois wanted no reminders of the material source of his wealth to intrude upon his own life, and so this obscuring of the means of production had been built into the urban fabric. The streets used by the industrial grandees to travel in omnibuses from their suburban villas to the commercial center cut through the grimmest of working-class areas, but those "main streets which run from the Exchange in all directions out of the town are occupied almost uninterruptedly on both sides by shops which are kept by members of the lower middle classes. . . . Even the less pretentious shops adequately serve their purpose of hiding from the eyes of the wealthy ladies and gentlemen with strong stomachs and weak nerves the misery and squalor which are part and parcel of their own riches and luxury."

Engels concludes: "I am quite aware of the fact that this hypocritical town-planning device is more or less common to all big cities. I realize, too, that owing to the nature of their business, shopkeepers inevitably seek premises in main thoroughfares. I know that in such streets there are more good houses than bad ones, and that the value of land is higher on or near a main thoroughfare than in the back streets. But in my opinion Manchester is unique in the systematic way in which the working class have been barred from the main streets. Nowhere else has such care been taken to avoid offending the tender susceptibilities of the eyes and nerves of the middle classes."[25]

If it proved so necessary, and so elementary, to shield from the mill owner's view the plight of workers in his own city, then it was almost certain that the dire situation of the Indian laborer would not be permitted to impinge on the consciousness of the industrialists, or the British public for that matter. What the urban plan of Manchester effected at home was even more efficiently achieved abroad through the filtering of information by the media and ideology of Empire. The humanitarian concerns of the liberal reformers for the conditions of the Lancashire laborer were rarely extended to the Indian plantation workers whose exploitation was the basis of the domestic industry. Manchester free-trade radicals like Richard Cobden and John Bright, who waged war against the Corn Laws for immiserating urban workers, were also in the forefront of the campaign to develop the Indian cotton supply. In that capacity, they paid lip service to the overtaxed plight of the *ryot*, but primarily as a rhetorical vehicle with which to push the local trade agenda of the Manchester industry. When public anxiety about the sweatshop conditions of the Asian laborer surfaced again, a century and a half later, a large part of it was fueled, as before, by concern about the loss of domestic jobs.

So too it was focused on the wretched circumstance of teenage women and children in the export processing zones of the offshore garment industry. Engels himself had paid particular attention to the gendered division of factory labor inside the Manchester mills. After the spinning and weaving machinery is installed, "practically all that is left to be done by hand," he noted, "is the piecing together of broken threads, and the machine does the rest." Since "this task calls for nimble fingers rather than muscular strength," it is lowly paid "women and girls alone who work the throstle spindles." Women, aged from fifteen to twenty, but rarely any older than that, also dominated the power-looms, "among the mules," and "in the preparatory processes," while children were to be found everywhere, mounting and taking down the bobbins, and squeezing between machines to gather up discarded material.[26] The manufacturers denied that these patterns of employ-

109

FRIEDRICH
ENGELS
VISITS THE OLD
TRAFFORD
MEGASTORE

ment existed, and that they were displacing higher-priced men from their livelihoods. Engels's moral condemnation of female factory work echoes still in contemporary anti-sweatshop literature. In 2001, for example, the National Labor Committee surveyed the working conditions of hundreds of thousands of young women employed in Dhaka's export garment factories, producing for the likes of Nike, Reebok, and Wilson. Compared to other countries they had visited, in Bangladesh, the NLC's Kernaghan and Briggs found "the greatest level of exploitation" they had ever seen. Descendants of the Bengali weavers whose livelihood was ruined by the rise of Manchester, these Dhaka women were "trapped in abject misery." Malnourished and abused, they toiled for up to eighteen hours a day in overcrowded, unsanitary workplaces: "By the time they reach thirty, most workers leave of their own accord, worn out, exhausted, sick and penniless—or management forces them out so they can be replaced with another crop of young teenage girls."[27]

Manchester and Dhaka had changed their roles. One can only imagine what Engels would have made of a visit to the Old Trafford megastore. In that most peculiar of emporiums, fans of a soccer club with origins as a factory-worker team pay exorbitant prices for cheaply produced goods that are sewn and glued in Asia by the same class of women and children who toiled in the original "workshop of the world." Many of the goods are tagged with "Made in Bangladesh" and "Made in China," the same countries that were once forced to import machine-made cottons and yarns from Manchester, after the decimation of the Bengali textile industry, and after the gunboat diplomacy that opened China's treaty ports to British concessions in 1842. Economic history can boast few examples with a more profound or ruinous irony.

Absolute Winners

At the postwar peak of his glory years with Blackpool, Stanley Matthews, the Wizard of Dribble, was probably the first soccer player to be endorsed for his signature. The company in question was the Wholesale Cooperative Society, one of the few quasi-socialist institutions to survive from that period. The

Co-op also manufactured and distributed the Stanley Matthews boot, the first modern soccer shoe, for which he was paid £30 per week in 1951. By the time I was old enough to play the game, the concept of the endorsed boot was becoming big business, and I was sold on the George Best boot—a garish blue-and-purple number, with unorthodox lacing that ran along the side, allowing for a smoothly polished top with which to launch deft passes or thirty-yard pile drivers at goal—at least if you were George Best. I soon learned that the design dragged down my performance on the field, but the boot looked snazzy enough to make up for it. There was already a yawning gap between the respective cultures that sustained the Matthews boot in the 1950s and the Best boot of the early 1970s. Matthews's fame as a sportsman had multigenerational appeal, and he was most renowned in middle age, retiring from First Division league soccer at age fifty. At that time, the local co-op store was still a customary place for working people to shop for clothing. Best was the first, multi-leveraged youth celebrity in the sport, and he retired at his peak at age twenty-seven after blazing a hipster trail through pop culture thirty years before the dazzling phenomenon that is David Beckham. The hirsute Man United star (dubbed the "fifth Beatle") was a

Sacred relics from Old
Trafford, Nevada Smith's
Public Bar, New York City
(PHOTO BY MARGARET GRAY)

1960s swinger with Carnaby Street fashion cachet, who started his own clothing lines and even owned two boutiques in Manchester. Naturally, his was the profile that companies would covet once they realized that sports figures could generate spin-off profit as consistently as pop stars.

By the time of Best's fame, sneakers and tennis shoes were an established part of the youth culture wardrobe, and they were obviously being used for nonathletic purposes. But it was highly unusual to see other items of sports clothing worn in daily life. Logo-heavy, lifestyle marketing was still far off. Disco mania in the late 1970s was responsible for introducing tracksuits into pop fashion, but it was the fitness-jogging craze of the 1980s that firmly established athletic wear as daily gear. The accompanying vogue for the trappings, if not the substance of, physical health also served as a launchpad for the mercurial rise of Nike. Hitherto confined to a marginal market—initially they were the select choice of marathon runners—Nike shoes became a vehicle of consumer identification for millions when the company's "Just Do It" campaign more or less shamed the public into exercising. The motivational campaign—which stylishly glorified individual effort as entrepreneurial gain, without too much of the pain, and suggested that the active life was a moral obligation—was critical in transforming Nike products into staple fashion items for those who at least wanted the patina of athleticism. "Just Do It" was a colossal success for the company, doubling its sales between 1987 and 1989, and it soon replaced Reebok, originally a Manchester-area company, which had established a stronghold in aerobic dance products, as the leading sports shoe manufacturer.

In the U.S., the moral obligation to be athletic, or at least to carry the appearance of being active, had long exercised its pull on the sports shoe trade. In a culture devoted to working constantly at the task of self-improvement, fitness all too easily became a compulsive goal of leisure time. This ethos helped drive the sales of early canvas-top sneakers like Keds, introduced by the U.S. Rubber Company in 1917; the "Chuck Taylor" All Star basketball shoe from Converse in 1923 (the best-selling athletic shoe of all time); and the blue-lined "Jack Purcell" sneaker from B.F. Goodrich in 1935 (later sold to Converse). All took advantage of Charles Goodyear's discovery of vulcan-

111

FRIEDRICH
ENGELS
VISITS THE OLD
TRAFFORD
MEGASTORE

ization, which molded rubber to cloth or other rubber components for a more permanent bond. Each, in turn, was widely adopted for nonathletic uses, taking on connotations that spoke to the national optimism of the American Way. Their appearance signified youth, health, and democracy long before the Puma, Adidas, and Nike sneakers became fashion items, expressive of similar virtues.

Another national attribute—the American taste for informality—played an important role in the adoption of sportswear (distinct from active wear) as fashion, notably in the periods following each world war. In the 1940s, when American designers were cut off from the orbit of Paris couture, they concentrated on designing sportswear for the domestic market with the limited materials at hand. Designers like Claire McCardell, who made dresses out of government surpluses of cotton weather balloons, helped establish casual sportswear as "the American Look" of the postwar period—functional, practical, and eminently modern. Garment manufacturers followed suit, moving from initially standardized lines to the bewilderingly diverse range of sports and sportswear products (Nike, for example, boasts 1,200 models of shoes in 3,000 styles and colors) that greets the modern consumer on today's retail shelves.[28]

Both of these tendencies—the activity ethic and the penchant for informality—have helped quicken the rate of casualization of dress, and everything else for that matter—including work, manners, food, and personality. At the end of the century, when the casual dress movement roared through corporate America, it was justified by its advocates on both counts. On the action front, it was promoted as a boost to productivity, especially on dress-down Fridays, introduced to counteract the slackening of the work rate. On the informality front, it was pushed as the no-collar style of American entrepreneurialism—libertarian and antiestablishment. Yet the factor that has driven casualization above all has been the restructuring of industrial production, especially the ease with which the manufacture of casual clothing—both sportswear and active wear—has lent itself to overseas relocation in low-wage export zones. Thus, "corporate casual" was not simply an expression of the anti-bureaucratic New Economy, it was also a response to a lavish marketing campaign launched by Levi Strauss in 1992, which bombarded 30,000 corporate HR departments with educational packets that promoted the virtues of casual wear in offices. The campaign was so successful that, by the end of the decade, one-third of all U.S. companies had gone casual five days a week, and fashion industry groups had retaliated with their own dress-up campaigns. Needless to say, this shift in habit had impact on jobs in the garment industry across the world. For each Banana Republic outfit, made in Saipan or Guatemala, that made its debut around the water cooler, a business suit, made by a union workforce, went unsold.[29]

That is not to say that multinational corporations have a free hand in shaping the clothing choices of the multitudes who have adopted casual dress as their global uniform. Youth who set trends are capricious tastemakers. They are relentlessly in pursuit of a fashion logic that outfoxes the rhythms of an industry seeking to package and market the very fabric of their lives. For over twenty years, this game of pose-and-run has been played fiercely among brand-conscious youth. The African American urban style connection is probably the best known, and the most influential, around the globe, partly because of its exploitation by Nike basketball shoe ads, ever pushing self-empowerment as a philosophy for overcoming the obstacles of race and class. Yet it was Adidas that first struck hip-hop gold, courtesy of Run-DMC, and it was not long before Fila was chasing the "urban market" through commercials awash with graffiti and inner-city street grit. Though it was in temporary synch with urban taste, peddling overpriced shoes to poor people turned out to be risky PR business, especially when stories surfaced about youth being robbed and killed for their Air Jordans. In the 1980s, the most lucrative marketing of sneakers was racially coded until it fell foul of community complaints about corporate exploitation.[30] Garment companies could not afford to ignore the basketball-driven street style engine, but they discovered there was a fine line between following and creating street taste. "Cool hunters" were employed to research shifting trends on the streets and test prototype products on the tastemaker kids to ensure they would have up-to-date, built-in appeal.[31] If it played well with the black kids, then thousands of white wanna-bes would buy in.

While other corporations needed the cool hunters to mine the commercial potential of musical and sports subcultures, Nike presumed to lead by example. Its ad campaigns evoked a ready-made insider knowledge that accompanied the brand in every niche market. Indeed, Nike's irreverent anti-advertising techniques could be extended to embrace wholesale anti-commercial sentiment whenever it was needed; as when Don Mattingly, in one baseball ad, remarks dryly, "I believe if Shoeless Joe Jackson were playing today, he'd have a shoe contract." In ads for the U.S. soccer market, the anti-commercial attitude was even more pronounced. They openly railed against the injustice of soccer's neglect by the insular sports media complex:

> Our football has no Primetimes nor Ministers of Defense
> Our football never stops, not for injuries, not for commercials.
> Our football championship isn't won
> By beating another city in our own country.
> It is won by beating every nation on earth.

In the same vein, Mia Hamm, ace in the pack of Nike's women's soccer sponsorship deals, is introduced in another ad: "The best soccer player in America . . . isn't good for ratings." Like Monica Seles, Sheryl Swoopes, and Gabriella Reese, her honesty and inner motivation are what make her an authentic Nike winner, and a perfect showcase for the huge suburban base that U.S. women's soccer commands.

Penetrating the consciousness of non-U.S. soccer fans was another matter, however. The storied brands and colors of famous soccer clubs could be bought off, but their fans proved to be shifty consumers, especially when soccer began to provide an unlikely breeding ground for fashion cults. In the "casual" movement of British fans, for example, flaunting designer brands became a way of life from the late 1970s. Post-punk working-class fans in Liverpool, Manchester, and London began to shape their identity around the most exclusive and expensive labels. Like the Mods before them, they looked mostly to brands on the Continent (Inega, Fiorucci, Ellesse, Fila, Dior, Lacoste, Tacchini) where their teams were enjoying unprecedented competitive success in European championships at the time. Their overseas "shopping" expeditions were soon supplemented by purchases (or thefts) of quality domestic brands (Pringles, Lyle & Scotts, Burberrys, Aquascutum).[32] Like U.S. inner city kids who adopted Ralph Lauren and other preppy brands far removed, in tone and purpose, from their own environment, casuals in dilapidated northern English towns donned the trappings of elite sports: ski anoraks, golf jackets, tennis and polo shirts, yachting waterproofs. The pursuit and adoption of new labels (Chipie, Stone Island, CP, Hackett, Henri Lloyd, Paul and Shark, Prada) was relentless, until the subculture became too mainstream or too solidly identified with the violence-prone supporter crews that were demonized in the 1980s as "mindless hooligans" in the British press.[33] These style wars were also played out with sneakers, and when manufacturers finally cottoned on in the late 1980s, and began churning out overdeveloped high-tops, taste on the terraces and elsewhere rapidly turned to old-school styles like Adidas Samba, Fila Tourissmo, Diadora Borg Elite, and Puma Argentina. Revivalist fever for classics began to drive the sneaker fashion market, and, along with the low-tech shoes of the anti-Nike companies (Airwalk, Simple, Van), came to challenge the technologically advanced ethos of Nike's high-performance product.[34]

Like all good subcultures, the casuals were a consciously spent force before too long. By the end of the 1980s, the movement had been tainted by the disastrous career of fan violence, and sidelined by the polymorphous energies of the rave revolution. In retrospect, however, the high-price elegance of the casual turned out to be a harbinger of the gentrification of soccer spectatorship. Each fancy label was another nail in the coffin of soccer's working-class terrace culture. After the Hillsborough disaster in 1989, the terraces were razed to make way for seating, and Margaret Thatcher's bid to domesticate the unruly male communalism of soccer crowds brought the game more fully into the world of middle-class mores and rules. In the 1990s, big TV money rapidly transformed the game (there had been no live coverage of soccer matches before 1983). The price of admission now cost an arm and a leg, and for those who wanted to avoid

115

FRIEDRICH
ENGELS
VISITS THE OLD
TRAFFORD
MEGASTORE

shelling out for a satellite TV subscription, watching soccer, especially away games, collapsed back into the male camaraderie of traditional pub culture.[35]

If nothing else, soccer's casual chic had proved to corporate marketers that expensive designer brands, even the most traditionally aristocratic labels, could be sold to low-income youth if only they were attached to a ruling passion in consumers' lives. Since few secular passions come anywhere close to the super-tribal allegiances fostered by a sport like soccer, fashion houses learned to take a practical interest in the clothing patterns of fans. Armani began to produce trainers, and Prada and other design houses opened their sport lines. The big names in casual wear were not far behind, and before long, they were producing clothing and shoe lines that drew directly on the influence of soccer. By the summer of 2002, when World Cup fever hit new retail highs, it was difficult to find any stores, in the upscale or discount market, that did not display this trend. The derivative soccer shoe, most identified with the global brand Diesel, quickly became an industry basic.

In some part, this outcome is simply an extension of patterns established with the introduction of designer jeans in the 1970s, when brands began to have impact on broad consumer trends. As consumer economies in the West bifurcated into value-added and discount markets, designer brands in almost every category of casual wear, even basics like T-shirts, became more and more of a staple in the former, exerting their pressure on the latter. Even so, it was a quantum leap to go from sports gear as streetwear to employing sport as an inspiration for haute garment design.

Yet the hybrid world of sport-as-fashion was an ideal expression of consumerism's appetite for high turnover. Sport, after all, is all about constant improvement and better performance. Insofar as those upgrades can be assisted by technology, then technical advances in materials and fabrics—remodeling and renovating—are part of the relentless pursuit of higher accomplishment. An operation like Nike, which often promotes itself as a technology company, succeeded, for a while, in synchronizing the rhythms of a whole industry to the periodic rollouts (several times a year) of its next-generation shoe technologies. Add to this stepped-up pace the increasingly fleeting fashion seasons—formerly only two, but now as many as four or five—and you have a cast-iron formula for product obsolescence. What is the impact of this escalating tempo on production workers? For some, the retailers' need for fast turnaround provides skilled, versatile work, close to urban fashion centers. In most cases, however, a system of high turnover and shifting product lines depends on cheap, manual labor. With less and less need for fixed, standardized lines, there is little incentive for manufacturers to invest in the machinery of mass production. It is much cheaper to turn to the immiserated of the earth to get the job done with their hands.

117

FRIEDRICH
ENGELS
VISITS THE OLD
TRAFFORD
MEGASTORE

A picture booth backdrop,
Dongguan, China

(PHOTO BY AUTHOR)

CHAPTER FOUR

Are the Chinese Losing China?

There is no place for workers now. Sometimes friends ask me, "Do you love your country?" I reply, "Of course!" But when they ask me, "Does your country love you?" I really have to think about it.

—A Chinese worker

THOUGH IT HAS A POPULATION of about 5.5 million, and is a significant point on the map of global production, Dongguan is hardly a well-known name, not even to urbanists who like to chart where smaller cities lie on the semi-periphery of the world system map. Nor is it even very recognizable as a centered city, since it is a combination of over thirty townships, each with some loose autonomy, in various states of turbocharged urbanization. Paddy fields and rural shacks lie cheek by jowl with long, low factory compounds carved out of the red earth and green hillsides; squat pockets of new housing abut high-rise business-class hotels; and chunks of the old village settlements are strewn around in between the voracious land development. Every so often, a decaying smokestack plant signals the former presence of a state-owned enterprise (SOE). Dongguan straddles the six-lane highway that connects the dreaming capitalist towers of Shenzhen in the south to the ancient trading entrepôt of Guangzhou on the Pearl River Delta, but it has none of the distinction of these other famous places. Yet it is much more typical of life and labor in the special economic zones of South China, whose open-door industrialization has been the engine of China's growth since Deng

Xiaoping declared them "windows on the global economy," in 1984, and later added the decree that "to get rich is glorious."

The range of products assembled and manufactured in Dongguan would cover all the major categories of a North American superstore, and in sheer quantity, amount annually to almost $20 billion worth of exports. Garments, toys, and electronics are foremost in terms of volume, but lately, some of the newly migrating semiconductor fabs have made their way there, to a location known as "Little Taiwan." Even more exotic products are alleged. Shortly after my arrival in town in the summer of 2001, on a brief visit to interview workers, I was told that a crime syndicate was mass-producing the recreational drug Ecstasy. The population was 70 percent migrant workers (*dagongmei*) primarily from China's poorest provinces, like Sichuan and Henan, and most of them were teenage girls, sprung from their family farms. The girls were not visible on the streets, however, since they lived in dorms inside the factory compounds, and were only allowed outside the gates for a short spell each day around lunchtime. Once a month, they had two days off, and a good deal of that time was spent hanging out in the lunchtime café zones around the factories.

Two of the girls I interviewed were on their days off, and were neatly dressed for leisure, their regulation work shirts left behind to dry on the balconies of one-hundred-square-foot dorm rooms that they shared with eleven other workers. They had been recruited by an agent in their village in Henan, where their families farmed peanuts, cotton, and wheat, and each had paid him 450 renminbi (rmb) to find them a job. Li You was working for a Taiwanese company making power supplies for computer products, and Gao Xiaoyin was employed at a Japanese-owned factory making photocopy machine components. Both of them spent twelve hours a day, seven days a week, working on assembly lines, one standing up, one sitting down. Every four hours, they had a ten-minute break, plus an hour and a half for lunch and dinner. Food and board cost them 50rmb, and their overall monthly wage was about 450rmb (about $50), which is slightly above Dongguang's minimum wage of 400rmb. They considered it dangerous to be outside in the evening, and so their entertainment was all in-house (TV, movies, the occasional dance), which saved money. Most months, they could save as much as 300rmb, to be sent back to their families in Henan or to put into their own savings.

Li You's fingernails were long on one hand, and cropped on the other—"It's the one I work with," she explained. "What are your thoughts when you work?" I asked her. "I can't afford to think. If I get distracted I screw up the line, and get fined 50rmb." Others in her village had told her that factory work wasn't all it was cut out to be, but she didn't believe them because she wanted the "outside world," in the South, to be a wonderful place, full of opportunities. It was too hot and arduous for her to work in the fields, and school had been boring to her. Now she wished she had studied more, and would covet the chance to acquire some computer skills. After several months in Dongguan, she was bored to tears, and wished she could get to a real city, like Shentzen or Hong Kong. As a migrant with temporary registration (like most of her co-workers, she was underage, and so she had a false registration card), she could not marry here, though she had little desire to

Li You and fellow workers, Dongguan
(PHOTO BY AUTHOR)

return to the family village, where she would be able to enter an arranged marriage. Gao Xiaoyin, also a "child of Deng" (born in 1983), phoned Li You and one other friend from the village every day to talk about their moods. "They are the only people I can trust," she explained. How could she see her conditions improving? She had heard about women workers from the same locality getting together to bargain over wages, but the worsening economy was making employment scarcer, and she thought she was lucky to have her job. "Girls don't generally make a lot of noise about such things," she added, "even though they know their rights."[1]

To compound the slowdown, it was low season, and so the number of floaters seeking work was unusually large. Two days later, in an industrial zone in Shenzhen, we talked to Tian Yan, in a lunchtime canteen, who was killing time before a job interview. With a feather-cut hairstyle, high platform shoes, flared pants, and a host of silver accessories, she looked fashionable, though she told us she felt ugly. This was important, as she pointed out, because "many factories only employ good-looking, light-skinned, girls who are tall and thin," and, in the month she has been out and about looking for a job, the sun had darkened her skin. She paid a labor agent 50rmb for four job opportunities, and showed up every Tuesday and Friday to see what was available. Her previous position was in quality control at a Hong Kong–owned factory that manufactured pagers and mobile phones, but she had gotten bored with the job, and had returned to her village to "worship her ancestors." When she returned to Shenzhen, jobs were scarce, and more and more workers had arrived in the area, desperate for employment. She wore a wedding ring on her finger "to ward off demons"—probably those who came in the guise of the Hong Kong businessmen who had made mistresses of some of her friends. What did she love most, I asked? Her country, her family or her self? None of them, she responded. Entertainment is what she craves, especially Taiwanese pop singers like Richie Ren, Chin Chyi, and Jimmy Lin, because they make her feel "modern," and that is why she can never go home again. All the same, her big anxiety was that she could not send any money to her family, a fact that clearly affected her self-esteem. Without her monthly remittance, her parents were in real trouble.

Worker dormitories,
Shenzhen
(PHOTO BY AUTHOR)

The ebullient proprietor of the café, who had shown an interest in us, could not help her out with a job, though he boasted that his employees earn over 700rmb. A resident, he knew full well how his interests were served by the household registration (*hukou*) system that excludes rural migrants from enjoying any privileges in the urban locations where they work. First of all, the export zones generated the need for a goodly amount of local businesses, like his own, which serviced the factories and their workers. Self-reliant individuals, like himself, therefore had options other than to rely on contacts (*guanxi*) with government officials. Local government officials charge companies a monthly fee for each temporary registration cardholder on their payrolls. This revenue, combined with business taxes, helps to fund public amenities—schools, hospitals—that are enjoyed by residents like himself but are inaccessible to the migrants whose labor makes it all possible. In addition, the worker dormitories run by the companies minimize the impact on communities of playing host to large migrant populations, and save local officials the social cost of policing shantytowns. On the other side, the remittance economy allows money to flow from the coastal cities to the provinces, and helps to sustain peasant families (80 percent of the nation's population) that Beijing has little chance of helping otherwise.

In the revolution's infancy, laboring was a heroic exercise of citizenship, and workers' sacrifice for the cause of nation-building was perceived to have clear returns in the form of lifelong security. For women, in particular, the freedom to labor was promoted as a vehicle of liberation from a feudal tradition of foot binding, arranged marriages, and general subservience. Ever since, the distinction of womens' labor has been manipulated to serve the dominant state program for nation-building. As elsewhere in the developing world, young women have provided the laboring backbone of the export economy, and their bodies have been subject to factory discipline to give meaning to the march toward modernity.[2] Female youth are no longer feted, as they were under Maoism, for their political evangelism and sacrifice for the motherland, but rather because their labor costs less.

However disillusioned by the reality of their new lives, the working daughters in Guangdong's export zones who have had a taste of the city generally do not want to return to the crushing poverty of their farms, or to the stifling roles they would play there in the household economy. Their desperation to stay in the South and eke out an independent life is clearly evident in the hardships they are willing to put up with in the factories. Labor-rights activists from the Asia Monitor Resource Center, China Labor Bulletin, Hong Kong Christian Industrial Council, and the New York–based National Labor Committee have extensively documented these conditions. Unbearably long hours, substandard food, cramped dorms, sadistic managers who beat and sexually abuse them, and pay that arrives months late, or sometimes not at all. Worst of all, arguably, are the health hazards that are a routine part of assembly jobs, where heeding environmental safety ranks even lower than labor rights on the scale of managerial priorities.[3] Sadly, it is in the toy industry—the target of massive concern about children's safety on the part of First World parents—that the range and intensity of workers' exposure to toxic substances on the job is greatest. Managers' reluctance to install basic protective technologies like extraction fans means that many workers directly inhale toxic fumes from poisonous glues and other toxic substances.

In the late 1990s, the international press seized upon two spectacular stories involving high death tolls—a spate of factory fires that incinerated workers locked inside, and an alarming increase in mining explosions. Less likely to capture attention is the daily toll exacted by routine lapses in regulatory oversight—maiming on the job, or respiratory and neural damage from toxic exposure. The only thing more tragic than these work conditions is the willingness of workers to accept them because they have so few alternatives, and because their employers have partially persuaded them that their jobs are a bridge to a modern way of life. It was not until November 2002, almost fifty years after the founding of the People's Republic of China, and largely in response to international media reporting on the escalating volume of industrial accidents and deaths (386,645 deaths from occupational illnesses in 2002) that the National Peoples' Congress introduced legislation on workplace safety.

The new laws stipulate that employees have the right to refuse illegal or risky work, and have the right to stop work and evacuate from a hazardous site. Yet there is little, in practice, that would prevent workers from being fired for doing so. On paper, China's labor laws are a model of worker protection, but they are rarely implemented. As I will argue in this chapter, this discrepancy has dire consequences, not only for the domestic labor force but for workers all around the world who are impacted by China's burgeoning export economy.

Chinese Characteristics

In *Globalization and Its Discontents*, Joseph Stiglitz's stinging broadside against two decades of the International Monetary Fund's (IMF) implementation of the Washington Consensus (fiscal austerity, privatization, and market liberalization), China is cited as the most prominent example of a developing country that got it right. Eschewing the IMF's shock therapy of fiscal discipline that has brought colossal distress to economies around the world, China, in Stiglitz's view, adopted a more cautious, homegrown approach. Beijing's gradual transition from state to market economy rested on a two-tier system, which insured prices for the production quotas of the command system while encouraging market prices for surplus production. Foreign investment was invited in the form of six different categories (wholly foreign-owned ventures, equity joint ventures, cooperative ventures, joint development, compensation trade, and imported inputs for processing and assembly, or "outprocessing"), and capital was made available to fund the local side of each venture. According to Stiglitz, the new economy was actively created, molecule by molecule, degree by degree, rather than thrown wide open to market forces to develop without constraint. Indeed, twenty years after Deng's decision to open up to international market trade, China was still dismantling its protective trade barriers.[4] By contrast, the looter's paradise of Russian privatization had produced a basket-case economy, distinguished by the abrupt stripping of state assets and the instant establishment of routine corruption.

Beijing got extra points in Stiglitz's book for having resisted the "colonial attitude" of the IMF bureaucrats, whose priority in every corner of the globe has been to protect foreign creditors and their investments. The implementation of Deng's flexible "one country, two systems" policy staved off any threat of a revival of the invasive arrogance of the Opium Wars. As a result, foreign trade with China does not exactly resemble the profitable terms and concessions enjoyed by the Western powers after the Treaty of Nanjing in 1842. Yet you would not have to probe far beyond the farrago of official statistics and communiques to find widespread evidence of plunder—on the part of citizens and foreigners alike—that approaches the measure of the semicolonial record. Stiglitz's gutsy portrait of a go-it-alone Beijing is quite a sanitized version of a system creaking with the kind of injustices—chronic corruption and ever-widening inequality—that are otherwise all too familiar in countries adjusted to fit the cookie-cutter template of neoliberalism. Only in China the scale, as always, is much larger, and China watchers are predisposed, as always, to be boggled.

Even though independent journalism in most parts of the country is severely hampered, there have been ubiquitous reports of managers selling off the profitable portions of SOEs for fast lucre. Corruption is rife at every level of the party bureaucracy, as local officials scramble to grease the wheel for foreign investors.[5] With the shuttering, or sale, of thousands of SOEs, workers who built the country's industrial base have lost their jobs along with most of the hard-earned social security—the iron rice bowl of guaranteed employment, pension, free medical care, and free schooling for their children.[6] 48.07 million workers were laid off from 1995 to 2000. One result is a surging wave of unauthorized worker strikes, sit-downs and bloody protests, posing a direct threat to party elites ever mindful of the history of dynasties being overthrown from below.

Another threat to social stability—Beijing's pervasive obsession—lies in the escalating unemployment figures (an official estimated 150 million) and the emergence of a vast "floating population" of migrant labor. Peasants (almost 80 percent of the population) faced with burdensome taxes and the loss of state subsidies under the terms of the WTO, have sometimes been reduced to selling their blood to survive, and have contracted HIV. In the factories of the special economic zones of South China, which boast one of the lowest wage floors in the world, sweatshop conditions have attracted the ire of human rights and labor rights organizations everywhere. "Made in China" has become a byword for the fierce exploitation of workers in export zones like those in Dongguan. Nor is the impact of these exploitative practices confined to China alone. The favorable terms that foreign investors can find there for manufacture are driving down wages throughout the region, undercutting whatever gains have been made in labor rights and conditions in other East Asian countries.

China's recent experience with SARS was an allegory of its pivotal role in the global economy. When China sneezed, the entire region's economy felt the impact. The explanation for this lay not just in the sheer size of its population, but rather in the marketization of its social services. After two decades of commercializing its state- and commune-funded health care infrastructure, the authorities had effectively gutted any existing national system of disease prevention. Praised in the 1950s and 1960s for its monumental progress in pioneering primary care in rural areas (resulting in the doubling of life expectancy), by 2000 China was near the bottom of the WHO public-health system rankings, both in terms of effectiveness and equitable provision. The SARS outbreak proved a threat to populations around the world precisely because the uneven impact of market liberalization on China's population had left the vast majority with no access to public health resources.

Beijing's determination to maintain a high annual rate of growth at all costs has spawned crises that clearly tarnish the shining example of economic rectitude sketched out by Stiglitz. Yet the mantle of resistance remains. Developing countries that have successfully bypassed the Washington Consensus, and that are forging their own alternative modernity, are few and far between. In many quarters, they earn kudos simply for trying. Even Asianists well to the left of Stiglitz advocate a hands-off attitude as recompense for the legacy of colonialism. Bruce Cumings, for example, agrees that China has displayed a "steady tendency, almost a textbook example, of how to introduce a developing country into the world economy."[7] How should outsiders respond? "Western humility," Cumings suggests, is the most appropriate stance to adopt, in the face of two centuries of humiliation visited upon the Chinese. "We have shaken China enough as it is": better to let China go its way. Even though we can "encourage a less dominant central government, the rule of law, and basic political rights for China's citizens," we should do so, he concludes, "without illusions that we will make much of a difference."[8]

It would be careless to ignore Cumings's caveat about humility. Even without the lesson about the legacy of Western imperialism, we should recognize that China, like any other sovereign nation, has the right to choose its own path of development. Can this autonomy be respected without consigning Western criticism of human and labor rights violations to the same domineering mentality that drove the Opium Wars? Can we acknowledge what is distinctive about China's exceptionalism while still advocating the right of workers to organize, to work in safety and sanity, and to be paid a fair, living wage? There is nothing essentially compliant about the former, just as there is nothing essentially imperious about the latter, yet the answer to these kinds of question bedevils the left in all of its debates about the impact of global trading. Whatever the outcome, to suspend our belief that "we will make much of a difference," as Cumings proposes, is to cede in advance the hope that these debates might be meaningful, or that activist pressure on the labor front could improve the dire situation of low-wage workers, both in China and elsewhere.

In the case of China, the silent humility advocated by Cumings would be a mistake. During the earlier upheavals surrounding collectivization, the Great Leap Forward in the fifties, the Cultural Revolution in the sixties, or even the household responsibility system that replaced the agrarian communes, the impact of Beijing's economic policies was mostly internal. In an era of global trading, this is no longer the case. The size of China's productive capacity and the potential scope of its labor reserves have a disproportionate effect on countries around the world. Just as American foreign policy, like it or not, is everyone's business, so too no one can afford to ignore what goes on in China's factories. Their low wage floor affects workers everywhere in the global sweatshop: in Juarez, Mexico; Bangalore, India; Seoul, Korea; and Los Angeles, U.S.A.

Yet there is another principle, less obvious perhaps, which might help us address the semicolonial legacy alluded to by Cumings. If we are to take seriously the impact of free-trade agreements that already exist or are in the works, then we must heed the proposition that trade is something that happens primarily between corporations, not the governments of nation-states. Trade can no longer be conceived or measured solely in terms of flows between countries, even though that is a staple of coverage in the business press. Investors and other business professionals may be reassured to know, for example, that Sino-U.S. trade chalked up $80.5 billion in 2001. But this statistic tells us nothing about how that trade operates; who provides capital funding, what chains of subcontracting are used, which labor markets are sought out and which labor practices are implemented. Governments, national or local, have a less consequential role to play in this process than do large investors, suppliers, or multinational corporations. Most nation-states have their own trade policy regulations, for sure, though they are increasingly dictated by organizations like the WTO or the World Intellectual Property Organization (the power to set tariffs, for example, has been drastically curtailed). So too rich countries still exercise a fair degree of direct control over the purchasing power of their own governments, though the choices of most others are dictated by debt-service stipulations. And, in China's case, the government regulates the currency exchange rate of the yuan, ensuring that exports are cheap. But to continue to envisage trade as a global map of intergovernmental flows is anachronistic to a fault. Not when corporations, which threw away their passports many years ago, already make up half of the world's 100 largest economies. Not when major contracting agents effectively control regional trade by supplying the transnationals, or by setting up their own firms to compete with the big brands. Not when key sectors of global production are located in export processing zones that are effectively quarantined off from the countries that host them, largely immune to the implementation of national labor and environmental laws. Not when government officials are subject to the caprices of corporate managers who relocate at the first whiff of increases in taxes, duties, minimum-wage levels, or environmental regulations. Not when the ideal manufacturing model for global corporations would be Jack Welch's fantasy of "putting all our production on a barge."

One of the sharpest lessons of the alternative-globalization movement has been to focus on corporate behavior, rather than to label nation-states as either good or bad. In many ways, this was the great leap forward that occurred in Seattle when progress on the new round of WTO agreements stalled, and when the movement earned its raucous pedigree. Much was made of the fact that organized labor and anticorporate environmentalists appeared to have joined together in protest for almost the first time in the U.S. Yet the harmonic convergence of Seattle was as much a product of serendipity as anything else. Six months later, at the A16 (April 16) action against an IMF-World Bank meeting in Washington, D.C., the two camps had fallen out of alignment. Four days before the anticorporate legions gathered to protest, the AFL-CIO establishment marched on Capitol Hill "against China" in a bid to pressure Congressional voting on granting permanent normal trading relations (PNTR) to Beijing—a vote that would clear the way for China's accession to the WTO. Labor leaders justified their decision to lobby against the PNTR bill by citing China's record of labor rights violations, but it put the AFL-CIO in the same corner as America First nationalists like Pat Buchanan (who spoke at the PNTR rally at the Teamsters' invitation on the same platform as John Sweeney), and right-wing policy hawks who have wielded human rights as an anti-Communist truncheon. China-bashing always has an audience on Capitol Hill, and Cold War vestiges within the AFL-CIO (from the anti-Communist activities of the American Institute for Free Labor Development, which cooperated with the CIA and other agencies to undermine left-leaning unions in Latin America and elsewhere) were strong enough to connect with that sentiment.[9]

This opportunistic alliance was a lucid example of how U.S. unilateralism in trade policy operates against the interests of working people. If the ostensible motive for the AFL-CIO's participation was to strike a blow for its members against the global sweatshop, the nature and conduct of the campaign left entirely the wrong impression. Choosing China as a target, instead of aiming at corporate control of the WTO agenda, was wrongheaded. It played into the hands of posturing policymakers, seeking, as ever, to secure advantages for U.S. multinationals in negotiating agreements with weaker, developing countries. It also reinforced the impression, abroad, that the American labor movement all too often thinks in protectionist ways (the AFL-CIO still has no fraternal relations with the Chinese trade union), and it undercut the efforts to distinguish labor rights, as advocated by the international anti-sweatshop movement, from the notion of human rights that is used by the North to protect its own unfair trading privileges. When John Sweeney made part of the AFL-CIO case on the basis that China had not ratified key U.N. Covenants on human rights, it was not the most shining moment in his presidency.

Challenging Beijing's qualification to fully integrate into the neoliberal version of world trade on the basis of its human rights record is viewed as especially hypocritical talk on the part of a nation-state that has consistently flaunted or violated international treaty obligations, which sanctions the widespread use of prison labor at home, and which maintains a system of capital punishment abhorred by all of its allies in the industrialized world. Every so often, Beijing publishes its own assessment of the human rights record of the U.S. The report, which makes for harrowing reading, is a detailed critique of the U.S.'s high rates of murder and violent crime; police brutality and discriminatory legal treatment, including the racist use of incarceration and the death penalty; shrinking tolerance for the poor, hungry, and homeless; continuing gender discrimination; and a consistent pattern of illegal intervention in the affairs of other countries, resulting in the infringement of the sovereignty of nations and the human rights of their citizens.

While China is habitually decried for human rights abuses, the Western powers have not held its East Asian neighbors (all vital Cold War dependencies) to the same criteria. For decades, Washington tolerated authoritarian rule in Korea and martial law in Taiwan, while the British turned a blind eye to the democracy lobby in Hong Kong. Accustomed to managing the economic and political development of the region from a distance, G7 elites have been shaken by the recent rise of Asian capital. Yet in China, Washington arguably faces its biggest challenge of all—a world-class "strategic competitor" with an economy that Americans depend on to supply almost every commodity item of their waking lives. As a long-standing member of the nuclear club, and one of the few remaining members of the Communist club, Beijing poses a unique challenge to U.S. dominance. Even though it is still officially a developing country, China's starkly independent path to modernization, combined with its ravenous share of world trade and investment, put it in a position to "say no" to the West. Predictably, this has generated its share of saber-rattling in Washington, and no end of bafflement about how to deal with a skyrocketing trade deficit.

Flagging the Way

In the spring of 2001, one of the first outbreaks of friction between Bush Administration hawks and the military establishment surfaced in the public farce involving a decision by the U.S. army chief of staff, General Eric

Shineskei, to buy his soldiers black berets from a supplier that used production facilities in China. This decision to kit the soldiers in black was part and parcel of the "transformation" of the armed services from a "Cold War legacy force" into lighter, more flexible units that could respond more quickly to "hot spot" activity around the globe. As Shineskei put it in a Department of Defense hearing, "We thought it important to have a symbolic and a visible demonstration that this army was prepared for change and undertaking it."[10] To make the move in time for the service's birthday on June 14 necessitated the prompt acquisition of over three million berets, and, if overseas suppliers were to be used, a waiver of the Berry Amendment, which requires the Pentagon to award all clothing contracts for the armed services to domestic suppliers. The order and the waiver went through, but they generated an uproar following the April 1 collision of a U.S. navy reconnaissance plane and a Chinese jet fighter off China's southern coast. When Beijing impounded the American plane for several weeks, the resulting face-off with Washington presented Deputy Defense Secretary Paul Wolfowitz with a grandstanding opportunity to countermand Shineskei and cancel the order. Henceforth, the famously hawkish Bush appointee declared, U.S. soldiers would wear "made in the U.S.A." uniforms only, and would wear nothing with Chinese content. The 600,000 berets that had been delivered to bases were recalled, but the Pentagon was unable to unload them on other federal agencies or to foreign buyers.

Thrown back on the resources of domestic manufacturers, the army found only one U.S. supplier—the Bancroft Cap Company in Cabot, Arkansas—with the machinery to make the one-seam berets.[11] Though Bancroft claimed to use "100 percent domestic wool in all of [its] yarns," the company imported tanned leather from Pakistan, claiming that there was "no leather market available in the United States." More public embarrassment followed, as domestic leather producers stepped forward to put the record straight.[12] The entire incident demonstrated the discrepancies that now exist between shows of patriotism and the realities of global manufacturing. Yet the beret flap was only a prologue to the drama that followed the attacks on September 11, when Americans rushed to purchase U.S. flags that turned out to have been made in Chinese factories.

Workers at companies like the Jin Teng Flag Company in Zhejiang province and Shanghai's Mei Li Hua Flags Company toiled around the clock to meet the explosive U.S. demand for Stars and Stripes in all available formats. Production of Chinese flags (for Chinese National Day) was put on hold as mainland producers rushed out 78 million of the 110 million flags imported into the U.S. in the last four months of 2001.[13] Medium-sized cloth flags produced by the Shanghai factories for a dollar were sold by American retailers for about fifteen dollars. Plastic "car flags" cost even less, but retailed for around twelve dollars.[14] Significantly, it was not the huge domestic markup but the foreign provenance and the middling quality of the flags that generated public outrage in the U.S. Devotees of the cult of Old Glory, which requires national legislation to detail exactly how the flag should be treated and flown (from the front bumper of a vehicle, for example, and never from the rear), kicked into high moral gear. Leading the charge were veterans groups and congressional grandstanders (like Rep. Ted Strickland [D-Ohio], who called for the banning of imported flags by introducing the Genuine American Flag Act). The "Buy American" flag crusade became the leading edge of directives from Washington to maintain consumption levels and stave off a deepening of the national recession.

America's domestic flag manufacturers seized the opportunity to band together and exploit the groundswell of public sentiment. One of their spokespeople, Greg Harris, president of Valley Forge Flag Company, based in Womelsdorf, Pennsylvania, stubbornly declared: "We have resisted the temptation to follow textile manufacturing overseas for the simple reason that an American flag has an element of patriotism that exceeds cost considerations."[15] If that statement were true, it would make his company almost unique among American firms, not to mention a champion of iffy business economics. However spurious, such commercial appeals to patriotism are pitched as if they transcend all of the normal concerns of business, including the price value of labor at home and abroad. In this respect, the flag appeal differed from traditional Buy American campaigns, whether undertaken by trade unions to preserve their members' jobs, or in the form, most recently, of anti-sweatshop policies, adopted by state and city governments and other institutions, that favor domestic manufacturers and forbid the use of sweatshop-prone suppliers.

Media coverage of the brouhaha revealed how much the U.S. depends on overseas production for the trappings of its patriotism. That Americans could not even count on their flags being made in the U.S. was either a mark of national shame or a sign of the global times. Yet the consequences were limited. Despite the saber-rattling that had accompanied the beret incident, the fierce chauvinism whipped up by 9/11, and the growing encirclement of China by U.S. regional military facilities, it is still unlikely there will ever be an all-out Sino-U.S. conflict, at least not as long as Wal-Mart's shelves are lined with Chinese-made sneakers, blouses, and toys with attractively low price tags.

Jumping the Straits

Shortly after the flag rumpus, there was another, less publicized, though arguably more portentous, story about flags that concerned the U.S. and China. In the spring and summer of 2002, the mainland PRC flag began to appear in Chinatowns in San Francisco and New York City, breaking with the universally observed code of displaying Taiwan's Republic of China (ROC) colors. The flag was first raised on the roofs of the two most conservative associations in San Francisco, the South China Benevolent Association and the South China Nine Rivers Charitable Association. The practice spread rapidly, reinforcing the impression that popular support for mainland-Taiwan reunification was surfacing openly, or at least that it was accepted as legitimate in the community.

If that was the case, then it was an appropriate response to the burgeoning traffic across the straits that had served as one of the hottest border zones of the Cold War, and still functions as a touchstone for the neoconservative hawks in the Bush administration. Like the U.S., Taiwan was finding it increasingly difficult to make national autonomy prevail over the powerful economic pull that Mainland China exacted on investors. Despite the pro-independence views of its premier, Chen Shui-bian, cracks in the anti-PRC posture had become gaping rifts as the manufacturing exodus and capital flight from Taiwan picked up speed. Unemployment had risen precipitously as Taiwanese industry began to suffer the same fate undergone by Hong Kong and Singapore in the eighties in response to the siren-like appeal of labor costs and high profit margins in China. After Taiwan's accession to the WTO (formalized at the same time as the PRC's), restrictions on direct trade links with the mainland were eased, dissolving a ban on trade, transport, and communications that had held up for over five decades. Soon, Taiwanese investors were clamoring for permission to join mainland political bodies like the National Peoples' Congress, even CCP (Chinese Communist Party) membership, that would give them a level of clout appropriate to their investments.

How will the resumption of direct investment affect labor conditions in Taiwanese-backed factories, both in China and overseas? For several decades the Taiwanese government has provided development aid for poor countries in return for diplomatic recognition. That policy, primarily aimed at restoring the 1979 loss of Taiwan's U.N. seat to the PRC, has included substantial business investment, in addition to funding for public highways, bridges, schools, and civic infrastructure. Taipei's cash incentives drew Taiwanese capitalists to low-wage export zones in regions like Central America, exploiting the desire of local officials for foreign investment at the cost of substandard labor conditions. Since Taiwanese capital props up the *maquiladora* system as part of an overt diplomatic mission, regulation of labor standards is a very low priority. In 2001, the Nien Hsing Textile Company, the world's largest manufacturer of blue jeans, was targeted by anti-sweatshop activists for its decision to fire union leaders at its Chentex garment factory in Nicaragua's Las Mercedes free-trade zone. Under strong international pressure from a coalition of student anti-sweatshop, trade union, and interfaith groups in the U.S. and Taiwan, Nicaragua's highest court ruled against the company, and reinstated the unionists in April 2001.[16] Astonishingly, it was the first time that a Taiwanese firm had been penalized by any government for its labor policies overseas. Yet workers in every corner of the global sweatshop know, and fear, the heavy hand of Taiwanese administration.

Workers in the export zones of South China are no exception. After all, most of the factories are owned by capitalists from Taiwan, Hong Kong, or South Korea. In some cities, Taiwanese managers are so numerous and powerful that their businessmen associations function like local governments, or even like quasi-embassies, since Taiwan has no diplomatic relations with China. For the most part, the associations operate beneath the law.[17] Among the workers whom I interviewed in the summer of 2001 in Dongguan, where the Taiwanese Businessmen's Association is especially formidable, Taiwanese (and Korean) bosses were the least popular among the available choices, combining a harsh regime of labor discipline with the lowest wages. Those from Hong Kong and Macau were marginally better on both counts, while Japanese managers were considered authoritarian but more generous with pay.[18] Though they are few and far between in Guangdong province, factories with U.S. and European management were known for higher wages and more humane work policies. Indeed, in 2001, workers at foreign firms earned a national average of 15,037 yuan ($1,816) that year, while those at Hong Kong–, Taiwan- or Macau-backed companies had an average annual salary of 12,547 yuan.[19]

Until recently, Taiwanese capitalists had to use indirect routes, mostly through Hong Kong, or offshore companies, to invest in mainland factories. As a result of Taipei's trade restrictions, the cost of doing business rose, and put further pressure on the wage floor. With the easing of that policy in 2001 by Taiwan's president, Chen Shui-bian, and the increasing de facto integration of Taiwan into the PRC's "one country, two systems," it remains to be seen how this will affect industrial life in South China, or Central America, for that matter, where the *maquiladora* sector has been losing jobs and foreign investment to China in significant numbers. A good portion of the world's production of computer peripherals—monitors, printers, scanners, mouses, keyboards, motherboards, and cables—already takes place in Taiwanese-owned plants in South China. Yet the most visible geographical impact of the newly relaxed investment laws has been on East China, and in particular in the Shanghai-Suzhou corridor, where Taiwanese investment is shifting, along with most of its high-tech, semiconductor industry, which until recently produced more than half of the world's computers and a quarter of the desktops. By 2002, more than 40,000 Taiwanese firms, including many of the leading makers of computer components, had shifted production to the mainland, along with an estimated $60 billion of investment.[20]

The flight of capital across the straits is not without its political pitfalls. Taiwanese investors live in fear of a military flare-up between Beijing and Taipei that could cost them dearly. With Taiwan's industrial base increasingly transplanted to the PRC, the island would be left with little in the way of leverage, and its investors could lose their mainland factories overnight. The Bush Administration has adopted a more confrontational policy in the region, openly stating that it will militarily intervene to prevent Taiwan's forcible integration into a unified Chinese state. In fact, the White House has explicitly threatened China with a U.S. nuclear strike if Beijing takes any steps toward consummating its "One China" policy. This commitment to U.S. military action is an effective repudiation of a strategic policy, pursued since the Taiwan Relations Act of 1979, of arming Taiwan to the teeth while formally recognizing Beijing's sovereignty over Taipei. Chen's "native Taiwanese" Democratic Progressive Party, which exploited the divided Kuomintang Party to take power in 2000, has been sufficiently emboldened by Washington's assurances to openly promote a pro-independence line. Yet the business establishment overwhelmingly favors de facto reintegration. Squeezed hard by the exodus of manufacturing, Taiwan's working class increasingly leans toward preserving the island's autonomy, and its farmers and fishermen staged the biggest street protest ever in Tapei to protest plummeting post-WTO prices for vegetables and fruit.[21] Nor are workers on the mainland well served by the rising friction. The more risky their investments are perceived to be, the less Taiwanese businessmen are likely to invest in their mainland workers' well-being, both on the job and off. The culture of production will be arrested in its current frontier mentality, with core labor rights recognized in name, but ignored at every turn.

From the U.S. point of view, Taiwan's independence is of little concern in and of itself, and its fate hangs in the balance of Washington's geopolitical interests in the region as a whole. The White House has made aggressive moves, in the wake of the events of 9/11, to secure U.S. access to oil and gas deposits in Central Asia. With new military bases in the Central Asian republics of Kyrgyzstan, Uzbekistan, Tajikistan, and Afghanistan, added to the Pentagon's access rights in Singapore, Thailand, Brunei, Indonesia, Malaysia, South Korea, the Philippines, and, of course, Taiwan, the American encirclement of China, a "strategic competitor," in the eyes of the Bush Administration, has put further political pressure on the economic situation. Unlike in the Cold War, when the socialist bloc supplied little that was vital to the West, the U.S. is increasingly dependent on its chief strategic adversary for the continued supply of technology products. If China's supply lines were withheld, the U.S. economy would surely falter. Even the SARS scare of 2003 had a serious impact on the supplying of companies and retailers in the U.S. With the escalating shift to the mainland of skilled, high-tech production, American economic security is further compromised.

The Taiwanese migration is only a part of what has become a region-wide stampede on the part of technology firms still struggling to recover from the Asian economic crisis, and newly hit by the post-bubble recessionary slowdown in business consumer demand. After decades of serving as the world's factory for low-wage production and assembly, China is now sucking in high-value industry from the region's other NICs—Singapore, Malaysia, Korea—in addition to Taiwan and fully industrialized Japan. Chinese universities are now churning out engineering graduates, who have business management training and English-language proficiency. The native know-how for high-tech crafts like chip-making and DVD design is establishing itself as rapidly as the specialized factory infrastructure is being imported from rivals in the region. The semiconductor and disk-drive industries that gave Taiwan, Singapore, and Malaysia a competitive edge are migrating to places where engineers are paid less than what an unskilled worker would earn in Taipei or Kuala Lumpur.

Blue-chip electronics brands like Toshiba, Minolta, Canon, Sony, Matsushita, Ericsson, Intel, Motorola, and JVC are also expanding their presence in China by snapping up the new graduate class at bargain rates—roughly a tenth of a domestic payroll in Tokyo or Seoul. With the price of their labor so low, these scientists will not be enjoying the lavish benefits extended to the much lionized engineers of Silicon Valley: stock options, permissive work cultures, self-management of schedules. Managers will feel little obligation to treat or regard these professionals any differently than they would a low-wage service worker in Singapore or Bangkok. Indeed, one executive of a biotech company described his scientist workforce (who earned the equivalent of $145 a month plus lunch) as if they were no better, though probably cheaper, than robots: "They respond to voice commands," he reported, "and are fully programmable artificial intelligence."[22] Nor will foreign engineers, like the returning Taiwanese, need to be so well-compensated in a country where their expat salaries allow them to live like royalty.

With China now offering even lower tariff rates under the terms of its WTO accession, there are few regional and global firms that will resist its combination of a low-cost, highly regimented workforce with special economic zones offering convenient ports, virtually zero land costs, subsidized loans, and negligible taxes. To move into some industrial parks in East China, foreign investors only have to pay the bill for clearing the land; everything else is taken care of, including the cost of relocating residents who lived there. Sealing the package is the fabled promise of China's own domestic market for consumer technology, growing by leaps and bounds, and unlikely to be saturated for decades to come. The lure of this package is proving irresistible to the high-skilled, value-added industrial sectors just as it had done, for the last two decades, to low-end production in garments, light manufacturing, and electronic assembly.

How will the migration of industry have impact on those jobs left standing in Asia's domestic economies? To compete with the mainland, the wage floor will have to drop even further, and new rounds of tax breaks will further deplete the national tax income and bite into programs. Having fought for decades to establish trade unions with the teeth to ensure a decent level of benefits and conditions, Korean and Taiwanese workers now see their hard-won gains slipping away along with their jobs. Employers wield the threat of China as an excuse to demand concessions, or to nudge their workforce into the informal economy. The Asian tigers, once the engines of the regional economy, may end up as satellite states, scrambling to retain some share of the high-value jobs, while other countries, like the labor-intensive export sectors in Thailand and Indonesia, will have to compete with China in a race to the bottom. The region as a whole is undergoing a massive adjustment to accommodate Chinese growth.

China's low production costs, high volume of foreign direct investment, and inexhaustible labor supply, have already made it unlikely that any other developing country can enter into, let alone claim, a competing share of the global market for low-wage, export-led growth. With the rapid penetration of skilled manufacturing and engineering, the same pattern may now ensue for high-wage and white-collar industry. Everything that can be made will be made in China, and sooner than anyone thinks. By all criteria, this is a fairly unique prospect in world history, and not one that many would consider desirable. What are the political and economic conditions that made such a prospect possible, and what are the chances of it all falling apart?

All Fall Down

Given the epic dimension of the nation's landmass and social demographic, its historical antiquity, and its complex network of links with ethnic Chinese overseas, it is no surprise that forecasts of China's disintegration are legion. In a country that has seen its share of dynasties toppled by peasant movements, expectations of prolonged CCP rule are not especially high, especially against the backdrops of the collapse of the state socialist bloc, the debacle of Tiananmen Square, and the implosion of Asia's economic boom in the late 1990s. For a traditional Cold War adversary, like the U.S., the desire for any such outcome is hotly promoted, and no more so than among policy hawks who harbor a vengeful memory over "Who lost China?" and who are pushing for "regime change" in Beijing by any means necessary.[23] In the wake of the "preemption" policies outlined in the Bush Administration's comprehensive document on the national security strategy of the United States (September 2002), PNAC's (Project for the New American Century) two co-founders, *Weekly Standard* editors William Kristol and Robert Kagan, reiterated their call for Washington to pursue a policy of "regime change" in China. PNAC's existence and its hawkish agenda were given a good public airing when it was revealed that they had prepared the blueprint for the war on Iraq, long before 9/11. Nor are destructive fantasies wanting among other regional or global competitors for whom China poses a massive economic threat. Lastly, there is always the Orientalist stereotype of "atavistic China," an inscrutable and insurgent mass force, which, as Cumings points out, always "seems to be lying in wait for the next trough in history's recurring cycle" to summon it up as a serviceable metaphor.

But not all of the predictions of decline can be dismissed as expressions of historicist or ideological kitsch. While the editors of the *People's Daily* may be correct in assuming that some of these "theories of collapse" are inspired by the desire of its rivals and would-be masters to knock China off its growth path, evidence of widespread unrest and instability is difficult to dismiss in this way. Protests and labor disputes have escalated in China since it began overhauling its state-owned industries. More than 120,000 protests were recorded by the Labor Ministry in 1999 alone, a massive increase of almost

Migrant construction workers,
Guangdong Province
(PHOTO BY AUTHOR)

30 percent from the year before. The following year saw another 12 percent increase to 135,000. In March 2002, the largest and most serious labor protests in a decade swept through China's northeastern "rust belt," when 80,000 laid-off, or *xiagang*, workers (still on payroll, but for token welfare payments) from oil fields and metal industries took to the streets en masse in Daqing and Liaoyang to demand back pay and better severance packages. Three months of sustained pickets and demonstrations captured the nationwide mood of industrial workers (erstwhile "masters" of the Communist state) whose livelihood and rights had been shelved by the sell-off of the more profitable SOEs and the dismantling of many others by managers on the make.[24] If their formerly privileged "iron bowl" status could be so brusquely overturned, private-sector workers in the export zones, most of them migrants in some form of indenture, had even less chance of decent treatment.

With the liberalization of trade required by China's accession to the WTO, there were widespread predictions, exemplified by Gordon Chang's much-discussed book, *The Coming Collapse of China*, that the coming wave of imports would throw even more SOE workers out on the street. Imported grain such as wheat, maize, and soybean, produced more efficiently at half the cost in the U.S., Canada, and the EU, will take an especially harsh toll on peasants no longer protected by tariffs and import quotas.[25] Who can say how many more of the country's 800 million farmers will be forced to join the floating population of urban migrants, already 130 million strong, who are treated with such disdain on account of their rural ways, weathered complexions, and dialects? Refugees from the agrarian labor pool (revealed, after decollectivization, to have a surplus of up to 150 million peasants), floaters are those who left their homes without official permission, and whose rural *hukou* registration restricts their rights in the urban regions beyond the meager diet that an employment contract temporarily affords.[26] Their migrant status makes them highly vulnerable to systems of bonded or forced labor. Though Beijing has announced the phasing out of *hukou* by 2005, it is not clear how forcefully this will alleviate the impact of such mass unemployment. On the one hand, floaters will be reluctant to give up their farmland (one of the few stable guarantees of peasant life) in return for an urban registration that does not automatically carry the generous package of public welfare, housing, and education benefits enjoyed by native-born urbanites. On the other hand, the public goods provision traditionally enjoyed by urban workers is fast eroding under the sway of marketization. Since 1958, *hukou* has served as a way of keeping peasants out of the cities, and in a state of second-class citizenship. Its demise comes at a time when the urban privileges of first-class citizenship are being degraded, especially for laid-off workers. For the time being, only those "drifters" with the most needed talent and educational capital are accepted as first-class city residents.

Market economists, pushing for greater privatization, have also taken a skeptical view of the foundations of the national economy. They see a system plagued by the oversupply (estimated at 75 percent) of manufactured goods, chronic retail price deflation, a mountain of nonperforming loans in the banking system (an estimated 37 percent of the 2001 GDP), low rates of profit, especially for SOEs, and rising government debt. By the standards of a fully capitalist economy, Beijing's deficit spending, its gamble of maintaining lines of state credit to inefficient SOEs (to stave off the social chaos that would result from their mass insolvency), and its refusal to introduce a workable bankruptcy law are widely seen as recipes for a fiscal crisis on a scale that would dwarf all others in modern times.[27]

Nor has there been much peace within the ranks of the political class. China watchers have long dined off analyses of the low-intensity conflict for factional influence and succession within the CCP. But the clash over recent theoretical shifts in party doctrine has been even more titanic than the upheavals that followed Deng's introduction of private economy reforms in 1978, 1984, and 1992. In a speech on July 1, 2001, to mark the eightieth anniversary of the Party's founding, former CCP President Jiang Zemin surprised even the most reform-minded by announcing that the Party would open membership to capitalist entrepreneurs. Proposed by Jiang as an "innovation" on the Marxist theory of labor value, the decision was widely viewed as a repudiation of the most basic Marxist principles regarding the distinction between exploiters and exploited.

Jiang laid the theoretical ground for the shift by outlining the new doctrine of "Three Represents," while on a 2000 tour of Guangdong province that echoed Deng's famous opening of the South. It called on the party to represent the groups who are at the cutting edge of business and culture, as well as the interests of the majority of workers. If the party were to represent the whole of society, Jiang's theory reasoned, then it had to recognize the interests and contributions of technologists and entrepreneurs, insofar as they are agents of the most advanced productive forces in society. While party cadres in thousands of government units around the country joined in the doctrinaire campaign to support the theory, left-wing dissidents within the party openly denounced the decision and the autocratic way in which Jiang had sought to enshrine the theory within the party charter. A "petition of 10,000 words," signed by fourteen senior CCP figures and circulated on the Internet, sharply criticized the moves, and a massive demonstration of opposition members in Tiananmen Square was narrowly averted.

Jiang's decision to admit members from classes such as private enterprise owners and managers, small businessmen and -women, white-collar professionals, and individual contractors, was backed by the decree that entrepreneurs should be educated vigilantly by the Party to be humane employers and philanthropists, and to reinvest a large share of their profits in expanding existing production. On the symbolically freighted Labor Day of 2002, the first domestic entrepreneurs were inducted into the party and honored with the label of "model workers." A year later, two foreign entrepreneurs were given the honor. Critics characterized these decisions as recognition of a theoretically impossible category—"red capitalists"—and asserted that the party had crossed the line with the induction, formally and irrevocably betraying the spirit of socialism by completing the transformation from a revolutionary party to a ruling-class party.

In reality, of course, it was a predictable step for Jiang and his reformers. Entrepreneurs dearly needed access to the party to safeguard their business environment, and senior party cadres needed the consent of business elites to push their reforms forward. Politically speaking, however, the decision had a huge significance. The conflicts it generated within party ranks were no longer a result of personal factionalism, as they had been in the heyday of Mao's periodic campaigns to flush out bourgeois elements from the party apparatus or in the Dengist period of transition to mixed economy. Now the conflicts were about which side of the increasingly polarized economic spectrum to occupy, with one wing of the party protecting its increasing reliance on business, and the other holding fast onto its accountability to its popular base.

In a liberal society, a multiparty system would emerge rapidly to make claims on these divergent interests. In China, no such prospect was on the cards. Yet the reasons had as much to do with Chinese nationalism as with state communism. In common with many other developing countries in the postcolonial world, a vigorous civil and political sphere had been suppressed in the interests of national unity and growth. The overwhelming focus on development and on catching up with more industrialized nations had been promoted at the expense of fostering opposition parties and a critical polity. Compared to the single-party rule that prevailed in many postcolonial democracies, state communism proved the more efficient medium for pursuing the goal of self-reliant modernization. Thus Mao selectively adapted the Soviet model of development, eschewing urbanization while adopting the cult of national productivity in heavy industry and agriculture. By extending the system of high production targets into the countryside during the Great Leap Forward, he was able to foster a national mobilization of the labor force at the provincial, peasant core of a country still intensely regional in its ways. The most perverse, and disastrous, expression of this drive were the thousands of steel furnaces that sprouted in farmers' backyards, consigning valuable kitchen utensils to the smelt in a massively flawed effort to contribute to Mao's announced goal of matching the volume of British steel production within fifteen years.

However vainglorious such campaigns turned out to be, when they were infused with the rhetorical zeal that attended Mao's mystique, they proved to be extraordinary instruments of national unity. Mao's authoritarian populism welded grassroots political fervor to the engine of productivity. The consistent objective was one of national self-reliance, and for China to forge its own path of modernization. Those goals were preserved under Dengism when populist politics ceded to technical expertise and orchestration of foreign capital and trade as the preferred instrument of progress. No less than under Mao, civil rights would be sacrificed in the interest of social stability; unyielding state control was deemed necessary for China to extend its march into modernity. In common with other developing countries, state managers declared that Western-style political freedoms had to be considered luxuries that only the advanced countries could afford.

The managers of the most vigorous Asian economies, however, added a regional spin to this credo by making the case for a distinctly Asian form of market economy. This "communitarian capitalism" was marked by firm respect for state authority, a disciplined work ethic, and a pervasive commitment to worker welfare that differed from the Western individualist model. Acceptance of the state's benign paternalism entails an alternative to the understanding of labor and other human rights that the West deems to be universal. State patriarchs like Singapore's Lee Kuan Yew, or Malaysia's Mahathir Mohamad, appealed to regional culture and history by infusing rapid capitalist industrialization with the Confucian ethos of loyalty to elders and gender hierarchy, ascetic work doctrines, and pious devotion to respectable family morality.[28] Most memorably, Mahathir has called this "not so liberal capitalism."

The Chinese approach to this model has been to indigenize it even further, while appealing to the leading role that ethnic Chinese entrepreneurs play in the region at large. Lee Kuan Yew has spoken of the "glow of Chinese fraternity, which suffuses a transnational network, linked by blood, kinship, and allegiance to the Chinese nation."[29] By relying on the shared trust of this *guanxi*-rich network, China's overseas trade in Singapore, Tapei, Bangkok, Hong Kong, Kuala Lumpur, and Jakarta will always be in the hands of those who have the mainland's national interest at heart. In this expanded, race-bound province of Greater China, it is hoped that the patriotic sentiment of businessmen of Chinese ancestry, amplified through male bonding, will moderate some of their more extreme proclivities for profit. Chinese, among the most mobile of migrant peoples, will have a spiritual and economic home for their mercantile affairs. In this way, capitalist development of foreign trade will make China's state even stronger, in ways that are still quite opaque to Western eyes.

This vision of Greater China augments Beijing's traditional justification for developing its private sector, now accounting for over half of the country's GDP. Economic development will steady the socialist state as it matures, according to one of Jiang's last declarations as president, over the course of the next century into the early phase of true communism. The "one country, two systems" model, where state-owned enterprise coexists with foreign or joint-venture firms, has produced record annual growth rates (an average 9.5 percent from 1980 to 2001), year in and year out, for over two decades. Its continued economic success, reflected in the national productivity statistics (even if they are never exactly reliable), and in the rising incomes of a significant portion of Chinese workers, may well offset its internal problems and contradictions, and confound those who adhere to one or another version of

Entertainment
at the mall
(PHOTO BY AUTHOR)

China's collapse. Equally, the unique composition of its economy, even now developing significant levels of domestic consumption for durable goods, complicates the view of those who insist—either with regret or glee—that China is now wholly a capitalist state (with its own stock exchange, its high ranking on *Fortune*'s list of the world's wealthiest young people, and its luxury lifestyles) that, twenty years ago, had no income gap, and now boasts one of the world's largest.[30]

Labor in Theory and Practice

Accustomed, as we are, to the staple fare of breathless Western media reports about the intrepid progress of capitalist penetration, it is sobering to consider how, or indeed whether, "socialism with Chinese characteristics" still makes a difference. Compared to ex-socialist states like Russia, and many other developing countries with an abundance of cheap labor and an export-driven economy, China's labor regulations are nominally very strong. As a result of recent amendments, the nation's Labor Law (revised in 1995) now mandates an eight-hour day, forty-hour week, paid vacations, and maternity leave. Overtime is voluntary, and is compensated at time and a half and triple for holidays, and child labor and racial and sexual discrimination is prohibited. These revised laws apply to all companies, whether state or privately owned.

So too the revision of long-standing trade union laws in October 2001 made it mandatory for all enterprises and other organizations with twenty-five employees or more to set up a trade union. In fact, unions are now required to represent workers in collective bargaining and labor disputes—the earlier law required them to do so only if their demands were "reasonable." Employers are now required to listen to the union's opinions on a range of matters, from business management to labor safety and sanitation. The amendments take away the right of an employer to terminate an employee on the spot, even for serious violations of labor discipline, and empower the union to appeal directly to the Peoples' Government if employers do not rectify their own "serious violations" of the labor laws. The revised laws still do not include the right to strike (as they did until 1982), but neither do they prohibit strikes, and when stoppages do occur, unions are now required to represent employees, and employers are required to accept their employee's "reasonable requests to resolve the dispute."

Skeptics who see these regulations as examples of Beijing's hypocritical lip-service to the "sanctity of labor" point out that the chances of their enforcement are extra-slim. In the private sector, most local unions are company unions, and the corrupt arrangements that generate graft for provincial party branch officials stack the odds heavily against workers getting any kind of fair hearing for their grievances. Competition for foreign capital is so tight that local Party branch secretaries and township committee bureaucrats will routinely ignore violations for fear of scaring off investors. Moreover, since independent unions are still prohibited, all unions must belong to the All China Federation of Trade Unions (ACFTU), an organization, with over a hundred million members, that is legally and institutionally tied to the government, and whose existence Beijing often uses as cover for responding to criticism of labor and human rights abuses in China.[31] Through the ACFTU the Chinese government is able to defend similar violations of trade union rights in other countries and support claims that principles such as freedom of association must be subordinate to social or cultural "values" or the level of development of each country. Like many national labor organizations, including the AFL-CIO, the ACFTU partakes of "state corporatism"—its collusion with the state in national unity leadership means it has a voice at the decision-making table in Beijing.

Some of the most diligent critics of labor rights abuse, like Anita Chan, argue that, for all its complicity, the ACFTU should not be regarded as a monolithic organization. It has been effective in pushing for labor law amendments, and it includes many officials whose genuine concern for worker rights is in direct conflict with the quietist stance favored by the central government. Moreover, pro-labor officials at the local level can make a real difference in mediating worker disputes, and the Federation has supported the publication of stories about labor abuses in party organs like the *Workers Daily*.[32] A report by an independent delegation of U.S. labor educators, who had been invited to China in 2002 by the ACFTU, concluded that it would be a mistake for the international labor movement to isolate the Federation. With the future of multinational labor agreements a paramount consideration, workers everywhere have a stake in what the ACFTU can achieve, in spite of its constraints and internal limitations. The record of the AFL-CIO's own collusion with the U.S. state apparatus is hardly an exemplary standard to hold up to the ACFTU, nor have U.S. unions played an insignificant role in anti-China sentiment on Capitol Hill. The delegation's report, which recommended that the AFL-CIO establish fraternal relations with the ACFTU while also reaching out to independent labor groups in Hong Kong, reflects the emerging wisdom of the U.S. labor movement that this kind of relationship is in the interest of Chinese and American workers, so intertwined are their prospects.[33]

At the level of party policy-making, the current and future condition of workers' rights is still discussed within the framework set by socialist ideology. Yet are these references to socialism of any practical use in safeguarding working conditions, or are they simply an insult to workers who have been stripped of many of the benefits of the iron rice bowl? Even though China may be socialist in name only—where socialism survives only as the living dead can do—rote expressions like "workers are masters of the state" can still serve the cause of workers. As long as bureaucrats have to use the rhetoric, it can still generate pro-labor sympathy and gains. Journalists in party newspapers, and policy-making cadres, in Beijing and the provinces, are obliged to fashion their prose in accordance with the language of workerism. A lingering sense of socialist responsibility has forestalled SOE managers, in some instances, from making their full quota of compulsory layoffs to meet the bottom line or the ruthless timetable set by privatization. Without the socialist rhetoric, as Chan argues, "what little is left of workers' moral authority will vanish."[34] However cynically they are manipulated or interpreted, the rhetorical survival of socialist goals prolongs the life of pro-labor opportunities.

Love Among the Ruins

Apo Leong, the director of the Hong Kong–based Asia Monitor Resource Center, cites an interview with an unemployed worker in Beijing: "There is no place for workers now. Sometimes friends ask me, 'Do you love your country?' I reply, 'Of course!' But when they ask me, 'Does your country love you?' I really have to think about it."[35] Here, perhaps, is a better parable for our neoliberal times than Jack Welch's barge. Long after our countries have stopped loving us, we still love our countries. Yet this wanton nationalist sentiment means something quite different to unemployed auto workers in Michigan than it does to Liaoning workers laid off by a graft-seeking state manager's decision to sell off the profitable part of his SOE.

Whatever shop-floor credence was extended to the famous dictum, "what's good for GM is good for America," threatened to evaporate when the auto factories began to relocate in the 1970s. Efforts to shore up the national consensus were made—renewed corporative competitiveness would make America strong again; NAFTA and other free-trade agreements would generate new kinds of jobs. This rhetoric made little headway within the blue-collar ranks. If anything, its xenophobic underbelly only supported the ugly conviction that "Mexicans or Asians are stealing our jobs." The mass layoffs of white-collar middle managers in the 1980s were experienced as a more serious breach of faith on the part of national authority figures, even if these were predominantly representatives of corporate America. Though the state played a critical role in deregulating the semi-contractual relationships between capital and labor, it was not perceived as an agent of betrayal. In the American version of nationalism, the thin state has no explicit demands or responsibilities. It simply encourages individuals to attach the risky pursuit of their own ideals to a baggy set of "self-evident" truths about the American way of life, and it guarantees protection for whatever contracts they have made to that end. In recent times, Americans who are most strident in expressing love for their country often harbor a fierce contempt for the federal authority of the state.

In a developing country with a strong, central authority, nationalism is cut from quite a different cloth. Nation-building in China has been driven hard by the state, and citizen loyalty is expected in return for the stability and the growth that the state provides. Mao carefully promoted the intimate fusion of country, people, state, and nation, and periodically relied on fomenting a wave of homespun evangelism to wash away any challenges to that union. His formula was one of popular self-determination, typified in the alternative paths (through the rural peasantry and not the urban proletariat) chosen for socialist development after 1949, and it was maintained in the successive modes of modernization that led up to and underpinned the reforms of Deng. While the vehicle shifted toward urban development and private enterprise, and while the intense politicization of the Cultural Revolution was forsworn, the formula of self-determination did not alter very much when trade and investment liberalization and state-mandated consumerism kicked in after 1992. To this day, the opening up to foreign capital has been justified as an expedient way of strengthening the state—which still owns over 90 percent of the land—and further reflecting the glory of the motherland on the rise.

China has long been seen, through neocolonial eyes, as everything that Western modernity is not. Consequently, the pace and shape of its development continues to be perceived as an extreme variation of, or an exception to, the "universal" template followed by liberal capitalist societies.[36] A more considered view is that while China's path to modernization has been unique, its end point—given the nature of its capitalist development—will prove not to be so atypical after all.[37] For the time being, however, the segregation of Deng's two civilizations—"spiritual socialist" on the one hand, and high-growth materialism, on the other—keeps at bay the sharpest contradictions between national-popular collectivism and incremental privatization. China's sovereign autonomy is thereby preserved, permitting all Western criticism, especially of human and labor rights violations, to be dismissed as neocolonialist.

Yet China's nationalist instincts can no more be ignored than can the swaggering chauvinism of the U.S. version. Their rolling and rattling affects all of us, albeit in different ways, and no one can let them well alone. Nor is the issue solely that of nationalism in one country. The businessmen and women who are hailed as part of Greater China have their counterpart in the vast enclaves of Chinese workers that can be found in cities and regions around the world. If the capital of businesspeople can be organized by appeals to their sense of kinship, then perhaps the international distinction of Chinese labor, which built the infrastructure (from railways to information superhighways) of so many other countries, might be mobilized in ways that could benefit workers more directly.

Finally, we must confront the reality of economic life in the age of the WTO. National interests still form the guiding framework for trade agreements (and military might can still be applied, when necessary, to seize assets), but it is corporations and banks that are driving development. They use the instruments of national states to build their profits and realize their investments just as brazenly as nation-states use them to build their growth statistics. Sooner or later, it will be clear who prevails in this game. Will China will be "lost" again, this time to foreign investors and banks, or will a popular insurgency deprive its leaders of the "mandate of heaven" that traditionally seals the social contract between the governor and the governed?

Conscious, as ever, of the lessons of history, the new Party leadership has taken some steps to shape the outcome. In the first Politburo "study session" after Hu Jintao's accession as CCP general secretary in November 2002, the focus was squarely on safeguarding the national constitution. Ever since then, Hu has promoted this new emphasis on the rule of law (*fa zhi*), as opposed to the rule of man (*ren zhi*), a distinction that presents a clear contrast with the elitist, market-driven policies of his precursor. The shift in focus toward legalism is, in part, an effort to reassure foreign investors that they can operate in a business environment that respects international law. On the other hand, this new emphasis, combined with Hu's populist vow to address the grievances of jobless industrial workers and overtaxed farmers, promises a new deal that would reign in the runaway corruption that has made China one of the most inegalitarian countries in the world. Of course, it costs very little to trumpet the rule of law, but if party leaders actually were serious about implementing the nation's labor laws, the impact on the global economy would be as far-reaching as the consequences of Beijing's studied neglect of these laws has been.

Electronic junk

CHAPTER FIVE

The Flight of the Silicon Wafers

JUST A FEW MONTHS after the 1993 bombing of the World Trade Center, I moved into a building twenty blocks north of that fateful site. Since my apartment overlooks one of the exit roads from the Holland Tunnel, which links New Jersey with Manhattan, I joked to friends that, if something truly apocalyptic happened in lower Manhattan—a serious ecological meltdown—I could escape by running through the tunnel to Jersey. The joke turned sour eight years later, when the area played host to the worst environmental catastrophe in U.S. urban history. To this day, however, not too many people remember the World Trade Center attacks that way. However bunglesome to those who watched closely, the cover-up of the environmental impact of the disaster proved effective enough to vanquish public scepticism.

In retrospect, it is astonishing that it took less than a week after September 11th for the Environmental Protection Agency to declare that the air and drinking water in lower Manhattan were safe, giving the go-ahead for employees to return to the financial district. Nothing could have been further from the truth, as Juan Gonzalez, the *Daily News*'s watchdog columnist, and virtually the only journalist in the city to follow up on the environmental consequences, uncovered in his investigative reports, and follow-up book, *Fallout*.[1] The story excavated by Gonzalez, along with other community-minded scientists and professionals, showed that federal and city agencies were well-informed of tests demonstrating disturbingly high levels of asbestos and heavy metals in dust and air samples, as far as a mile north of the site. Indeed, there was ample evidence of widespread contamination that posed high risks to public health.

In Gonzalez's estimate, the witch's brew released by the incineration of the buildings' contents—the equivalent of a small American city—included from 400 to 1,000 tons of asbestos, 200,000 to 400,000 pounds of lead, ten to twenty-five pounds of mercury, millions of pounds of plastics with PCB content, unquantifiable volumes of deadly dioxins, furans, and many other carcinogens like chromium and benzene. Fed by a massive fuel and oil spill of as much as 200,000 gallons, the underground fires that burned for four months generated pollution levels higher than the hellish oil fires of Kuwait during the Gulf War, and all in one of the more densely populated places on earth.[2] The cover-up by government agencies of this public health crisis was an instinctive response on the part of authorities dedicated to protecting the financial engines and property values of lower Manhattan. Yet their reaction had debilitating long-term consequences for the rescue and recovery workers who worked at the site for weeks without adequate protection, and for all employees and residents who would develop the infamous World Trade Center Cough.

What Gonzalez and others discovered is that regional authorities sought to allay public anxiety by simply creating ad hoc "benchmarks," or "screening levels," for exposure to toxic substances for which no EPA safety standards existed. The absence of such standards is a scandal in and of itself. Even if they had existed, no risk assessment could have adequately applied to a person's synergistic exposure to the many potential combinations of chemicals released from the crematorium-like site. Perhaps the nearest equivalent would be the "clean room" of semiconductor fabrication plants, where the interaction of hundreds of compounds puts these "fabs" high on the list of the most hazardous industrial workplaces. Indeed, one of the contributing factors to the risk assessments of Gonzalez and others was the impact of the simultaneous incineration of up to 50,000 computers, servers, and mainframes within the Twin Towers.

As many as 1,000 materials, many of them hazardous, are involved in the production of a computer work station; each cathode ray tube monitor contains from four to eight pounds of lead, along with quantities of cadmium and vanadium; mercury in switches, beryllium in motherboards, PCBs in older transformers, brominated flame retardants on printed circuit boards, and PVC in cables and plastic casings that releases highly toxic dioxins and furans when burned. Among other things, the World Trade Center's noxious stew was a by-product of the age of information, and a vile reminder of the physical and chemical foundation of the Promethean technologies that had lately starred as the alchemical stuff of the New Economy.

All through the 1990s, Wall Street had been on a voracious roll, riding a bubble that fed off hot air generated by the go-go rollout of new technologies. The places where these new toys were made and the graveyards where they ended up were far away, out of sight and out of mind. Nor would you be likely to find any such references to the material manufacture of computers among the evangelical pronouncements of the digerati whose heady prose helped to drive the tech boom. Little mention of the workers employed in semiconductor production and electronic assembly who incur lasting damage to their health, or the massive ecological footprint generated by each silicon chip, and even less of the e-waste scavengers in the poor regions of the world whose desperate livelihood it is to recover chemical compounds from the plastic casings of discarded computers. The environmental security of the world's rich countries depends on exporting these toxic processes. Yet, however well-managed, this North-South trade is seldom a one-way flow; the toxins are imported back to the North in consumer commodities and food products made where labor is cheap and environmental regulation is weak. This is the "boomerang effect" cited by Ulrich Beck in his influential book, *The Risk Society*. It is a consequence of the global character of environmental problems in an economic system that overproduces complex chemical, genetic, and nuclear risks.[3]

Though wealth and power can mitigate the impact of these hazardous by-products, no one, ultimately, is immune, as was demonstrated by the disaster in lower Manhattan, or countless others in the making. The World Trade Center attacks were not only an example of political blowback—the progeny of decades of interventionist U.S. policies overseas—they were also a kind of environmental blowback. The ingredients of the toxic soup that enveloped some of the richest real estate in the world had been designed with the expectation that their poisons would be disposed of in the world's poorest backyards. In the aftermath of the attacks, those who had benefited royally from the unequal geography of the tech-stock boom found their own trading floors contaminated by carcinogenic waste that should have ended up in electronic junk heaps picked over by impoverished peasants in South China.

Ironically, the greatest economic impact of the attacks was borne by low-wage garment, restaurant, and service workers in Chinatown, the most densely populated residential neighborhood near to Ground Zero. Three quarters of the workforce were temporarily unemployed after 9/11, and 65 percent of the garment factories in the neighborhood closed in the following year.[4] Overall, the toll of unemployed there was greatest (10 percent of the city volume), the levels of assistance and media visibility were lowest, and information-sharing about air safety was virtually nonexistent. Residents in the northern half of the community, who reported an alarming increase in asthma rates, were excluded from the EPA testing and cleanup zone. Government agencies set up no forums to gauge the impact on the residents, nor were there any expectations that the health or the opinions of this community would play a role in decision-making to remedy the crisis, let alone to rebuild the downtown infrastructure.[5] The premium placed on the labor and safety of Chinese workers in the citadel of world capitalism was not significantly different, as I will argue, from the neglect visited on their kinfolk 6,000 miles away.

In recent years, much of the initiative of anti-globalization activists has been aimed at hammering clauses on labor rights and environmental standards into world trade agreements. Yet decades of tension between environmentalists and labor advocates has not made it easy to push on both sets of issues with the same energies and resources. Conditions in the high-tech industries, the topic of this chapter, provide all the evidence one would need to make the case that it is both foolhardy and ruinous to separate the two.

The Dirty Secrets

Most high-tech machines are designed in anticipation of being outdated by the market within a few years. Given the accelerating tempo of product cycles, where do most of our barely used computers go to die? According to "Exporting Harm," an influential 2002 report prepared by the Seattle-based Basel Action Network (BAN), and the San Jose–based Silicon Valley Toxics Coalition (SVTC), between 50 and 80 percent of electronic waste collected for recycling in the United States is sent overseas.[6] It is sold primarily as mixed scrap to wholesale brokers who ship it to Asia, mostly to China. In other industrialized countries, this practice is constrained by the 1989 Basel Convention on the Transboundary Movements of Hazardous Wastes and Their Disposal, which encouraged national self-sufficiency in waste management, and the subsequent Basel Ban Amendment, which prohibits the export of hazardous waste from OECD to non-OECD countries. These are two of the many international environmental agreements that the U.S. has refused to ratify. As a result, the bulk of the country's computers that are discarded and consigned to "recycling"—12.75 million in 2002—can be found being hammered to pieces in e-waste processing centers like Guiyu, in the southern part of Guangdong province.

In a 2001 investigation, BAN found village soil in Guiyu that contained 200 times the level of lead considered hazardous, and drinking water that was 2,400 times over the World Health Authority lead threshold.[7] The BAN team estimated that 100,000 of the region's villagers were employed in dismantling computers with their bare hands, picking apart and processing silver, gold, palladium, platinum, and other precious components like solder, chips, and copper cable, before burning the units' remnants in open pits or acid baths. Guiyu's ponds and granite-lined canals that had been used for centuries to irrigate rice fields were found by investigators to be filled over with broken monitor glass and other unrecycled plastic e-waste. Unable to use their polluted groundwater, villagers drank imported water from twenty miles away. Exposed to an environment not unlike that of an open incinerator, they suffered chronic respiratory and skin complaints, and had reported many new cases of leukemia. In response to the publicity generated by BAN's exposé, Chinese authorities launched a crackdown on illegally imported e-waste in June 2001, and urged exporting countries to take responsibility for their wastes.[8] Ever since 1996, when Beijing prohibited the import of solid wastes that are unusable as raw materials (under the Law on the Prevention and Control of Solid Waste Pollution to the Environment), China has been a leading proponent of the international ban on e-waste exports.

But as long as farmers fail to eke a living wage from their paddy fields, and local officials profit from the e-waste business, and as long as nations like the U.S. officially condone the exports, the trade will continue. Nor would there be too many objections from the neoliberal master economists of free trade. Who could forget the leaked internal memo written by Lawrence Summers when he was chief economist at the World Bank in 1991?: "Just between you and me, shouldn't the World Bank be encouraging more migration of the dirty industries to the LDCs [least developed countries]?" Summers summed up the mentality of his peers when he went on to note: "I think the economic logic behind dumping a load of toxic waste in the lowest wage country is impeccable and we should face up to that. . . . I've always thought that underpopulated countries in Africa are vastly underpolluted; their air quality is vastly inefficiently low compared to Los Angeles or Mexico City." Even if we grant Summers the benefit of the doubt about his professed irony, the "economic logic" of his infamous memo has been effectively implemented by the leading institutions of the Washington Consensus, backed by the U.S. Treasury Department, where Summers was subsequently employed before ascending to the presidency of Harvard University. According to this consensus, developing countries should exploit whatever comparative advantage is available to them, including lower environmental standards, to build up their export industry at the expense of production of local needs and community health.

The international toxics trade is no longer what it was, since several EU countries have taken steps to strengthen regulation, but the U.S. has increasingly acted to oppose any new laws and weaken existing ones. For example, the Office of the U.S. Trade Representative was enlisted by the industry to lobby against the pending passage of European legislation aimed at resolving the e-waste problem through the principle of extended producer responsibility.[9] Despite the U.S. efforts, which proved successful in stopping an outright ban on all toxics from the production process, the European parliament passed the legislation (Directive on Waste from Electrical and Electronic Equipment) in May 2001. As a result, after 2004, untreated e-waste will no longer be accepted at landfills; recycling and recovery figures will be set; some toxic materials are to be phased out of electronics production; and producers will be held responsible for waste disposal.

But however progressive, the legislation will lack international clout without similar efforts by the U.S. to regulate its e-waste sector, and there is little sign of movement there. In addition to being the only developed country to ignore the Basel Ban entirely, the U.S. took the explicit step of exempting e-waste, under amendments to the Resource Conservation and Recovery Act in 1994, from the minimal American laws that do exist to protect importing countries. Where, formerly, exporters needed the "prior informed consent" of receiving countries before shipping out waste, now all that is required is a bill of lading that claims the cargo is bound for "recycling." While the EPA's policy is that all hazardous waste should be recycled, the law offers no guidelines and no regulatory teeth for determining how and where that vaguely termed process should be carried out. In the case of any materials containing hazardous waste, recycling generates considerable amounts of pollution, even when it is executed with optimal, or appropriate, technologies, and by workers with special training. Moreover, there are always residues, which require final disposal in someone's backyard. Where labor is dirt-cheap, and the technologies and protection are nonexistent, recycling is a potential death sentence to the human recyclers and their immediate environment. For most of us, domestic recycling is a feel-good exercise, even though we have little idea of how, or how much, of our carefully separated waste is actually treated in responsible ways. There is less ambiguity about the commercial "recycling" of e-waste through export. The chances of its being dumped as a life-threatening burden on some of the world's poorest people are astronomically high.

U.S. federal and state e-waste regulations are partly responsible for the practice of exporting the problem because they generally transfer the disposal costs onto municipal taxpayers rather than onto the producer. When it comes down to how much taxpayers are willing to pay, legitimate U.S. recyclers, who offer a living wage and benefits, are placed at a severe competitive disadvantage with the export recyclers. Increasingly, the only domestic means of matching China's wage floor is to employ prisoners at less than a dollar an hour, which is the high-growth option that many privatized prisons are adopting as a way of generating easy profits. Nor is this policy being opposed by states with progressive environmental policies. In California, where CRT monitors are now banned from landfills, the low-cost solution of prison labor, where neither OSHA's occupational safety standards nor the Fair Labor Standards Act are applicable, is now actively being pursued, over and against the cost of public investment in improving recycling technologies. In 2003, Dell was the first top-brand company to contract with "high tech chain gangs" of federal prison inmates, charged with manually smashing open the leaded glass of cathode ray tubes at work stations that had been designed with little concern for their protection.[10]

As long as e-waste can be cheaply disposed of downstream, among prisoners and peasants whose health is held at a low premium and who have not benefited in any way from the active life of the products, there will be few incentives to alter the upstream sources of the problem in the design and manufacturing of new technologies. Yet the most appropriate solutions lie upstream, with clean, or green, production, backed by regulation that places unequivocal responsibility on producers for the entire life cycle of their products. Poisonous inputs have to be phased out, and testing protocols have to be altered to screen all new chemicals in order to preempt any further harm. Above all, the acute wastefulness that characterizes an industry "governed" by Moore's Law (the number of transistors on a silicon chip doubles every eighteen months) must be reduced by more flexible design. Groups like the SVTC and BAN argue that the planned obsolescence mandated by these eighteen-month product cycles will alter only when manufacturers are finally required to take back all their consumer products once they are "outdated," and dispose or retrofit them for reuse.

The alternative is an ever-growing mountain of e-junk—an estimated 315 million obsolete computers in the U.S. by 2004, with 1.2 billion pounds of lead stored inside them, not to mention the DVD players, high-resolution televisions, and digital flat-screen monitors, traditional television sets, and VHS players that are now produced and marketed with the certainty of high turnover and low life expectancy. In an advanced consumer civilization, citizens have long been accustomed to the psychology of a throwaway culture. Yet even this psychology has not been able to keep up with the challenge of electronic product obsolescence. As a result, consumers will hold on to outdated computers and other high-tech toys because we cannot bring ourselves to acknowledge that the gadgets for which we forked over thousands of dollars became worthless within a couple of years. It is a peculiar form of guilt, and it constitutes a massive problem-in-waiting for the municipal waste stream, already contaminated by toxic runoff from early generation e-junk, the fastest growing component in solid waste landfills nationwide (accounting for 70 percent of the heavy metals, and 40 percent of the lead).

Can some of this guilt be converted into consciousness, or even action? Pressured by an international network of activists,[11] the European parliament has taken far-reaching steps, and in liberal-minded American states like Massachusetts and California, where CRT monitors are now banned from landfill disposal, citizen action is beginning to bear fruit in e-waste legislation. Some manufacturers (Dell, Gateway, HP) have voluntarily offered takeback programs under certain conditions, and for a hefty charge to the disposing consumer (Sony began collecting and recycling its own products free—but in Minnesota only). So too the Clean Computer Campaign, run by SVTC, is gaining ground with each new coalition partner (as diverse as Materials for the Future Foundation, the Southwest Organizing Project, and SEIU's Justice for Janitors campaign). Yet, as environmental justice activists have shown again and again, hazardous waste is always likely to run downhill, on the path of least resistance, to a poorer, receiver community, either at home or abroad. Establishing manufacturer responsibility is certainly more effective than pressuring strapped local governments to shoulder the burden, even if those costs are likely to be passed on to consumers. However, with the increasing internationalization of production, it will not be easy to make manufacturers accountable for their suppliers, especially when the brand-name giants, like their peers in the garment industry, can legally disown responsibility for what happens further down the chain of subcontracting.

Patterns of Flight

These days, China is not only importing e-waste, it is also attracting semiconductor fabs that are the cornerstone of high-tech manufacturing. Each new silicon-age factory brings its own hazardous ecological footprint. If the chemical risks faced by downstream recyclers and their villages are a grave cause for concern, they are not substantially different from those that affect factory workers who manufacture electronic components. No more than in the case of e-waste, China will be assuming environmental burdens that more developed countries have decided are too costly to bear.

Semiconductor manufacturing uses more highly toxic gases (including lethal ones like arsine, boron, and phosphine) and chemicals than any other industry; its plants discharge tons of toxic pollutants into the air, and use millions of gallons of water each day. In Santa Clara County, ground zero of the silicon revolution, there are more groundwater contamination and EPA Superfund sites (twenty-three) than anywhere else in the U.S. The prevailing public perception is that these are light manufacturing workplaces, and that the famous "clean rooms" protect bunny-suited workers from the chemical components of manufacture. In fact, the clean rooms are designed to keep silicon wafers free from human contamination, and not vice versa. The bunny-suits prevent particles of dust from employees' clothing from ruining a wafer, but they do a poor job of protecting workers against skin contact with corrosive solvents and other chemicals. The constantly recirculated air (to prevent new infusions of airborne dust) that workers breathe is often thick with chemical vapors.

The risks harbored by such workplaces are legion, and are multiplying daily, since chemicals new to this relentlessly innovating industry are rarely subject to toxicological assessment before they are introduced into the manufacturing process. Contrary to the Semiconductor Industry Association's (SIA) official position that the industry ranks among the nation's safest manufacturing industries, many critics estimate that microchip workers suffer industrial illnesses at three to four times the average rates for manufacturing jobs in industries like petrochemicals, paper, coal, steel, petroleum, plastics, and rubber. Studies have consistently found significantly increased miscarriage rates and birth defect rates among women working in the chemical handling that is often part of the jobs.[12] The more common and well-documented illnesses include breast, uterine and stomach cancer, leukemia, asthma, vision impairment, and carpal tunnel syndrome. In many of these jobs, workers are exposed to hundreds of different chemicals in varying combinations. Very little occupational health research exists that analyzes the impact on the human body of combining multiple compounds, and research on reproductive hazards, in particular, has been seen as a women's issue and is therefore underfunded and underreported.[13]

Nonetheless, corporate managers are increasingly alarmed about the volume of lawsuits brought by employees who blame miscarriages or birth defects on workplace hazards. The plaintiffs include former employees who have children with no arms or legs or reproductive organs. In many states, workers' compensation laws prevent employees from suing their companies for injuries, but courts are increasingly upholding the rights of their offspring to litigate. Children have begun to sue their parents' employers, on the basis that workplace toxins cause prenatal damage.[14] These prenatal cases are a recent addition to the swelling flood of litigation directed against employers who made no effort to inform workers of the risks of handling chemicals. For example, a 1998 class action lawsuit in Santa Clara, brought by former IBM employees, many of them prematurely deceased, was based on an incidence of cancer clusters (and brain cancer deaths) that is about 2.5 times that of the general population. Part of the plaintiffs' argument was that the cancer rate increased with the duration of employment.[15]

Such cases are almost always settled out of court. Industry lawyers are well-aware that any cooperation on their clients' part with efforts to study cancer and birth defects among semiconductor workers will entangle these brand-name companies in an endless series of legally imposed compensation payments. A 1998 industry-wide study, initiated and funded by the EPA's Common Sense

Initiative, along with California's Department of Health Services, was thwarted when semiconductor manufacturers, led by Intel and IBM, pulled out, even though the program promised to safeguard the privacy of workers and companies alike. A press leak from Intel spokesperson Tim Mohin generated widespread media scrutiny: "To participate in a project like this would be like giving [legal] discovery to plaintiffs. I might as well take a gun and shoot myself."[16] Indeed, there are obvious economic reasons for the overwhelming resistance to scientific study of the problems on the part of the major chip manufacturers and the SIA. The SIA's science advisory committee, set up in 1999 in response to criticism, took two years just to complete a feasibility study on whether further epidemiological research was needed. The committee's report, delivered in October 2001, was not made public. In yet another delaying tactic, the SIA announced in March 2002 that the report had recommended that it "conduct a preliminary review to determine if it is possible to conduct a study of health risks in the semiconductor industry."[17] Yet again, the U.S. trails behind European efforts. In Scotland, for example, Phase II, a health and safety organization, was able to demonstrate high cancer rates among Silicon Glen employees of National Semiconductor through a government-sponsored study in 2001.[18] Lawsuits were subsequently filed by the employees.

But the ecological impact of the microchip factories affects more than facility workers. According to the SVTC, the resources used in producing just a single six-inch silicon wafer include 3,200 cubic feet of bulk gases, twenty-two cubic feet of hazardous gases, 2,275 gallons of deionized water, twenty pounds of chemicals, and 285 kilowatt hours of electrical power. (As chips get smaller, even more energy-intensive processes are required to make them clean and pure.) The waste produced by that single wafer include twenty-five pounds of sodium hydroxide, 2,840 gallons of waste water, and seven pounds of miscellaneous hazardous wastes.[19] Multiply those numbers by the number of wafers produced in a week (up to 5,000 in a large facility), and you have some idea of the massive volume of pollutants capable of poisoning the atmosphere and the aquifer in and around a semiconductor plant. The polluted groundwater plumes and Superfund sites that spread out from some of the most infamous semiconductor complexes are well-known in Silicon Valley. Santa Clara

County residents live with cancer risks, ranging from 47 to 1,543 times higher than the threshold goal established by the Clean Air Act.[20] Entire residential communities have been slowly poisoned by contaminated aquifers and river basins. Some have sought legal redress, like the south San Jose neighborhood of Los Paseos, where residents experienced health problems and birth defects after leaks from a Fairchild Semiconductor plant poisoned their groundwater in the mid-1980s. Such suits have added to the legal monster that companies increasingly face among a population awakened to the risks of hosting the industry, and increasingly aware of their right to sue the offenders.

The industry response has been multifold. Wherever manufacturing has stayed in northern California, the potentially carcinogenic jobs have been allocated to immigrant workers with little, if any English skills, and who are therefore unlikely to be aware of their legal rights in the event of workplace hazards and injury.[21] So too the IT industry has adopted a tiered structure wherever possible, employing temps, or spinning off and contracting out services and operations to keep down direct labor costs and to protect the core companies from any liability. Just as important, the SIA and the leading manufacturers have been effective in keeping unions out of the industry. In fact, high-tech is the least unionized of all goods-producing industries. While 56.2 percent of steel workers, 54.6 percent of automobile workers, 43.8 percent of telecommunications workers, and 23.7 percent of workers in durable-goods manufacturing overall were unionized in 1993 in the U.S., only 2.7 percent of workers in electronics and computer equipment belonged to unions.[22] The mid-century strength of the industrial unions was the major factor in introducing safer exposure levels and monitoring equipment for the first wave of industrial chemicals. Union power began to wane just as synthetic chemicals made their appearance in industry, resulting in a lack of worker protection and safety standards for handling a whole new generation of industrial materials. Compounding the problem was the fierce libertarian culture of the IT industries, which has kept unionization to a bare minimum. As a result, employees know they have little protection against being fired if they decide to blow the whistle. Not surprisingly, OSHA reports a low level of employee complaints, relative to other manufacturing industries.

But by far the most common response is to export the health and safety hazards. Rather than fund research to develop low-impact, environmentally benign techniques of manufacture,[23] companies began to move their fabs from northern California to the Southwest in the early 1980s, where sparse union activity combined with weaker environmental and safety regulations and a lower wage floor ensured the continuation of business as usual. The tax breaks that Intel and others were offered by New Mexico and Arizona were lavish enough to compensate for the potential dearth of water supply in the semiarid regions to which they were lured. As a result, low-income communities near Albuquerque and Phoenix became the first destinations on the "toxic flight" route path. Many of the "dirtier" processes of high-tech production were relocating overseas, in search of even lower standards, accelerated by any signs of an organizing drive or occupational health lawsuit. Following the corporate pattern of using contract manufacturers, U.S. and Japanese companies steadily relocated their fabrication lines to the European low-wage periphery of Scotland, Ireland, Hungary, Poland, and the Czech Republic, and to Asia, where Taiwan and Malaysia became production centers for third-party suppliers. In countries like Thailand, Indonesia, Vietnam, Mexico, Panama, Costa Rica, and Brazil, modular industries like the printed circuit board sector joined long-established export assembly operations, where the lowest paid workers use solders and solvents that are almost as toxic as those handled by chip workers. With skilled labor increasingly available at low prices in developing countries like China, it is only a matter of years before the geography of high-tech global production resembles that of the garment industry's race to the bottom.

Everywhere along IT's toxic flight routes, the same trails of environmental ruin can be found. Where manufacturing is concentrated in industrial parks, often exempted, by state managers, from national jurisdiction over environmental monitoring, regulation is likely to be industry-friendly. Competition among parks for investment results in even weaker standards. Employees in these parks pay the price for the exemption from national environmental laws granted to their employees. Toxic waste from multiple facilities is routinely dumped in the water supply, making it difficult to single out offenders. All the same, a group of former RCA workers in Taiwan's Science-Based Hinschu Industrial Park have filed suit against the company, alleging that contamination of ground and drinking water at the company's facility (shuttered in 1992) was responsible for some 1,375 documented cases of cancer among former workers, including 216 deaths.[24] Even if they are unevenly implemented, many Taiwanese regulations are far more stringent than their U.S. equivalents. For example, American manufacturers and their suppliers are required to recycle up to 75 percent of their water by Taiwanese law, whereas no such provision exists in the U.S., nor in China, where they are migrating. Like Europe and Japan, Taiwan also requires manufacturers to participate in take-back disposal programs.[25]

Taiwan built its industry as a supply hub for major U.S. and Japanese computer brands, producing low-value components and high-value niche products. In turn, Taiwanese manufacturers subcontract to low-end operations in South China and, increasingly, to new fabs in East China. In effect, the industry has a supply web that stretches across several countries, and management of this supply chain, wherever it exists, is notoriously ineffectual. The further down the chain, the thinner the profit margins and the less chance of finding any kind of environmentally or socially responsible oversight. If only for PR purposes, firms at the top, which depend on their brand name to compete, are more likely to be attentive to problems in waste and production. Their names cannot afford to be tarnished. But most companies in the chain compete on cost and performance speed, and their names are virtually unknown. In response to criticism, the core companies insist that they cannot be held accountable for the practices of every firm with which they do business, especially when the same firm is supplying several others, all with different compliance rules. Yet it is telling that any efforts to mount independent monitoring schemes usually run into resistance from these core companies when it comes to revealing their suppliers' names and locations.

In the absence of industry-wide binding standards, and in light of structural difficulties of enforcement, what are the prospects for cleaning up high-tech, especially in developing countries where the worst impacts occur? In a critical survey of the industry's problems in five developing countries (Taiwan, Malaysia, India, Thailand, and Costa Rica), the Nautilus Institute, in conjunction with other corporate accountability organizations, called for regulators to mandate corporations to disclose information about their suppliers. The report concluded that no serious monitoring of conditions can occur on the basis of the voluntary internal auditing that companies favor.[26] Nor, it should be added, in response to the Nautilus report, will any serious disclosure occur without a strategic campaign of activism directed at leading-edge companies whose profits depend on brand recognition.

Because the global garment industry shares many structural features with high-tech manufacturing, the model for such a campaign already exists in the anti-sweatshop movement. Anti-sweatshop groups have a proven record of successes (and near-failures) at pushing manufacturers to adopt workable codes of conduct that respect worker safety, union rights, and a living wage. So too in the technology sector, groups like the SVTC have petitioned companies like Intel, GTE, and Motorola to establish codes of conduct. But the high-profile media strategy of targeting brand names has generally not been used by semiconductor activists. There is no reason why the vulnerable brand names of AT&T, Phillips, Intel, IBM, Hewlett Packard, Toshiba, Samsung, and Fujitsu cannot be publicly shamed in the same way as Nike, the Gap, Guess, Phillips Van Heusen, and Disney have been tarnished by consumer campaigns and boycott threats. Because there is so little difference between their respective products, and because their product cycles are so short, brand-name recognition is all-important in driving sales of technology we do not need. As a result, the top brands have a ubiquitous presence on the advertising landscape, which makes them particularly vulnerable. Above all, it is important not to underestimate public outrage, especially among higher-income technology consumers who can afford to assuage their conscience. Unlike clothing, consumption of high-tech goods is not yet a daily necessity, but the rate of market penetration in the last twenty years has been phenomenal. The potential for inflaming public consciousness lies largely untapped.

There are several reasons why semiconductor activism has been relatively weak. Unlike garment labor activism, which has been funded and supported by trade unions with long traditions of expertise in the field, there is virtually no organized labor in the technology industries. The fight against the garment sweatshop was a historic milestone in trade union history, and the recent campaigns have been on the leading edge of the resurgent U.S. labor movement. Nothing comparable exists in high-tech workplaces that emerged in a climate intrinsically hostile to the principles of trade unionism. Indeed, high-tech industry lobbyists have been zealous leaders in efforts to undermine the existing protections of labor legislation. Employee codes of conduct and workplace monitoring, whether carried out internally or independently, are better than nothing, but they are poor substitutes, in the long run, for effective union regulation. Add to this the special treatment afforded to microelectronics by state managers, all too aware of the industry's strategic importance in the global economy. Many nations assess their competitive standing in world trade by the growth of their advanced technology sectors, and so regulatory authorities are often sidelined in the stampede to develop a high-tech presence.

An even greater obstacle to activism is the public perception that high technology is a clean, even green, industry. In the public mind, the computer is still viewed as the product of magic, and not industry. The fact that we can repair our own car but not our computer does not help. As a result, the process of manufacturing is obscured and mystified. The vast majority of users are largely unaware that their machines contain so many harmful substances, and are likely to believe, erroneously, that miniaturization consumes less resources.[27] So too the utopian rhetoric that surrounds these overhyped technologies strips them of their material underpinnings. In the public mind, when workers are associated with high-tech, they are the engineer whiz kids of Silicon Valley, with much-lionized jobs and incomes, not low-wage temps and Third World teenagers.

It is time to change those perceptions. Corporate icons in the electronics worlds must be put on notice that their brands will suffer severe PR damage unless they begin to accept cradle-to-grave responsibility for all of the constituent operations, no matter how remote, from which they reap their profits. The public appetite for anticorporate outrage should not be underestimated. The qualified successes of anti-sweatshop garment organizing came as a surprise to many seasoned activists, long accustomed to being shut out of the media, and beaten off by the swaggering indifference of corporations. In the case of information technology, the time may be ripe for capitalizing on the sympathetic climate for calling the brand kingpins to order.

Triumphant UNITE members

(PHOTO BY TERU KUWAYAMA)

CHAPTER SIX

Strike a Pose for Justice:
The Barneys Union Campaign
of 1996

THE DAYS ARE OVER when union pride alone could sustain an audience for commercial entertainment. The high watermark remains *Pins and Needles* (1937–1941), the famous musical revue sponsored by the ILGWU and performed by garment workers, which turned into one of the longest-running musicals in Broadway history. This immensely successful production, which irradiated the popular show tune with overtly political lyrics ("I'm on a campaign to make you mine/I'll picket you until you sign/In one big union for two," and "Sing me of wars and sing me of breadlines/Sing me of strikes and last minute headlines"), was a full-blown extension of the vibrant culture of union organizing and working-class solidarity that had flourished in the course of the 1930s. While nothing since has matched this feat— Hollywood's one-off feel-good (*Norma Rae*) or feel-bad (*Matewan*) features don't rate—the tradition of drawing on entertainment and showbiz to lend some spice and dash to labor campaigns has far from died off. Sometimes, when it's done right, it can make all the difference.

Under the Stars in Chelsea

If you were standing on a certain street corner in Manhattan's gentrifying Chelsea neighborhood on an unseasonably chilly April evening in 1996, you would have witnessed one of the most striking uses of that tradition. The New York fashion world's fall shows ("Seventh on Sixth") had just wound down. But there is one more runway show in town: "Seventh on Seventeenth," on the street corner synonymous, since 1923, with Barneys—a New York institution in retail that had grown, mercurially, from its rag trade beginnings into the largest men's clothing store in the world, and then shot off, at a tangent, into the air-kissed stratosphere of chic taste in the course of the 1980s decade of greed.

By 7:15 P.M. on this Saturday evening, there is quite a scene to behold. From a brightly lit catwalk mounted on a flatbed truck, speakers are pumping out house music anthems, as the models begin to strut, sashay, and swirl on stage. The people in the crowd, numbering in the hundreds, and hemmed in by police street barricades, cheer wildly and strike up chants more appropriate to a football game than a fashion show. One by one, the models either don or expose clothing and caps bearing the insignia of UNITE, the garment union. Emcees reveal each model in turn to be a Barneys worker, with their very own workplace concerns to parade in public:

> "Here comes Michael. This fierce, fun-loving contract negotiator [in a long blond wig, with tight gabardine pants and a UNITE T-shirt tied up around his midriff] is fighting for all our concerns to be heard. Work it, Michael!"

> "Next up is Kelley [in a little white dress with high black boots], our blond bombshell, who is worried about job security because her job might be cut in half. Was her dress cut in half?"

> "A big hand for Timothy from the cosmetics department, queen bitch for glamour. Here to show unity—it's a family affair—is his sister Sharon [with silver coat, boa, and white go-go boots] and Chanel poster puppy Bon-Bon, his puppy. He [in a full-length sharkskin overcoat, the pooch painted green] is a firm believer in an ironclad contract as long as management can no longer be trusted."

"Come on up, Efron, a seasoned union veteran [all black from head to toe] who wants to be assured our health and pension plans remain secure in our union contract. Work it, homie!"

"Please welcome Philippe, a popular Parisian from couture [in bhanji-style streetwear] who is against mandatory overtime because he needs to get his beauty sleep. He looks like *he's* been sleeping for quite a while!"

"Here comes Brenda [in leather jacket and miniskirt]. This Puerto Rican party girl has one problem—productivity! Well, *she* sure looks productive tonight!"

"Step up, Matthew [in classic unstructured Armani]. He is one of the

Barneys
union workers
fashion show
(PHOTO BY TERU
KUWAYAMA)

top producers in his department. He fears merit-based increases because he knows *he* won't get one!"

"Loretta, our babe from Brooklyn, is in the house [hair slicked back, in a double-breasted pimp suit]. She says she's never seen such unity at Barneys. We are stronger than ever and will not be ignored."

"Next up is Erving, an up-and-coming designer [in a sparkly vest and pinstripe pants] who wants to make sure that non-selling employees get a fair increase. Work, girl, work!"

"Sure to bring the house down is absolutely fabulously fierce David [vogueing to the max in a see-through organza dress, festooned with UNITE buttons, and with full flamenco plumage on top]. With more hair colors than Linda Evangelista, David worries about stock levels and how they affect compensation, not to mention keeping his manager happy. *He* certainly looks happy, doesn't he?"

"Lastly, we have Gaston [in full Naomi Campbell drag, with a silver body sheath] who makes RuPaul look soft. Gaston is concerned about fair-pay increases and transfer procedures, and he knows that, yes, we are Barneys, but we are also UNITE."

Across the street, more soberly garbed employees from Barneys legal and management ranks look on, amused and astonished as the "fragrant MCs from cosmetics," whip the crowd into shrill appreciation of the vamping models-for-a-day and the union name. Even louder is the announcement that it is the workers who truly represent the company: "We are Barneys! We are Barneys!" Weary from weeks spent with lawyers and corporate hardballers in the fractious negotiations following the company's filing for Chapter 11 bankruptcy protection, the managers and lawyers pause to wonder if they themselves represent Barneys any longer. Far from providing comic relief, albeit at the expense of the svelte fashionistas to whom the company now caters, the runway show is a stark reminder of union strength and the role that these employees have insisted on playing in the bankruptcy proceedings that will decide the future of their jobs. For the last seven days, union employees at Barneys's three Manhattan stores have been working without a contract, and this show is the culmination of a public campaign, aimed directly at store customers and neighborhood residents, to win job security, fair compensation, and sound agreements on health and pension benefits, overtime rates, productivity standards. The campaign has included ads in trade organs like *Women's Wear Daily* and the *Daily News Record*, lunchtime rallies and leafletting outside Barneys's lush Madison Avenue uptown store, and posters all around town heralding tonight's event:

What's in Fashion This Year? A Fair Union Contract!
See Real Cool People in Real Hot Fashions!
Get the Inside Scoop on Life at Barneys!
Strike a Pose for Dignity!
April 6th
Don't Miss "7th on 17th"
Under the Stars in Chelsea!

Everyone agrees—this is a unique way to put contract demands in the public eye. But there's more to this event than a routine round of contract negotiations. Just before the models strike a pose, Fred Kaplan, manager of Local 340 (ACTWU), addresses the crowd: "We will not take a backseat to the insurance companies and the banks!" The workers certainly know what he is talking about, but so do many New Yorkers, who have been voyeurs of the messy legal spectacle of a famous business partnership gone sour.

The bankruptcy petition centered on a nasty dispute with partner Isetan, the Japanese department store giant, landlord of Barneys's three flagship stores in New York, Chicago, and Beverly Hills, and financier of its expanding empire of provincial outposts of taste in Seattle, Dallas, and Troy, Michigan.

Keeping company with Isetan were a host of creditors, from construction subcontractors to big-shot designers like Hugo Boss and Donna Karan, left holding millions of dollars' worth of unsecured invoices. A bankruptcy court judge had recently barred the company's attempt to evict the union's Amalgamated Insurance Fund from the creditors' committee. Barneys workers, through the union, had a high stake in the outcome of the bankruptcy filing and were not about to be ignored. It was not just the fate of the Pressmans, New York's most famous retail family, that hung in the balance. Six hundred workers, in jobs that had been union for over forty years, stood to fall along with the storied owners of the clothing empire.

But before I explain how this came to pass, let me clarify a thing or two about the scene that evening. Among the crowd were a host of residents from Chelsea itself, lately established as New York's youngish and upwardly mobile gay male neighborhood of choice. Many were from Splash, the club opposite. In fact, the runway show, minus the UNITE schmattes and labor voice-over,

A well-dressed
campaign
(PHOTO BY TERU
KUWAYAMA)

pretty much resembled amateur drag night at any one of a legion of gay clubs in the city. It was a simple extension of baseline gay club culture. In addition, the show was an extension of workplace culture. Every holiday season, management organized a runway event—called "Christmas Kick-off"—solely for employees, and primarily to build unity and loyalty among them. The theme of the event was to model a new line, but it mostly involved drag roles in skits and spoofs of the usual high-fashion rituals. Management took part, playing roles like Patsy and Edie from *Absolutely Fabulous*, while employees did drag impersonations of over-the-top Barneys customers. The high jinks of these affairs were combined with a lavish breakfast for the entire workforce. So too the extravagant holiday parties the Pressman brothers threw for workers had their performative elements. In other words, some of the models on the runway that night were doing repeat performances of roles they had pioneered in a much safer, nonpolitical environment where workers mingled with management in a festive, almost saturnalian setting.

There was an easy continuity, then, between "Seventh on Seventeenth" and queer-inflected practices within the workplace and within the neighborhood itself. Of course, the overlay of union pride and partisan commentary gave them quite a different meaning and design, and a shiny element of political genius lay in this transformation of purpose. It took real courage to move the runway from the protected sanctuary of the store into the public hubbub of the street. Yet these worker-models were taking it all in their high-heeled stride.

Could the same be said from the perspective of the union? This was exotic territory for an industrial union with its roots in the loft-and-tenement sewing and cutting shops. UNITE, sensing that the Barneys campaign was going to be pivotal, not only within the retail business but also from a public relations angle, had lavishly backed Local 340's efforts, providing three full-time organizers and extensive media support for public outreach. While the idea for the runway event and for other internal tactics had come directly from workers themselves, UNITE, the result of a recent merger of the ILGWU and ACTWU, lent its newly strengthened resources. Even though the reports published in the UNITE newspaper did not record that "gay" strategies had proven effective in the campaign, there was a palpable buzz at the union's

Seventh Avenue headquarters that this campaign was breaking new ground in some way that wasn't fully understood at the time.

Was there any recognition, on any side, of the pioneering use of gay culture in the campaign? If so, it did not translate directly into contract demands that benefited specifically queer employees (very much in the majority in the Barneys workforce) in the form of same-sex domestic partner benefits. For a while these benefits were on the table, but Barneys and the union decided to establish a new health fund, and, according to the manager of the local, Fred Kaplan, "we didn't want to start a new fund with levels of benefits that had no history." In addition, the company, while receptive to the idea, was reserving the right to review all benefits if challenged on a discrimination suit, as sometimes happens with domestic-partner benefits that exclude straight couples (who can legally marry). "Since we didn't want to divide the workforce," Kaplan and the committee aimed, ultimately, "at the greatest good for the greatest number." Katherine Kirsch, a UNITE organizer who worked on the campaign, recalled that the workers themselves did not assign a high priority to these benefits at the time. They were more ready to push in 1999, when the contract was up for renewal, and when the benefits were finally secured. (It also took until 1999 for UNITE staffers to enjoy these same-sex domestic-partner benefits, which they won in contract negotiations between the staff association, the Federation of Union Representatives, and officers of UNITE).

The Barneys workers, it appeared, were ahead of the bargaining curve in putting a queer foot forward with their campaign tactics. The runway on the street may have been a simple expansion of their daily, often theatrical, labor in selling style, but the queer tactics it embodied brought results for the whole workforce, gay and straight. Why did they prove so successful? The answer lies in the story of what Barneys had come to be.

Rise and Fall

No Bunk, No Junk, No Imitations. This was the sales motto that Barney Pressman adopted when he set up shop as a discount, used-clothing store in

1923, using the $500 he redeemed from pawning his wife's engagement ring. At that time, the neighborhood was solidly working-class, and tied to the thriving Hudson River waterfront, a world away from the genteel setting of the uptown emporia of taste like Saks, Bergdorf Goodman, and Bloomingdale's. In the classic mold of the first-generation Jewish garment entrepreneur, Barney peddled and wheedled his way to success by selling basic men's clothing in all sizes to all comers at bargain prices. By the time his son Fred took control in the early 1960s, Barneys was selling more men's suits than any other retail store in the world.

A color-blind tastemaker who turned his back on the cut-price religion of his father, Fred steered the store onto the path of upward mobility by preaching his own theology of style. Classier merchandise, much of it bought from exacting Italian tailors still working in a preindustrial environment, began to set the profile for a more discerning customer. Ironically, the neighborhood itself was now in the throes of deindustrialization, with its deserted lofts and warehouses abutting an abandoned waterfront. Customers, now more WASPy, or Euro-friendly, and not at all from neighborhoods like Chelsea, were drawn to the store by the new designer ethos. While well-established in ladies' fashion, designer wear represented a new mode of consumerism in men's clothing that would come to supplant the traditional retail manufacturer and transform the entire industry. Fred introduced the names of Brioni, Cardin, Givenchy, and, most infamously, Armani. Expanding the retail space by leaps and bounds, he also added departments like the Underground—dedicated to rococo hipster gear gussied up from the rock 'n' roll counterculture—and, in 1970, the International House, which exclusively featured European and Japanese designer wear set off in individual boutiques. Nothing like this had been seen in American men's stores, and the Barneys name quickly became synonymous with a new self-consciousness about masculinity that prized individualist flourishes over the mass cult of suit-tie-and-hat conformity. As the 1970s wore on, Fred's store also acquired a reputation for serving the prosperous.

The third-generation sons, flashy Gene and bottom-liner Bob, took this ranking into the realm of the opulent. The steep rise in Barneys status began with Gene's introduction of pricey women's couture and ended with the mother-of-pearl shelves, silk dressing-room curtains, goatskinned and platinum-leafed walls, and Carrara-marbled floors that graced the flush uptown palace of Barneys Madison Avenue store, decorated for a king's ransom, and built by a Pharaonic army of laborers working around the clock. Gene and Bob's reign began with Azzedine Alaia's dresses for those who "could never be too rich or too thin," and ended in a blizzard of Prada bags, Manolo Blahnik heels, Valentino coats, Comme des Garcons shirts, Dolce and Gabbano underwear, Lang pants, and Gucci shades for those who could not afford to be seen without the right items and accessories. Under the sway of the Studio 54 aesthetic, disco prince Gene's departments became a mecca for the mix of Eurotrash, gay underground, and self-glamorizing yuppie hipsters that came to rule Manhattan's high life in the 1980s and early 1990s. Not the uptown bourgeoisie, but the cultural elites that bubbled up from the rapidly gentrifying downtown arts, media, and lifestyle scenes. In no time, the styles and attitudes concocted for these downtown beneficiaries were hungrily emulated by the city's young finance capital entrepreneurs.

This, at least, was the Pressman family story about Barneys, imaginatively recounted in Joshua Levine's recent book, *The Rise and Fall of the House of Barneys*.[1] But what did these sea changes mean if you were an employee? Arguably the most famous, and most highly paid, was Simon Doonan, the acerbic satirist and protégé of Diana Vreeland, awarded directorial control over the design of the store's famous windows from 1984 onward. Doonan's biting, and often bitchy, *tableaux vivantes* served to broadcast the new shockist attitude associated with the store. The usual camp celebrities made de rigueur appearances: Bette Midler, Cher, Jackie Onassis, Nancy Reagan, Liberace, Louis XIV, Queen Elizabeth II, Barbara Cartland, Martha Stewart. But pride of place, as figures to be ridiculed with punk bravado, was reserved for the patron saints of cultural conservatism, like Margaret Thatcher, Dan Quayle, Jesse Helms, Tammy Faye Bakker.[2] Of all the sins of taste to be pilloried in Doonan's hierarchy, homophobia ranked among the highest. To be hip to this aesthetic you had to aspire to be fabulous, which meant being gay or

gay-friendly. Doonan brought a decisively queer, though somewhat unforgiving, sensibility to the public image of Barneys. Increasingly, this sensibility
reflected the world outside. Chelsea had become the latest desirable gay
male haven, with rents and prices to match, and an insider culture with a distinctive look and esprit de corps quickly branded as "Chelsea Clone."

Inside the store, the new buyers and tastemakers established the color
black as the universal rule of thumb in every wardrobe item—put together in
austere, minimalist ensembles. The cult of black quickly extended its sway,
almost like the Holy Roman Empire, all over the global fashion map. The
nature of the labor expected of the selling employees had also changed.
Retail clothing, no less than couture designing, has always been heavily
staffed by gays and lesbians. While the ability to do the "emotional labor"
required in fitting and selling clothes has traditionally been seen as a queer
talent, these personal skills had been exercised discreetly, and were indistinguishable from the service ethos of gentility. As Barneys made its way up in
the world, it drew more and more openly gay employees into the selling
ranks, and with the opening of the Underground and the International
House, discretion was no longer a virtue on the sales floor. As in the chic
restaurants that studded the gentrifying belts of the city in the eighties, service employees who were identifiably gay were not just a business asset, they
would become an economic necessity. What sold clothes to the hipoisie in
this new environment was a frankly camp, though still restrained, behavior,
combined with a posture of *folie de grandeur* that verged on parody. At
Barneys that blend was perfected for the benefit of customers who needed to
be persuaded that their high-end purchases could be worn as a charm to
ward off the demons of bourgeois respectability. The attitude that Barneys
sold was woven from the cloth of queer labor in more ways than one.

By the mid-1990s, the temple of taste was in serious financial trouble. The
women's department had bled money from the outset, the provincial stores
had flopped, and the sumptuous Madison Avenue store was sucking
Seventeenth Street dry. When the Pressmans sought bankruptcy in January
1996, the writing was on the wall, and workers were galvanized in their cam-

paign to renew and strengthen their contract. There was talk of layoffs and reorganization and much uncertainty about the future. The union needed a highly visible strategy to unite the entire bargaining unit. A membership meeting was called, and workers came up with a bold new tactic, designed to win over customers and clients in a way that simply picketing outside the stores would not.

Soon, customers who visited the stores on Tuesdays began to notice employees wearing swatches of red against the severe backdrop of basic black—a tie, a handkerchief, a scarf, a T-shirt, socks. Some actually wore red, from head to toe. It could have been a new trend, so customers took notice. But the red, it was explained, signified unity with the union campaign, and it was the workers' way—through a stylistic flourish—of communicating their contract concerns to customers and management. Why red? To represent the union's colors, and also to contrast with black, though the precedent of AIDS ribbons gave the color some additional resonance.[3] Some of the men in cosmetics went a little wild with their nails, lips, and cheekbones. While this sort of thing could pass, on an individual basis, without too much comment at Barneys, the spectacle of an entire workforce united by the color of union loyalty sent a powerful message to management. "The unity was very visible," recalled Elba Liz, a rank-and-file member at the time. "It showed we were out on a mission to bring the contract home. Coming into the store and seeing our brothers and sisters wearing red, gave us an energy and sense of pride. And it made the workers want to be more active. . . . A lot of the workers knew they had a union but they didn't know what it was to be organized, if you will. Getting involved in the process like this made all the difference."

Katherine Kirsch, the main UNITE organizer, agreed. "Rather than having a small minority being active, the overall sense of ownership helped to build the union from the bottom up." In addition, "outrageous was part of our goal, it sent a message to management that we were willing to go wacky on them." Kirsch confesses that she had wondered if some of the top-selling employees would identify, finally, as workers: "They have their own client books and have some bargaining agency as individuals. I was amazed to see workers, earning as much as $95,000 who sell $2,000 Armani suits, and who wear these suits, chanting *Union! Union!* out there on the street." It helped that the tactics didn't associate the union solely with "drudgery and militancy," and the employees, who established authorship of the campaign, "felt free to be who they were (or weren't) on the picket lines." Tyler Mayo, a rep from the cosmetics and fragrances floor, recalls: "We were friendly and direct, not militant, not mean, and our issues were made very understandable to the public."

Contract negotiations began to get sticky, and it looked as though an impasse might be declared, at which point management would be permitted to implement the last offer. One of the workers in cosmetics suggested the runway show as a public event that might break the impasse. The models, it was agreed, would be able to address the concerns that were still on the negotiating table. Not only was the show scripted by the workers, the fact that it expressed their own identity helped to intensify their solidarity. For many of the employees, the pride in their public flamboyance was part and parcel of their pride in the union, both during the runway show and in the immediate impact it had on management when negotiations resumed three days later. Liz explained: "They really were working the runway, and didn't mind at all that people recognized them as homosexuals, because they were open about it, and felt good about themselves. And every time we went to the table and came back with something we had gained just because of that, it gave them even more ownership and pride. They were happy because 'We got this' *and* 'I was all that.' 'We got to be out there,' and so 'we got it because of my flamboyance.' It was a very proud moment for them."

According to Liz, who served on the negotiation committee and went on to take a position with the local, "management was shocked. They said, 'How did you do all of this?' A few days later, we got job security, and productivity was up for discussion, and the compensation system was negotiated on our terms. We brought the contract home." In fact, the compensation system proved so lucrative that the increase in commissions outpaced the increase in sales, and had to be renegotiated three years later. Especially satisfying were the solid increases that were won for non-selling employees. Straight workers were more likely to be employed in the non-selling ranks, and so here was an example of how overtly queer campaigning was directly benefiting straight workers.

Staving off the threat of a strike was a relief to management, but nothing could stem the heavy losses. After showing a deficit of $97 million for the fiscal year ending in August 1997, the company closed, and auctioned off the Seventeenth Street store, along with many of its national outposts. Ownership quickly passed from the Pressmans to its unsecured creditors and two so-called "vulture funds," which specialize in investing in distressed companies' debt. When a reorganized Barneys finally emerged from bankruptcy protection after three years, it was a different creature. With the imposition of the new corporate environment uptown, and much more conventional management, workers quickly realized that the camp ways were no longer encouraged. But the legacy of the 1996 campaign did not die. When contract renewal negotiations started up in 1999, workers revived Red Days, this time on Saturdays. Management tried to exploit the tactic by placing an easel at the front of the store, advising customers to open a Barneys credit card if they "saw red." Peeved that management had tried to co-opt their actions, the employees quickly switched to yellow. The most fashion-conscious among the rank and file had to swallow some pride to wear this color, and at least one had to fit in two appointments in a tanning booth before his pale, white skin could carry the yellow. Leafletters outside the store handed ingoing customers yellow balloons with smiley faces. Carried inside, much to the chagrin of management, the balloons revealed, on their flip side, "NO MORE PAY CUTS."

By the time it returned to Chelsea in the form of the smaller Co-op branch, Barneys was no longer quite what it was, for its workers, owners, and customers. But the lesson of 1996 and 1999 was worth lingering over. These campaigns were as creative as anything dreamed up in the course of the company's colorful history. The tactics deployed grew directly out of the culture of the workplace, and drew upon specific features of queer labor that the company had employed for its own benefit during the glory years of Barneys. So too the public and the press responded in kind, rising to the support of this artful expression of workers' concerns. Management was impressed by the ingenuity of the tactics, while the kindred enthusiasm of straight workers, in the less spectacular jobs, demonstrated how queer tactics can bring justice for everybody. All in all, there had been little to distinguish gay pride from union pride. Tyler Mayo, the cosmetics rep who worked his way from floor rep in 1996 onto the negotiating committee in 1999, put it this way: "We are gay and part of the union at the same time. We don't work at Barneys because we are gay, and we're not gay because we work at Barneys, but these all happened to be simpatico at one and the same time, and they are part of the whole picture here."

Campaign slogan for UAW members at
the Museum of Modern Art, New York
(STICKER)

CHAPTER SEVEN

The Mental Labor Problem

IN THE WINTER MONTHS OF 1998–1999, Local 802 of the American Federation of Musicians (AFM) succeeded in organizing, and securing a contract for, the part-time jazz program faculty in the Mannes College of Music at the New School University. Among the seventy adjunct teachers represented by the union were some venerable musicians from the world of jazz, including Chico Hamilton, leader of the famous quintet, and seasoned virtuosos, like Benny Powell and Jimmy Owens, who have played with the Count Basie and Duke Ellington orchestras.[1] Hired from year to year, often for chronically low compensation, and without any benefits or pension plan, these faculty looked to the oldest of the craft unions in the arts (founded in 1896) to muster support from community leaders and elected public officials and to win recognition from their employer through the National Labor Relations Board. The day the musicians' contract was signed, the New School also offered pensions and benefits to 3,000 other nonunion adjunct faculty members. While this offer was clearly aimed at forestalling any further unionization, it also exemplified the old labor maxim that "justice for one is justice for all."[2]

This campaign, named Justice for Jazz Artists (with its echo of the legendary SEIU Justice for Janitors campaign of the early 1990s), may have been a microscopic landmark on the increasingly busy landscape of academic labor, but its significance radiated in many directions. In the AFM's first bid to represent musicians as teachers, the local ran what its chief organizer described to me as a "real, large-scale corporate campaign" by using the arena of public opinion. His comment conveyed pride in the newfound strength of the organizing department, which was only three years old and therefore dated from the 1996 election of the Sweeney-Trumka-Chavez-Thompson directorate of the AFL-CIO. In the course of the campaign, organizers appealed to the public perception that jazz greats had been denied their due desserts, historically and to this day.

Among all arts workers, jazz musicians arguably have the most visible profile as artists whose work has been most lionized by all classes of audience, and whose personal compensation has been most blatantly discounted. Indeed, the contract helped to remedy the local's own, long neglect of jazz musicians in New York City. The New School's own credibility, as an institution with a progressive pedigree, most recently soiled by headline-making student protests over the paltry minority representation on its faculty, was put to the test by this bargaining unit of primarily African American musicians. The profile of these seasoned working teachers also refuted the more typical image of underpaid adjunct faculty as fresh-faced Ph.D.s facing the first, albeit prolonged, obstacles to their professional ambitions for full-time employment. Most striking of all, the campaign yoked together artists and academics in ways that gave rise to some friction over whether a musicians' or a teachers' union ought to be representing the adjuncts.

While sectors of the performing arts have been unionized for several decades, and faculty sectors of the academy since the 1960s, both professions have been resistant, historically, to industry-wide organization, retaining a craft culture of flexible, if not exclusive, bargaining, each in its own distinctive ways. However disparate their solo career traditions, the artisan jazzman here shares the same position and predicament as the professional academic whose labor has been degraded and de-professionalized in recent years. What are the circumstances that have accelerated this degradation, and are they only economic in nature? Is there something about the sacrificial labor traditions of artists (in the broad sense of the term, used throughout this chapter) and academics that can clarify the common plight of their labor in the current economic landscape? In this chapter, I will review how their shared work mentality has become increasingly serviceable to the new neoliberal world of labor. They offer an entrepreneurial profile that fits well with the self-managing employee identities that are encouraged and prized in the flexible economy. No longer on the margins of society, in bohemia or the ivory tower, they are providing a rationale for the latest model of exploitation in core sectors of the information economy, and pioneering the workplaces of tomorrow.

The Cost of Idle Curiosity

Try to imagine the response to such union campaigns on the part of the original founders of the New School in 1919, among whom were Progressive titans like Charles Beard, Herbert Croly, Wesley Clair Mitchell, James Harvey Robinson, Thorstein Veblen, and John Dewey. They certainly supported the extension of education to trade union members, and indeed, the New School established ties with the Workers Education Bureau of America. But the prospect of union organization among faculty would have been as distasteful to these scholars as the entrenchment today of an expansive administrative bureaucracy with the managerial capacity to dictate every root and branch of collegial policy.[3] They conceived the new institution in large part because the wartime policies adopted by their previous university administrators had demanded a fealty to college and state that offended their fierce devotion to intellectual independence. Indeed, the Columbia University administration went so far as to reorganize its departments into military corps (the medical corps, the legal corps, the language corps, the economic and social service corps, etc.), and dismissed two faculty for their "antiwar" sentiments, prompting Beard, and later Robinson, to resign in a blaze of publicity.[4] Launched as a clear alternative to the elite ideal of service to God, country, and capital, the fledgling New School (disastrously, as it happens) would have no president, trustees, or bureaucratic cohort to constrain the free exercise of the intellect.

One of the strongest renditions of the scholarly ideal of faculty governance appears in Veblen's own "memorandum on the conduct of universities by businessmen," *The Higher Learning in America*. In this 1919 volume, the Progressive aversion to corporate trusts and capitalist inefficiency merges with the customary repugnance of the scholar-gentleman for a narrowly vocational approach to learning. Veblen relegates the utilitarian application of knowledge to the domain of purely pecuniary gain identified with the Vested Interests (his euphemism for the ruling class), and he finds trustees and senior administrators everywhere in collusion with those interests. *University Control*, a similar, though less enduring, book by the psychologist James McKeen Cattell, one of the faculty fired at Columbia, analyzes a nationwide survey of responses to the growing plight of micromanaged faculty, snared between "the Scylla of presidential autocracy and the Charybdis of faculty and trustee incompetence."[5]

The university ideal, according to Veblen, should be the pursuit of "Idle Curiosity," and any treatment of knowledge as a "merchantable commodity" is a desecration of an exalted calling.[6] Neither is Veblen's university a fit environment for training students to pursue legal or business careers. Above all, Veblen's book spotlights his withering opposition to the penetration of academe by the techniques of business salesmanship and advertising—all too familiar today as the corporatization of higher education in an advanced stage, with its sharp market orientation and its managerial premium on cost-effective delivery of risk-free educational product. By way of contrast, his passion for Idle Curiosity is the direct scholarly equivalent of "art for art's sake," so quarantined from the world of "wont and use" as to render its devotees ineffectual as economic or social actors outside of the cloistered sphere over which they hold some sway.

This ideal of disinterestedness helped pave the way, as David Reisman later pointed out, for a "cult of incompetence" among modern academics: "proud of their inability to preside at a meeting, or turn in grade lists on time, or to remember appointments or the names of students, or to write memoranda not tainted by irrelevance."[7] It is a cult whose devotions still flourish today, but is increasingly observed only by the securely tenured or tenurable, who are already a minority in many institutions of higher learning. In its heyday, this cult was most assiduously observed in colleges patterned after the model of elite East Coast institutions living off their legacy of pre-Jacksonian colonial hierarchies.[8] The customary garb of their Anglo-identified faculty directly expressed their distance from the worldly uniforms of commerce. Indeed, the long-suffering tweed jacket of the academic and the highbrow writer evolves directly from the attire of the English country gentleman who does not dirty his hands with city trade. While many alternative forms of sartorial affiliation have flourished in recent years, university intellectuals will generally not wear business suits unless they hold higher administrative positions, and, when they are not aping faded gentility, they will opt, like most other arts professionals, for downwardly mobile apparel.

Unlike fellow Progressives (Morris Cooke, the influential reformer of the engineering profession, unflinchingly recommended tenure abolition and academic Taylorism in his 1910 report, *Academic and Industrial Efficiency*), Veblen railed against the advent of cost-effectiveness in his dreamy precincts of academe *at the same time* as he called for more efficiency in industry. In the world of factories, he argued, it is the financial captains and the Vested Interests who are wasteful and who sabotage the productive potential of the national economy. But for the Veblen of *The Engineers and the Price System*, the solution did not lie in industrial democracy, in the shape of labor power-sharing. The caste of practical intellectuals that he lionizes—the engineers— promises to deliver a more efficient system of production, preempting, among other things, the need for industrial workers to organize their interests against the wasteful exploitation of labor for profit. Though they do not fully know it, Veblen suggests that the engineers are actually in control of the system of production, and if only they could be true to their professional scientific ideals, they could effect a peaceful, but revolutionary, transition to a more rational economy and society.[9] Within Veblen's academy, the faculty hold a similar position, but their potential lies in resisting, as opposed to quickening, efficiency. Like the engineer, the scholar would be loyal to science and not beholden to business interests, and if only the customs of Idle Curiosity were properly observed, the Taylorist model of productivity quotas could be kept safely at bay.

Even in his day, Veblen's faith in the pure and generous spirit of the scholar was out of synch (and quite at odds with the midwestern agrarian traditions of his own educational background). But it would not become an actual *liability* to the material well-being of the academic workforce until much later in the century. In our time, the legacy of this "impecunious" credo has not only failed miserably to stave off the worst incursions into the academy of corporate rationalization. Through its studied neglect of money matters, this ideal may also have actively contributed to the proletarianization of large sectors of Veblen's profession, a sizeable percentage of whom now earn compensation at or near the poverty line.

A Great Divide

Before I expand on this claim, let us consider the lot of musicians in the year when Veblen's book was published, for it is the common conditions of academic and artistic labor that I am pursuing here. By the end of World War I, the AFM had already accomplished a great deal. The union had set the first wage scales for orchestras traveling with grand operas, comic operas, musical comedies, and similar attractions. It had lobbied for congressional reform of copyright law and, in its first wave of protectionist ardor, for curtailing the unregulated admission to the U.S. of foreign musicians willing to work for lower wages. Its members had been hard hit by the wartime cabaret tax and then again by Prohibition, but a much bigger threat lay in the introduction of recording technology on an industrial scale, which was rapidly changing how music was produced and heard. The commercial explosion of the player piano was a harbinger of how new technologies would affect the livelihood of performers. By 1916, 200,000, or 65 percent of the pianos produced in the U.S., were mechanized, and the roll industry that serviced the player-piano boom was the most significant factor in the music industries as a whole.[10] It was a business that announced the redundancy of live piano accompanyists—a career only recently boosted by the spread of silent movie houses.

Radio broadcasting of recorded musical performances further reduced the number of job opportunities for live performers, and, very soon, the canned music of talking pictures put thousands of theater-pit musicians out of work.[11] The forward march of cultural industrialization had begun in earnest, and the musicians, actors, singers, dancers, and others who had crisscrossed the postbellum landscape in hundreds of small performing companies now faced an uncertain future in the age of Vitaphone and Movietone. Traditional commercial forms of theater, vaudeville, and circus would take a beating, and their more popular, and hence lucrative, audiences would be poached away by the millions. Despite the efforts of the Music Defense League, organized by the AFM against movie exhibitors and radio broadcasters, the Depression, and the popularity of the new media and sound systems, took a further toll. The voracious spread of the jukebox followed, displacing even more musicians. By end of the 1930s, AFM turned to union militancy and threatened strikes against the radio and recording industries. A controversial union-enforced ban on recording endured from 1942 until the AFM's power was drastically curtailed by the Taft-Hartley and Lea Acts.[12]

Not only the conditions of employment but also the conditions of artistic expression would be decisively altered by industrialization in the 1920s and 1930s. Practitioners of the high-culture genres, cut off from a popular consumer base and catering more and more to an educated and well-heeled cognoscenti, would eventually drift into the quarantine zone of the state-subsidized, or nonprofit, sector. There, a full-blown cult of artistic license would flourish, sponsored, in the postwar years, by a Cold War policy establishment that diligently promoted the superior civic liberties of the West. The nonprofit enclave proved to be a fecund environment for the psychopathology of the late Romantic artist, living hand to mouth and visibly chafing at the comforts, however scant and short-lived, provided by a medley of corporate, government, and bourgeois patrons. By contrast, in the commercial sectors of film, radio, TV, journalism, and recording, cultural workers, beginning in the early 1930s, would accept a more stable and increasingly union wage in exchange for the partial surrender of their artistic autonomy.

The great divide between the high arts and popular culture has, of course, been discussed to death (including by this author) as a measure of changes in the aesthetic life and mass social organization of modern times. The corresponding change in the nature of cultural labor has received much less attention. Even within the literature that could be grouped together under the heading of cultural policy, the lion's share is given over to the "funding problem" of the arts, such as changes in the sources and traditions of patronage and institutional money supply. By contrast, there is relatively little focus on the "labor problem" of the arts.[13] Among the exceptions to this rule I have chosen to briefly outline two quite different, but not untypical, approaches to this topic of cultural labor—the cultural discount and the cost disease.

The Cultural Discount

In the first approach, the cultural labor problem figures primarily as the challenge of maintaining a steady supply of workers willing to discount the price of their labor for love of their craft. This might be characterized as the culture vulture's version of "how difficult it is to find good help these days." The most incisive version of this thesis can be found in San Francisco Foundation executive William Kreidler's useful account of the rise and decline of the nonprofit arts foundation. Central to Kreidler's analysis is the principle of the *cultural discount*, by which artists and other arts workers accept nonmonetary rewards—the gratification of producing art—as compensation for their work, thereby discounting the cash price of their labor.[14]

In the nineteenth century, Kreidler points out that it was the model of individual proprietorship that characterized most theaters, orchestras, opera companies, performing arts impresarios, and many museums. The separation between high and low, or elite and popular, as Lawrence Levine and others have shown, was much less distinct in this period.[15] While these for-profit proprietorships had to meet the test of the marketplace to survive, they were still heavily subsidized and sustained by the willingness of cultural workers to accept deeply discounted compensation for their labor. Indeed, it is fair to say that the largest subsidy to the arts has always come from workers themselves. To this day, all such workers, even those employed on market-driven contracts, tend to earn compensation well below that commensurate with their skills and levels of educational attainment. The rough justice of the marketplace does not seem to deter the chronically discounted. Indeed, and largely because of artists' traditions of sacrifice, it often appears to spur them on in ways that would be regarded as self-destructive in any other economic sector.

Kreidler observes that, lately, arts organizations have begun to worry about the depletion of this discount labor supply. Today's youth, he suggests, are less attracted to the ethos of public service or service to the arts that equates to personal sacrifice, an ethos that was more appealing to relatively affluent, white baby boomers in the post-Kennedy period at the height of nonprofit funding of the arts. As that funding pipeline has sharply reduced its flow, and as leisure time has declined radically for most people in the U.S. in the last two decades, the arts economy faces an uncertain future. The older proprietary models have mostly been subsumed by the commercial culture industries, and the traditional dependence on volunteer, discounted labor to support the arts can no longer be taken for granted. Subtle improvements in the money supply, he concludes, are not likely to offset the long-term impact of labor attrition.

Since Kreidler assumes that the status and levels of comparative compensation enjoyed by artists have not changed significantly since the entrepreneurial heyday of the nineteenth-century arts proprietor, the root of the current arts crisis must therefore lie in the "selfish gene" pool of the boomer parent. Although he does not identify the problem in quite this candid way, it is not unfair to see his conclusion as akin to parental indictments of Gen X apathy. The labor crisis of the arts can thus be laid at the door of youngsters who will not commit to an ideal higher than their own self-absorbed, material interests. Presumably the moral calling of the arts is not well-served by a generation distinguished by its cultivation of types like the world-class slacker or the IPO-seeking dotcommer. If we flesh out this line of argument, we can almost hear the grouchy tones of the parental scold, chiding the listless off-spring with mawkish tales about his own hardships of yore, nobly borne in cold-water apartments and fixtureless lofts. Kreidler's description of the cultural discount is a very useful contribution, but his belief that sacrificial labor is morally sustaining for youth is little short of a recipe for exploitation. Reasoning that appeals to the moral fiber of generational temperament may be consoling, especially to those above the boomer waterline, but it will not provide a cogent assessment of the state of cultural labor. Not when the percentage of employees identified as artists, in national labor statistics, is higher than ever. Not when the principle of the cultural discount, as I will shortly show, is more and more utilized on a semi-industrial scale in sectors of the knowledge industries.

The Cost Disease

A second kind of explanation of the labor crisis, with proven historical impact on arts funding, has been advanced by arts economists. Professionally challenged by evidence of productive activity that does not observe the all-powerful laws of market supply and demand, liberal economists have been drawn to offer a structural explanation for the "income gap" between the arts and other professions. One influential example was offered by William Baumol in a 1966 study of the performing arts co-authored with fellow Princeton economist William Bowen. With the help of their faculty spouses, who did much of the empirical research, Baumol and Bowen set out to reveal how and why the performing arts have failed to keep up with the impressive productivity gains, measured in outputs per man hour, that have been recorded by other sectors of American industry in the course of the century.

For their purposes, they propose to assess the labor cost per unit of the arts as if the arts functioned like any other service-sector industry: "It is helpful to treat the arts, not as an intangible manifestation of the human spirit, but as a productive activity which provides services to the community: one which, in this respect, does not differ from the manufacture of electricity or the supply of transportation or house-cleaning services."[16] Viewed from this angle, Baumol and Bowen find that the performing arts do not behave at all like other sectors of the service economy, primarily because they cannot, by their nature, exploit the productivity gains that come with advances in technology. In terms of its technological conditions of production, a contemporary performance of *Macbeth* is not substantially different from its Elizabethan equivalent. "It will be seen," Baumol and Bowen write, "that the tendency for costs to rise and for prices to lag behind is neither a matter of bad luck nor mismanagement. Rather, it is an inescapable result of the technology of live performance, which will continue to contribute to the widening of the income gaps of the performing organizations."

While the costs of performing will continue to rise without an increase in productivity, Baumol and Bowen conclude, more auspiciously, that productivity in other sectors of economy will provide workers with more leisure time to consume and participate in the arts, and thereby alleviate some of the economic pressure. This cheerful rider, so indicative of the mid-1960s American climate of chipper expectations, would have a much more consequential echo in Bowen's infamous report on a different service profession, twenty-three years later. His 1989 study of graduate education forecast widespread tenure-track job openings in the professoriat by the middle of the 1990s and may have bootlessly lured thousands into doctoral programs with its misconceived assurances of a buoyant future in college teaching.[17]

Baumol and Bowen's 1966 arts forecast foundered almost as quickly as the education one offered by Bowen in 1989. A decline in the leisure time available to the general U.S. workforce set in from the early 1970s and has not been stemmed, not even by the boom economy of the 1990s, which only triggered even higher levels of performance anxiety. Overwork, as opposed to joblessness, became the most chronic feature of the labor landscape. Nonetheless, the impact of the 1966 study helped to fuel the clamor for increased state funding for the arts, revived that same year, after a hiatus of almost three decades, with the creation of the National Endowment for the Arts. Baumol's "cost disease" model, as it came to be known (the cost disease condemns the cost per live performance to rise at a rate persistently faster than that of a typically manufactured good), provided empirical support for state intervention in the arts, and subsequently became a staple principle of welfare economics.

But his cost disease does not apply solely to the arts. It is shared, he points out, by other "stagnant sectors" like health and education, whose capacity to provide services is impaired by increasing relative costs.[18] Handicapped from the outset by the cost disease, the arts, in Baumol's opinion, can either join the productive sector—by emulating the culture industries in their adaptation of advanced technologies—or hew more and more to the model of social services, like health or education (or national defense for that matter), which produce a subsidized public good under the heavy hand of bureaucratic supervision.

In some respects, both of these outcomes have come to pass. The institutional divide between the high and low arts has continued to blur, and more and more live performance has come to serve a merely promotional function for cultural product available to remote consumers in some other technologically mediated format. So too, as George Yudice has analyzed, the new profile of the artist as a glorified social service worker has supplanted the autonomous avant-garde innovator as a fundable type, increasingly sponsored through local arts agencies. The all-purpose artist-citizen, whose work can help to preserve rural and inner-city communities at risk and stimulate efforts to revive their economies, is increasingly viewed as a means to create jobs through cultural tourism, to promote urban renewal through the competitive siting of museums and arts centers, to save teenagers from substance abuse, or generally to enhance public education through an infusion of communicative skills.[19]

New Model Workers

In the steady withdrawal of federal support for the arts, Yudice sees a new phase of governmentality. Released from its lingering Cold War obligations to fund and promote the "free world" artist, the state began to forge and broker model partnerships between government, corporations, and nonprofit foundations and groups. Akin in some ways to the liberalization of health and education services, this new profile for the arts as the poster child for civic activity extends not just to new kinds of application—"from youth programs and crime prevention to job training and race relations," in the words of "American Canvas," a 1997 NEA report by Gary Larson. It also includes the new kinds of sponsors or "partners that arts organizations have taken on in recent years, with school districts, parks and recreation departments, convention and visitor bureaus, chambers of commerce, and a host of social welfare agencies all serving to highlight the utilitarian aspects of the arts in contemporary society."[20]

In the same year as the "American Canvas" report, the American Assembly (a leadership policy group drawn from the private and public sectors) coordinated a conference and a report on the public purpose of the arts that proposed a similar set of principles:[21]

1. "The arts help to define what it is to be an American"—by advancing democratic values and American pluralism at home and abroad, and reaffirming national identity in general.
2. "The arts contribute to quality of life and economic growth"—by strengthening not only the economic livability of communities, but also the prosperity of the nation at home and abroad.
3. "The arts help to form an educated and aware citizenry"—by promoting cultural diversity, educational competency, and freedom of inquiry in an open society.
4. "The arts enhance individual life"—by encouraging individual creativity, spirit and potential, and by stimulating "release, relaxation, and entertainment."

Like the NEA report, the American Assembly document proposes an expansion of the potential roles on offer for artists in a newly fluid civic sphere where private and public can no longer clearly be distinguished. One of the political outcomes that Yudice discerns is the soft management of dissent—the traditionally adversarial artist is accommodated through the offering, and voluntary embrace of, partner status. Under this arrangement, time-honored traditions like *épater la bourgeoisie* and bash-the-bureaucrat will be retired, since this new profile does not *require* artists to bite the hand that feeds them as proof of their free will in a liberal society.

Under Tony Blair's New Labour administrations, this bureaucratic dispensation toward artists was more firmly established through the policies of Chris Smith's Ministry for Culture, Media, and Sport. *Creative Britain*, Smith's blueprint for cultural policy, asked artists to play more functional roles in society: assisting in the improvement of public health, race relations, urban degradation, special education, welfare-to-work programs, and, of course, economic development. Above all, the new policies required funded arts activities to show a good return on investment (ROI, in MBA shorthand). Naturally, most working artists saw these functions as more appropriate to entrepreneurial social workers than to conventional art makers, and so a vigorous public debate ensued about the pros and cons of adopting the arts into the machinery of social and economic policy.[22]

If this arts profile does indeed herald a new kind of arrangement of public authority that triangulates state, corporate, and nonprofit sectors, the service-ability of the artist's flexible labor is even more indicative of the moment. Since flexible specialization emerged as a leading industrial principle, the number of artists employed in the general labor force (defined in decennial U.S. Census data and annual Bureau of Labor Statistics (BLS) reports as eleven occupations: artists who work with their hands, authors, actors and directors, designers, dancers, architects, photographers, arts teachers, musicians/composers, etc.) has swelled from year to year. According to the NEA's annual summaries of BLS tabulations, this number more than doubled from 1970 to 1990, showing an 81 percent increase in the course of the 1970s (while artists' real earnings declined by 37 percent), a 54 percent increase in the 1980s, a slight decline in the depression of the early 1990s, and a renewal of growth ever since, crossing the threshold of two million in 1998. In 1997, artists were enjoying a growth rate in employment (at 2.7 percent) that far outstripped the general workforce (1.3 percent) and even that of other professional specialists (2.4 percent).[23]

These are impressive numbers, but they do not tell a simple story. To figure in the BLS survey, "one must be working during the survey week and have described that job/work as one of eleven artist occupations." Respondents are asked to describe the job at which "they worked the most number of hours in the survey week." Artists working more hours in other jobs outside the arts are classified as employed in those other occupations. By 1998, these amounted to an additional 330,000, for a total of 2,280,000 artists employed in the workforce.[24] Randy Martin points out that these requirements gloss over the verifiable existence of full-time jobs within that occupational sector: "One works in an occupation, a sector, but has the flexibility to remain unattached. The artist can secure an identity for a day's wage, but the rest of the week remains unsecuritized."[25] Because of the high degree of self-employment, and because they are most likely to have other jobs to support a creative trade that habitually employs them for only a portion of a workweek, employment and earnings data on cultural workers have always been unreliable. Even in the most highly unionized entertainment guilds, where the majority of members cannot find work on any given day, the dominant employment model is casual employment on a project-by-project basis. Loyalty is to the guild or craft or union, rather than to a single employer.[26]

There is clearly more going on here than the sleight-of-hand interpretation of statistics to paint a rosy picture of job creation in the arts. The numbers reflect the expansion of economic sectors devoted to the commercial and nonprofit trade in culture, with the consequence that more and more people are able to sustain a living from the arts as a primary occupation. Many of these jobs sprang into existence because culture is perceived as value-adding, and thus increasingly offers a return on investment. Culture has become a major stimulant to urban economies in particular, and a controversial instrument of urban regeneration. Whether for purposes of tourism, or to boost property values of marginal neighborhoods, or simply to satisfy the consumer tastes of urban professionals, every city of middling size now claims its own artsy district, modeled after Manhattan's SoHo, with bohemian status conferred on the neighborhood's nonconformist residents. An entire urban policy initiative, called Creative Cities, has sprung into being, centered on the role that cultural ideas can play in regenerating not just the image, but the economy of ex-industrial cities as a whole. Northern cities like Glasgow (architecture and design), Sheffield (music), Liverpool and Manchester (music) are the most salient British examples that stand out from the much broader heritage tourist economy. In the U.S., cultural policy is increasingly a central component of urban policy, not only in cities with a traditional pool of creative workers—San Francisco, New York, Los Angeles, Seattle, Boston, Austin—but also in those, like Newark and Pittsburgh, which have suffered from the impact of deindustrialization.[27]

In addition, however, there may be a more general trend that supports the BLS figures. Whether or not we can verify a proliferation of new jobs, the "mentality" of artists' work is more and more in demand, and is steadily being relocated from its traditional position at the social margins of the productive economy into roles closer to the economic centers of production. Indeed, the traditional profile of the artist as unattached and adaptable to circumstance is surely now coming into its own as the ideal definition of the postindustrial knowledge worker. What is the profile of this new kind of worker who behaves and thinks like an artist? Someone who is comfortable in an ever-changing environment that often demands creative shifts in communication with different kinds of employers, clients, and colleagues; who is attitudinally geared toward work that requires long, and often unsocial, hours; who dedicates their time and energy to distinct projects, rather than to a steady flow of production; who exercises self-management, if not self-employment, in the execution of their work; and who is accustomed to a contingent and casual work environment, without overt supervision or judgment from above.

The best example of these employment patterns could be found in the New Economy companies that emerged in urban downtown centers from the mid-1990s. Borne along by the boom in Internet services, these new media start-ups capitalized on a surplus of creative labor and depressed real estate prices to recruit and nurture a neo-bohemian workforce that satisfied the profile of the "fast company" in a creative ferment, throwing off innovative ideas from a nonconformist mold. In *No-Collar*, my ethnographic study of two of these companies, I observed the efforts, on the part of company managers, to develop templates that could standardize the fitful rhythms of creative labor.[28] This involved the attempt to fashion a business that imitated all of the attributes of artists—their habitats, lifestyles, clothing, work patterns, and custom individuality—and incorporate them into a tempo and a work temperament that could be recognized by clients as a reliable industrial process. The disposition of artists to undertake sacrifical labor was a blessing to a start-up economy that demanded of its workforce a legendary outlay of time and energy on the promise of deferred bounties: most employees in the new media industries invested a massive share of "sweat equity" in the mostly futile hope that their stock options would pay off. More important, even, than this apprenticeship in sacrifice was the flexibility of artists' work patterns to a corporate economy that had placed flexibility at the heart of its restructuring efforts the last two decades.

In the workplaces I observed, employee concentration on the job was variable, often erratic. It was a style of work (which the casual observers could easily misconstrue as goofing off) where stints of inspired self-application alternated with vivid socializing, and with those intervals of undirected play and dreamy indolence that Henry James once called the "unstrenuous brooding sort of attention" that is required to produce art. Employees were not producing anything that Henry James would have cared to acknowledge as art, but they were doing their work in a way that he might have recognized. Company managers were faced with the formidable task of trying to accommodate these spasmodic rhythms. Play and recreation were encouraged in the workplace because they were perceived to add value to the work product. Employees were encouraged to work as and when the spirit took them, on the premise that ideas and creativity were as likely to surface at home or in other locations. In return for ceding freedom of movement to employees along with control over their work schedule, a no-collar company exercised the right to collect returns from areas of their lives that lay far beyond the physical workplace. A traditional industrial model derives value from workers where and when the company can control their labor. In the realm of no-collar work, the goal is to extract value from any waking moment of an employee's day. In this way, the most free of all impulses—the most unmoored of all thoughts—could become snared in the work process.

In these knowledge companies, the ethos of creative autonomy was lavishly supported by the principle of self-management. While this precept released employees from the indignity of constant supervision and other work rituals of subordination, it also required them to shoulder the full brunt of risks and responsibilities that are ordinarily borne by middle managers. Self-directed employees were newly vulnerable, experiencing the kind of raw exposure to the market that would ordinarily have been mediated by organizational higher-ups. The result of this liberalization of the workplace was not unlike the liberalization of the economy. It had been accompanied by a stripping away, or shredding, of layers of protection and social insurance against risk and insecurity. In the absence of safeguards and protections, the ultra-humane workplace could easily turn into a medium of self-exploitation—with bottomless seventy-hour-plus workweeks, and a dissolution of all boundaries between company and personal time.

The Internet industries of the New Economy hosted a fusion of work traditions drawn from the technology industries, on the one hand, and urban bohemia, on the other. They offered an advanced profile of the neoliberal world of work, where the worker, like the traditional artist, is a freelance thinker, operating in a deregulated environment that has banished stifling bureaucracy. In return for the opportunity to pursue personally gratifying work, the liberated individual takes over, from state institutions or company organizations, all responsibility for his or her economic survival and welfare. The creative entrepreneur is no longer alienated; there are no structures to be alienated from.[29]

Artists Cannot Afford to be Rewarded Well?

Capitalist history is full of vicious little time warps, where archaic or long foresworn practices and conceptions of work are reinvented in a fresh context to suit some new economic arrangement. The "sweating" system of putting out work to competing contractors in the nineteenth-century garment industry was disdained as a preindustrial relic by the apostles of scientific management, yet this form of subcontracting is now a basic principle of almost every sector of the postindustrial economy and has emerged as the number-one weapon in capital's arsenal of labor cost-cutting and union-busting. So too the ethos of the autonomous artist, once so fiercely removed from industry's dark satanic mills and from the soiled hand of commerce, has been recouped and revamped as a convenient, even alluring, esprit de corps for contingent work in today's de-structured knowledge industries. Indeed, the "voluntary poverty" of the déclassé bohemian artist—an ex-bourgeois descendant, more often than not, of the self-exiled Romantic poet—may turn out to be an inadvertent forerunner of the discounted labor of the new industrial landscape.

How does the legacy of these nineteenth-century traditions enter into the analyses of the cultural economists? In their 1966 study, Baumol and Bowen have little to say about the impact of Romantic artist mythology, except to note that the parlous condition of artist compensation "seems only to elicit apathy from a public whose responses have been dulled by the stereotyped and somewhat romantic notion of the engarreted and starving artist."[30] In considering arguments against government support of the arts, they also refer to the

> antediluvian manifestation that poverty is good for the arts and stimulates creativity. "We want to develop a hungry theater" said one witness at the [1962] House Hearings on economic conditions in the performing arts, who went on to assert that only a hungry man feels compelled to say "what's in him."[31]

Antediluvian this may well be, yet popular wisdom is full of gimcrack rationales for paying people less than they deserve. Many are distorted hand-me-down versions of formerly principled positions about the worth of labor and the dignity of expression. Others are more candid judgments about the expendability of workers. When they circulate as common sense, they do have some real impact on net income levels, but not in a way that the empirical economist can safely measure. These nuggets of ideology are often at their most antediluvian when viewed from the perspective of the rational science of neoclassical economics, which cannot break down their influence on labor markets into hard numbers. Who could compute the impact of popular prejudices about race and gender on the kind of heavily segmented work that women or immigrants are expected to take on, at depressed wage levels? Yet market supply and demand cannot explain alone those features of labor segmentation that consign women and immigrants to specialized locations in the secondary labor market.

It may be worth taking the time, briefly, to review some of the history of what Baumol and Bowen refer to as the "antediluvian manifestation" of the starving artist. Ever since the name of the artist was attached to artworks, patrons have been extracting personal prestige and profit from their own association with the labor of art. In part, to maintain and inflate this prestige, artistic labor was elevated to a rank above and beyond the mere workmanship of craft and trade. It was the royal, papal, and noble patrons of the Renaissance who, for their own gain, invented the concept of the artist-genius in emulation of alchemists who, through their craft, might turn the dross of mere custom into the gold of lavish repute. Traces of this precapitalist prestige survive in those successive phases of patronage characterized by the bourgeois public, the mass market, and the state subsidy (nation-states can claim status on the global landscape on the basis of the great artists they have produced). As for the work of art itself, Marx's distinction between the value of labor and labor power—the value added to a product, in this case, primarily the artist's name—is extremely consequential. The autonomous artist, who emerges in the nineteenth century as a solo entrepreneur working for a largely anonymous public audience, can benefit, in principle, from the surplus value that the name adds to his or her labor. But the name's value tends to increase with the formal estrangement of the artistic soul from the bargaining and haggling of the marketplace. Any taint of mercenary involvement with market supply and demand can diminish the worth of that name.

For the most part, then, this surplus value accrues in reality to the publisher, dealer, promoter, producer, or owner-manager. To say the least, it is in their own pecuniary interest to endorse their clients' remove from matters of commerce. The personal agent emerges as the artist's best shot at recouping some of this value. When literary agents first sought to strengthen writers' bargaining power in the literary marketplace of the late nineteenth century, publishers complained that this "philistine" intervention disrupted the sacred bond between writer and publisher.[32] Yet these agents were realizing their clients' labor power in much the same way as fledgling trade unionists. (In bargaining for hours and wages, the unionists were also accused of "intruding" on the benevolent capitalist's relationship with his workers.) Did the result amount to the cheapening or commercialization of culture, as publishers had warned? To some degree, yes, but nowhere nearly as much as the behavior of publishers themselves, already covetous of the popular market, and well-primed to pattern the book trade in the mold of the mass media industries that would dominate the twentieth century.

The noble ethos of the unattached artist was conceived in the struggle to break free from aristocratic patronage and was clearly compromised by the simultaneous birth of a mass commercial audience from the womb of the bourgeois public. Most fatefully, from the perspective of the artist wage, this ethos was soaked in the full torrent of Romantic thought about the separation of art and culture from the commodity production of industrialization. As the industrial division of labor everywhere sought to convert artisans into machine operatives, artists recoiled from being treated like any other trade producer. At the very least, the artist would be an independent skilled worker producing a marginal commodity of taste, but the higher calling of the Romantic imagination demanded something more. The artist was called on to represent, if not wholly embody, those imaginative qualities, skills, and virtues that industrial civilization was systematically destroying. Ironically, then, the artistic sensibility that was so opposed to utility could not afford to be directly rewarded by trade, yet the commodity value of the artwork rose in direct relation to the artist's remoteness from trade. In time, the highest value could be attached to the work of those—Van Gogh is the quintessential example—who were most detached, reclusive, ignored, or pauperized by bourgeois society. To some degree, this value could appreciate in inverse proportion to the depression of their labor value while alive. As the moving

legacy of Romantic ideas collided and meshed with the evolving arts economy, a curious, and perhaps unique, condition of labor emerged. *The artist
cannot afford to be rewarded well.* High-caliber compensation proves fatal to
the peer appraisal of an artist's achievement; pecuniary neglect, by that same
token, translates into cultural credit.

With the subsequent development of urban, bohemian quarters in low-
income districts, this formula would have a geographical basis in the rent
economy of the industrializing city and would endure through several
decades of suburban flight and urban renewal until the waves of gentrification finally washed over its center-city habitat. The special condition of artistic labor, however, persists in all sorts of vestigial ways. Aside from its
increasing use as a rationale for flexible labor in the new postindustrial workplace, in its traditional form it may well serve a general function in a capitalist society as an alleviator of liberal guilt for living in an exchange economy
that puts a market price on everything. This social sanctioning of discounted
arts labor is quite distinct from the pro bono work built into the pricing system of other, more highly paid, professions like the law. Alpha professionals,
like lawyers, occasionally work for free because they can afford to do so, or
because their complicity with structural injustice would otherwise be too
conspicuous. This is no less the case for the highest-paid arts workers in the
commercial sector, like pop musicians, whose continued regard often
depends on high-profile appearances at benefit concerts where their fees are
seen to be waived for a higher cause. But artists in general are expected, and
are therefore inclined, to put in time gratis for love of their art in contexts
that would require overtime pay for most other workers.

To compound matters, there persists an ingrained prejudice on the left
against being well-paid occupationally, whether in the arts or in the academy.
According to this reasoning, an underpaid intelligentsia can identify more
readily with those living in low-wage conditions or abject poverty. Material
self-denial and voluntary poverty are the monkish markers of conscience and
left-wing integrity in a reward economy. Compassion and commitment may
well flow from this posture, but they are hardly dependent on it. Ultimately,
there is something quite patronizing about this ascetic credo, redolent, as it

is, of middle-class fantasies about the lives and aspirations of working people. Nothing could be further from the raw thrust of ameliorative laborism, typified by Wobbly chieftain Big Bill Haywood's pronouncement (when asked about the fat cigars he smoked) that "nothing's too good for the proletariat."

For a modern version of Haywood's bravura, consider the priority placed on "getting paid in full," which has been a constant strain in hip-hop, and never more so than in the quixotic materialism of today's alpha rapper scene. The champagne-and-Bentley fantasy of the high life may be a crass nouveau riche version of American success, but it cannot be divorced entirely from the claim for reparations for almost a full century in which black artists had been robbed blind of their rights and royalties by the music industry. Golden-age rappers from the late 1980s were perhaps more articulate about the reparations claim than today's gilded celebrities, but the industrial streamlining of rap's genres in the intervening years has only made the choices more limited. Sustainable careers in hip-hop are ever harder to come by. Top-billers tend to be commercial champions for only a short period of time before they fall to fresh contenders (which rapper can honestly envisage a career in the mold of B.B. King, earning a livelihood from performing at a ripe old age?). Rappers who enjoy the limelight temporarily are obliged to be conspicuous consumers; their flaunting of wealth is a kind of potlatch, and they lose their status if they cannot spend flamboyantly, even if the habit threatens to drive them prematurely into poverty. Even as they fill the swaggering role of cartoon figments of the casino capitalist imagination, they must remind us that the choice between "selling out" and preserving one's artistic purity has never been an equal option for black performers, and was only really adopted as a litmus test of integrity by advocates for a white rock fraternity who elevated it to an unlikely, and mostly impractical criterion of faith for most working musicians, let alone African American ones. Yet the search for music untouched by the taint of lucre goes on, rather like the search for undeveloped beaches. Deprived, since the "discovery" of the Delta bluesmen, of a supply of domestic primitives, well-meaning liberal rockists (Paul Simon, Sting, David Byrne) have patronized Third World musicians hitherto remote from any direct contact with the dollar economy. Ry Cooder's *Buena Vista*

Social Club of Cuba's aging, "forgotten" legends is the most recent, and perhaps the best, example of this search for purity of performance unsullied by high exchange rates.

The bohemian option has always been much less meaningful for artists of color. In communities with a history of being starved of any kind of resources, voluntary poverty is not generally regarded as a virtue, and least of all as a heroic, or romantic act of self-invention. Whenever a black bohemia has emerged, as in the case of the bebop jazz enclave, it was almost instantly converted into super-bohemian capital by white emulators like the Beats, hep-cats, and street-corner juveniles of the 1950s. By contrast, material success for black artists has been much more closely tied to status for those few who can rise above the competition. The often blunt focus on compensation—it's all about the Benjamins—contrasts with the predominantly cultural prestige that the white indie artist is trained to extract from the thin wages of bohemia. That is why getting paid in full has had to mean as much to the rapper as the stage conventions of "keeping it real." That is why the militant "rebel without a pause" of late 1980s hip-hop, who came the closest to meeting the romantic profile of the rock rebel, was still expected to be up-front in expressing opinions about the terms and conditions of his recording contracts. No surprise, then, that it was Chuck D, the paragon of the rebel without a pause, who was one of the first recording artists, a decade later, to make a preemptive strike against the industry by seizing on MP3 as a way of outfoxing the majors by bypassing traditional distribution routes.[33]

Or take a performer like Prince, whose profile came much closer to trading on rockist credentials. When Prince changed his name (and inscribed "Slave" on his face) as a protest against his Warner Brothers contract, he was doing something that appealed directly to race consciousness, and for which there was little precedent within the conventions of bohemian glam rock. By contrast, at the ultra-rockist end of the spectrum, musicians stand to lose credit among their fans for negotiating too visibly and brazenly with industry suits. Prestige is tied to the artist's safely quarantined distance from the haggling of the marketplace. Clearly, this is a legacy of the conventions of the Romantic artist, most fully embodied in the rock troubadours of the early

1970s, but whose bloodlines run all over the performance map, and whose trappings can take the rural form of populist sharecropper denim just as effectively as the urban form of déclassé velvet. One aims at the cosmopolitan stance as fiercely as the other is determined to be provincial. The cosmopolitan (David Bowie, Jimi Hendrix, Patti Smith, Jim Morrison) glorifies personal deliverance from the social constraints of class consciousness and morality. The provincial (Bob Dylan, Bob Marley, Tracy Chapman, John Cougar Mellencamp, Bruce Springsteen) gives voice to generic anthems that register the shared yearnings of the multitude. Virtuoso expression vies with genre interpretation. But these are not simply choices among modes of performance, although they have become very effective commercial marketing profiles. They are also profiles of labor, symbolizing the kind of work that artists are expected, or imagined, to do in society, and so they borrow accordingly from history's wardrobe.

Yet the model profile of today's musician carries more weight because it is indicative of the increasing centrality of the artist in the economy as a whole. For an example, one need look no further than the self-fashioning, materialist rapper who is required to flaunt the lavish status-seeking rewards that come with his professional success. There are very few rap lyrics about the regular jobs that most African Americans do for a living. When rappers tell stories about work, they almost always focus on the romance, or the tragedy, of the informal economy. The most significant rhymes, however, are about making a living from hip-hop itself—the golden-age classic being Eric B. and Rakim's "Paid in Full." Being a rapper is not exactly a representative profession, but the genre's own self-consciousness about rap as a form of livelihood is very much a sign of the economic times. Yes, it is an expression of traditional concern about the double-edged career opportunities that African Americans have had through the music industry, but it can also be taken as a brazen expression of the go-for-broke, winner-takes-all individualism that has made artists the darlings of the new economy.

The Service Ideal

The short-lived, but iconoclastic, series of New Deal federal programs that directly employed jobless artists and writers was an instructive point of origin for many of the new modes of mental labor. What was the consequence, if any, of the formerly quaint idea that artists would be targeted by poor relief programs in much the same way as unemployed welders and construction workers? By the mid-thirties, the Depression landscape of breadlines, soup kitchens, and shantytowns had flattened out the élan of bohemia and closed off patronage routes and avenues of income. The proverbial "starving artist" was suddenly no different from the man in the street, struggling to survive. Their social and economic predicament were one and the same. Both needed a living wage. Although its programs barely survived through the end of the decade, Federal Project Number One of the Works Progress Administration (WPA), begun in 1935, organized relief for tens of thousands of artists, writers, actors, and musicians, and parlayed a legacy of semipublic support into the nonprofit infrastructure of foundations, museums, and universities in the years following the war.

While its primary aim was simply to put food on the table, this New Deal for the arts was conceived in the ferment of intellectuals' allegiance to the cause of organized labor. The opportunity it offered to promote radical causes inevitably stirred up a hornet's nest among grandstanding members of Congress who oversaw the demise of the programs in a spasm of premature McCarthyism, beginning with the House Un-American Activities Committee's liquidation of the Federal Theater Project in 1939. Unlike the *proletkult* aesthetic endorsed by those artists and writers who leaned toward the strictures of Comintern policy, there was no single aesthetic agenda observed in the work produced under the WPA programs. In many respects, then, they were a social democratic alternative to the bureaucratic cultural policies administered under state communism and promoted overseas by the Comintern. Insofar as they may have resulted in partial accommodation with the state, they were a relatively inexpensive way of appeasing the political opposition of influential voices, and, in this respect, anticipated the state's subsequent embrace of intellectuals during the Cold War.

For some critics, especially those, like Harold Rosenberg, in the *Partisan Review* circle, the WPA programs ruinously emptied out the bohemian ideal, drawing artists in from the more radical margins of society and placing them on a domesticated path toward professionalization.[34] This first step in the bureaucratizing of the arts threatened to compromise the ideal of the autonomous artist. Even worse, the academic ghetto lay ahead. For those, like Rosenberg, who hewed fiercely to the credo of the unattached radical, the independent mind would be a fatal casualty of the transition from the WPA's weekly government wage to the state college's tenure-track salary.

But it was the inexorable rise of the culture industries that had a much greater impact on the profile of cultural labor, while posing an equally grave threat to the value system of key liberal intellectuals like Rosenberg, Clement Greenberg, and Dwight McDonald. Michael Denning argues that the coalescence of Popular Front activities within the commercial culture industries gave rise to something quite new—the "emergence of modern mental labor."[35] With highly successful unionization drives in radio, film, recording, and journalism, performers, writers, and artists could not help but further their sense of common cause with workers organized, after the CIO model, in the great industrial unions of the day. Reinforcing that common cause was a spate of cultural production influenced by Popular Front values and politics.

One result of this arts unionism, Denning observes, is that the traditional division between mental and manual labor was eroded. Older ideas about artistic and intellectual work began to dissolve in the face of the new white-collar cultural trades, while congeries of new corporate forces came to the fore, both competing and collaborating with state agencies to manage mental production, distribution, and consumption on a mass scale. C. Wright Mills would later describe this as the "cultural apparatus": a vast semi-organized network of institutions, where "arts, science, and learning, entertainment, malarkey, and information are distributed and produced. It contains an elaborate set of institutions; of schools and theaters, newspapers and census bureaus, studios, laboratories, museums, little magazines, radio networks. It contains truly fabulous agencies of exact information and of trivial distraction, exciting objects, lazy escapes, strident advice." Mills saw this "cultural apparatus" as a direct result of the "overlap between culture and authority," and its raison d'être depended on the use of "cultural workmen for the legitimation of power."[36]

Unlike those in the *Partisan Review* circle, Mills had little nostalgia for the erosion of the bohemian ideal of the unattached artist, nor did he share their sniffy contempt for the commercial products of mass and middlebrow culture, but he more or less shared their views about the use of commercial culture to legitimate power. For all the differences between the major schools of leftist commentary about commercial popular culture—whether the Frankfurt School, the New York Intellectuals, or other tendencies represented by Gramsci, Mills, the New Left, and the Birmingham School—their critiques all rested on a common view of the culture industries as instruments of mass consent, hegemony, and/or social control.

What is striking about Denning's shift of emphasis is that he reminds us that the rise of this new cultural apparatus was also an *opportunity for labor.* Culture, in its new industrial context, was now a product of mass labor, and the politics of labor to which it gave birth bore many similarities to the conditions of industrial unionism. Just as important, however, the workers involved—screenwriters, actors, musicians—could exert a direct political influence on the shape and content of the product. (Teachers and journalists would follow in this mold.) Cultural workers could seek to politicize the product of their labor in a way that autoworkers could not do so readily. This was something relatively new in the annals of organized labor. As a result, the history of commercial culture is one of perpetual compromise, concession, truce, and arbitration both on the side of labor bargaining and also in the business of content bargaining. The reputation of "liberal Hollywood" (not entirely a right-wing invention) stems from both angles of this new politics of labor. In Baumol's analysis of the arts economy, he cites the high level of unionization as an obstacle to efficiency in a sector where independent craft functions are "carefully protected" by each union local. On the other side, we are all too well-aware of the ceaseless efforts of many cultural workers to give their artistic product a liberal or progressive slant in the face of systemic pressure to reinforce the capitalist value system.

Intellectuals in the Cold War period devoted a good deal of time to declaiming on the stultifying impact of "mass culture." For critics who had been weaned on workers' causes in the 1930s, it is astonishing how little attention they paid to labor's involvement in the culture industries. Virtually no one saw this development as a fit topic for extended commentary. Even C.L.R. James, who keenly followed the record and progress of labor, and who, in *American Civilization*, saw the American entertainment industry as part of the most advanced industrial state of popular civilization, did not necessarily see the culture industry's workplaces as "labor's workplaces." The closest he came was in drawing an analogy between the bargaining process of capital and labor and the process of negotiation hashed out between the industry's owners and the mass audiences of popular culture over the politics of content. Uncomfortable with the view of the Frankfurt and *Partisan Review* critics that moguls and bankers frankly use popular culture's content to affirm capitalist values, James believed the bosses would not dare to impose their political views. Indeed, part of their compact with audiences is the unwritten agreement not to do so.

> The general public accepts, or to be more precise, appears to accept the general political ideas, standards, social ethics, etc. of the society which is the natural framework of the films as they are produced today. Whenever possible a piece of direct propaganda is injected, but the C.I.O., the great strikes, capital and labor, war and peace, these are left out by mutual understanding, a sort of armed neutrality. If those who control films dared in ordinary times, to give their view of these problems in films, for instance, they would empty the movie houses. The large masses of the people would not stand for any employer view of unions in films. In totalitarian states, the state does exactly the opposite. It uses the film, the popular film, to the limit. In fact the film is merely an arm of the government.[37]

Echoing the Cold War climate that was coming into being in 1950, James depicts the state of affairs as a "sort of armed neutrality." The accord he describes in film was not unlike the postwar compact between capital and labor. In return for capital's recognition of basic bargaining rights, and its offer of high wages in return for high productivity, the labor movement had accepted the general framework of capitalist society.

The Cold War added a new, international dimension to the uneasy truce to which James was alluding. For almost forty years, the cultural policy that accompanied Cold War "armed neutrality" was tied to a massive exercise in state propaganda. For the purpose of this policy, it was essential that American artists were no longer the "federal workers" of the New Deal programs. They were now to be ambassadors of freedom, and were promoted as such by the various CIA fronts, like the Congress for Cultural Freedom, set up to win the battle for minds. Artists were sent out on world tours by state agencies to put the best face on liberal, capitalist values.[38] In contrast to the proletarianization of the artist in the WPA of the 1930s, the Cold War required the revival of the credo of the autonomous artist. This time around, the autonomy in question was not from commerce, as in the Romantic version, but from the state censorship more prevalent in the socialist states. As for cultural workers in the commercial industries, they could be seen to belong to "free" trade unions, at least after the Communist presence in the labor movement had been purged. All of this was presented as the antithesis of the unfree mental labor of the socialist bloc and its Third World client states.

But by far the most extensive development on this front, and of the welfare state in general, was the massive expansion of the national higher-education system in this period. The state thereby bought itself a dependable research arm, especially through defense-related funding in the sciences. Corporations were able to have their basic research funded and future employees trained at public expense; and the "herd of independent minds," as Rosenberg once described the intelligentsia, was brought under the purview of academic deans and other responsible institutional shepherds. Such developments dealt the U.S. immense advantages in the public-relations game of the Cold War. However expedient to the corporate liberal state, these advantages were won in the name of academic freedom and the democratic extension of education to the lower middle class and portions of the working class.

When the American labor market took its flexible turn in the early 1980s, and union organizing eroded as a fundamental right, blue-collar unions took a direct hit, but white-collar and professional organizing was still on the rise. The new knowledge industries, either comprising the higher-education sector or in corporate parks built around a university research complex, provided a natural union base for salaried employees with less and less control over their own workplace. In the 1990s, the corporatization of higher education set in for real, and casualization began to take a heavy toll on institutions nominally built on tenure, academic freedom, and faculty governance. The tenure-track appointment, hitherto a staple contract in the profession, would soon become a highly privileged exception to the rule. Professional academics, long accustomed to regarding their workplace as a non-worldly realm, beholden to different rules and standards from those observed in more "secular" employment sectors, had a rude awakening. In no time at all, it seemed, higher education had became one of the more advanced examples, among the professions, of the adjunct contract workplace, where a large percentage of its part-time labor force was soon struggling to earn any kind of living wage.

A Volunteer Low-Wage Army?

The rapidity with which the low-wage revolution swept through higher education was clearly hastened along by conditions amenable to discounting mental labor. For one thing, the willingness of adjuncts (whether as graduate students or postdoctoral employees) to accept a discounted wage out of "love for their subject" has helped not only to sustain the cheap labor supply but also to magnify its strength and volume. Like artists and performers, academics are inclined by training to sacrifice earnings for the opportunity to exercise the teaching craft. While other traditional professional industries, like law or medicine, depend to some degree on intern labor, none rely economically on the self-sacrifice of their accredited members to anything like the same degree.

Employers have long relied on the existence of a reserve army of unemployed to keep wages down in any labor market. Institutions of higher education have now entered this business with a vengeance. In addition—and this is the significant element—their managers increasingly draw on a *volunteer low-wage army*. By this I do not mean to suggest that adjunct and part-timer educators actually invite their underpayment and lack of benefits or job security. These conditions are, first and foremost, a direct result of managerial policy. Nor are they inactive in protesting and organizing for their interests. Like the jazz musicians at the New School, they are forming unions and bargaining units (my own institution now boasts the largest adjunct union of any private university). Rather, I choose the phrase to describe the structural eventuality of being trained in the habit of embracing nonmonetary rewards—job gratification is self-actualizing—as compensation. As a result of this training, low compensation for a high workload can become a rationalized feature of the job. In the most perverse extension of this logic, underpayment can even be interpreted as proof of the worth of the academic vocation—as the ultimate gauge of the selfless teacher and/or the disinterested seeker of knowledge.

Vestiges of the amateur ideal of the scholar are a contributing element. Indeed, one of the uncommon privileges traditionally enjoyed by academic scholars was the right to pursue their work in full ignorance of its economic underpinnings. Money matters were considered too vulgar and trivial to be understood, let alone handled, by faculty. Such pecuniary concerns befouled the noble quest for knowledge and truth. No doubt, this customary feature of the profession has made it easy for power to shift inexorably to managers and administrators, whose ready grasp of fiscal affairs renders their decisions unassailable by faculty members. Ultimately, the comfort offered by job security in the form of tenure was a recipe for complacency on the part of those who might have resisted the casualization measures, much earlier and more vigorously. Submission to the selfless, disinterested devotions of the scholar's calling almost inevitably led to the sacrifice of younger "apprentices" on the altar of an anachronistic faith.[39]

In the restructured economy of the American higher education system, the net result of this professional ethos has been rapid deprofessionalization, not the revival of Veblen's virtuous ideal of Idle Curiosity. It has contributed, directly or otherwise, to policies of casualization pursued in the name of belt-tightening and aimed at redistributing academic work out of the realm of regular tenure-track lines. Two generations of scholars now form a semipermanent cadre of independent contractors, with little or no prospect of advancement into regular, full-time employment. For most graduate students, as Marc Bousquet points out, the attainment of a degree is not the beginning, but the end of their teaching career; they are not a product, but a by-product, of graduate education; their degree holding is not a credential to practice, but rather it "represents a disqualification from practice."[40] As for regular faculty, their salaries have stagnated against the average wage, and they retain control over a profession that can no longer ensure, or control, its

NYU graduate students win their campaign for a union, 2002 (PHOTO BY SCOTT SUMMER)

means of reproduction. Increasingly, their job security serves as window dressing for a system designed to ensure a continuous flow of cheap, easily replaceable labor.

What forms of self-rationalization motivate adjuncts to contribute so selflessly to a workplace where they are regarded as untouchables? Comparing their organizing efforts to a process of recovery from codependency, Mickie McGee describes how she and her fellow "teachaholics" and "ad-junk-ties" diagnosed the early symptoms of their "high-functioning addiction" as a way of understanding their need to unionize. They came to realize that their selfsacrificing love of teaching, combined with the intoxicating fantasy of universities as cachet-rich havens from the marketplace, had led them into a spiral of addiction and self-exploitation.

McGee recalls "the damage that adjuncting did to my life":

> Somehow, in spite of my adjuncting habit, I'd managed to become pregnant. My partner and I were thrilled. At that point, my teaching habit was so all-consuming that we'd all but given up hopes of ever starting a family. I was expecting and I was delighted. But still I wouldn't give up my teaching habit. Even in the final months of the pregnancy, when my doctor urged me to remain in bed to control pregnancy hypertension, I couldn't do it. Fearful that I'd lose my classes, or seem "unprofessional," I was in the classroom, dizzy with high blood pressure, the week before my daughter was born, not surprisingly by emergency C-section. This was insanity. This was an addict's insanity."[41]

In some respect, the peripatetic life of the part-timer, offering her skills hither and thither (a large majority are female), on one freeway exit after another, is germane to the eccentric work schedule of the traditional academic, who commonly observes no clear boundaries between being on and off the job, and for whom there is often little distinction between paid work and free labor. For the professionally active full-timer, this habitual schedule means that she can take on a range of tasks and obligations that will easily fill out a sixty-hour workweek.[42] For the part-timer, desperate to savor the prestige of being a college teacher at an institution with brand-name cachet, the identity of being a switched-on, round-the-clock thinker, eager to impart knowledge, and in a position to freely extend her mental labor, feeds directly into the psychology of casualized work and underpayment. The industrial worker, by comparison, is not beset by such occupational hazards.

What we see here is the fabrication of a model "flexible employee" out of the cloth of the profession's nonconcentric habits and beliefs, a worker whose customary training in the service ideals and irregular routines of mental labor can be roundly exploited by cost-cutting managers. In this way, we can see how and why fundamentally characteristic features of the academic work style, like those of artists, whom I earlier depicted, conform to the demands of a contingent labor profile. Most fateful of all, perhaps, is the elective ingredient of this recipe for exploitation. Again, I do not mean to suggest that individuals are drawn toward this predicament, nor indeed that they are directly responsible for their own exploitation. For the most part, the patterns of casualization chosen by academic managers have more or less emulated the policy behavior of corporate managers. (Partly, as a result, graduate students have been able to win legal recognition for their perception that they hold the status of an employee.) Nonetheless, I am proposing that academic labor has been casualized in ways that directly complement the habits and compulsions of the academic work mentality, and this has made it all the easier to accomplish. It is in this respect that we can speak, structurally, of a volunteer army of underemployed, low-wage contract labor. As part of its ceaseless search for ways to induct workers in their own exploitation, capital, it might be said, has found the makings of a *self-justifying,* low-wage workforce, at the very heart of the knowledge industries so crucial to its growth and development.

It is no small irony that artists and academics, who would have been borderline, even oddball, features of an older labor landscape, are now more like exemplary figures, occupying frontline positions on the leading edge of neoliberal penetration. With the relocation overseas of core manufacturing, value-adding sectors have become key to First World economies. Artists and academics are value-adding paragons. In the past, their work traditions and privileges have been marked by an impermeability to the mainstream rhythms of industrial process. Now, their customary work life increasingly lies at the center of industrial attention. Indeed, it may come to serve soon as a core industrial personality of the early twenty-first century.

In this respect, it is hardly surprising that higher education has become a battleground for labor. Too many bullish forces in the corporate sector see higher education as a huge, untapped market for selling goods and services on the basis of the prestigious brand names of universities. At the primary and secondary levels, the spoils of the public school system have long been coveted by "education entrepreneurs," touting the "discipline" of the marketplace over the "inefficiency" of the public realm, and normalizing the rhetoric of corporate management—the public as customer, education as competitive product, learning as efficiency tool. Remember Lamar Alexander's declaration, shortly before becoming George Bush's secretary of education, that Burger King and Federal Express should set up schools to show how the private sector would run things.[43] School-business partnerships opened the door not just to total quality management but to every corporate huckster looking for ways to promote and build brand loyalty in the "K–12 marketplace." Tax-supported school vouchers and union-free charter schools were introduced respectively, as the fast and the slow track toward privatization. If your local high school hasn't yet been bought out by McDonald's, many educators there probably already use teaching aids and packets of materials, "donated" by companies, that are crammed with industry propaganda designed to instill product awareness among young consumers: lessons about the history of the potato chip, sponsored by the Snack Food Association, or literacy programs that reward students who reach monthly reading goals with Pizza Hut slices.[44]

In addition to serving as magnets for corporate sponsorship, the economy of scale and the fiscal autonomy enjoyed by many institutions of higher education allow them to function like corporations in their own right. On the labor front, they have adopted many of the same tactics of union-busting, downsizing, and outsourcing, and they hire the same antiunion law firms. In their respective campaigns against graduate-student organizing, NYU, Yale, and Columbia all retained the notorious legal firm Proskauer, Rose, which openly advertises its antiunion services on the company Web site—("With respect to union relationships, we counsel clients how to avoid, and where appropriate, resist union organization among employees"). In addition, the modern, neo-corporate research university is no longer simply a vehicle, as it was in the Cold War period, for socializing the costs of training, research, and technological development on behalf of capital.[45] Far from serving as a money-launderer for the Department of Defense's permanent war economy, the research university has now become a site of capital accumulation in its own right, where the profitability of research and teaching programs and the marketability of learning products is fast coming to the fore as the primary driving force behind academic policy at many institutions. Corporate sponsorship increasingly buys faculty and entire research programs, while the patenting and selling of online courses promises a bonanza of low-cost yields.

In many cases, cost-cutting employment policies are also instruments for establishing administrative control over curricular content. Recently digitized programs of distance learning, for example, were eagerly championed by administrators and state legislators itching to switch their fixed investment in temperamental bodies and impetuous minds over to the sleek machinery of digital pipes with mega bandwidth. In a milieu where education is viewed as a product to be delivered without risk, it is easy to see how the most compelling corporate vision would be that of the wired, tenureless university, where contract hands prepare or administer online courses pumped out to a remote, disaggregated student body. Faculty attempts to establish control over online instruction are not simply struggles to stave off the automation of jobs, they are also frontline battles in the culture wars over the right to determine and influence curriculum.[46]

While the economic payoffs of digitized instruction appear to be self-evident, these technology-assisted programs have less to do with increased efficiency or cost-effectiveness than with control over the workforce and, potentially, the curriculum. The elimination of the social and cultural services ministered by full-time, flesh-and-blood faculty inevitably results in a sharp drop in the quality of education. Any cost-benefit analysis of online instruction should have to assess the challenge of delivering a product of comparable quality. Based on this criterion, no one has ever been able to identify clear gains in productivity or cost-effectiveness from the computerization of work. I am referring here to the phenomenon of the productivity paradox, an IT update of the technology trap first identified by business economists in the fledgling years of automation forty years ago. As economist Robert Solow put it, in a famous throwaway line, "You can see the computer age everywhere except in the productivity statistics." "Downstream benefits" have not exactly flowed from the habit of throwing "upstream" money into IT systems, applications, upgrades, management, and maintenance that do not serve the practical needs of businesses or other employee organizations. Promotional hype, technological obsolescence, communication overload, and widespread downtime outages caused by worker sabotage are only some of the factors that inhibit productivity.[47] The economic failure of many online programs (NYU threw away $25 million on its version) was not simply a casualty of the downturn in the Internet economy. It also stemmed from a miscalculation of the economic benefits to be won over and against the high, and therefore unproductive, cost of widespread faculty resistance to the idea of virtual education.

Second Thoughts

With or without its virtual arm, how efficient will the newly restructured academic sectors prove to be in servicing the labor markets of industrialized knowledge? Higher education is in a pivotal position in this regard. Not only is it now a massive anchorage for discounted labor among its own workforce, it is also a training site, responsible for reproducing the discounted labor force among the next generation of knowledge workers. Are educators contributing involuntarily to the problem when they urge students, in pursuing their career goals, to place principles of selflessness (public interest or collective political agency or creative expression) well above the pursuit of material security? In an economy so heavily under the sway of neoliberal business models, is it fair to say that this service ideal invites, if it does not vindicate, the manipulation of inexpensive labor?

Fifteen years ago, this suggestion would have seemed ludicrous. Labor freely offered in the service of some common benefit or mental ideal has always been the informal economic backbone that supports political, cultural, and educational activities in the nonprofit or public-interest sectors. Selfless labor of this sort is also a source of great pleasure. The world that we value most—the world that is not in thrall to market dictates—would not exist without this kind of donated effort. But what happens when some version of this disinterested labor moves, as I have suggested here, from the social margins to core sectors of capital accumulation? When the opportunity to pursue mentally gratifying work becomes a rationale for discounted labor at the heart of the key knowledge industries, is it not time to rethink some of our bedrock pedagogical values? Does the new landscape of mental labor demand more than the usual call for modernizing the politics of labor? What is to be done with the anxiety generated by such questions?

First and foremost, we must remember that the problem lies not in how people choose to operate within an economy, but rather in how that economy is structured to limit their choices. As ever, the educational system is playing its role in creating and rationalizing the gulf between those in the de-skilled lower tiers, destined for low-wage service sector jobs, and those in the skilled strata, who are tracked into credentialed fractions of the mental labor economy. Currently, managers of national and global economies tell us that education is the only passport to economic mobility or security in a knowledge society. And yet people with advanced degrees are waiting tables, driving taxicabs, or functioning as Microserf temps, while most service jobs in the secondary labor market (with absolutely no prospect of advancement) require little more than basic literacy accompanied by a modest facility in pleasing customers. In the academy, just as in the neoliberal economy as a whole, there is no shortage of work, only a shortage of decent jobs. The accumulation of real skills means little in a system that underproduces real jobs. In the Fordist era of the two-tier labor system, it was the simple presence of trade union power, and not gaps in skills, that separated the decent high-wage jobs in the primary labor markets from those in the low-wage secondary labor markets.

The education system (both at the high school and collegiate levels) is overdeveloped in relation to the needs of an economy that will only provide so many meaningful jobs that pay a living wage. Accordingly, there exists a cruel disconnect between the managerial promises and the opportunities on the ground. While this disparity generates its share of social discontent, the expectations raised by these promises play a crucial role in regulating labor markets. In the sectors of mental work I have looked at here, the prospect of meaningful work provides a rationale for de-professionalizing while helping to maintain a degraded labor market that disciplines and sets the wage floors of those precariously positioned in the core segments immediately above. In addition, and at a time (quite distinct from the Fordist era) when creative gratification is more and more touted as an obligatory feature of the realm of no-collar work, the collective educational capital that once stimulated and supported consumption and leisure time is more and more invested in gray areas of unwaged work that the new cultural economy is creating. For example, Tiziana Terranova has outlined the role that free labor played in creating the Web site infrastructure of digital capitalism and in contributing directly to its development, as in the Open Source model of software improvement, where corporations now take advantage of amateur users to locate bugs and suggest refinements and upgrades.[48] All in all, the creation of the World Wide Web has been the most massive, uncoordinated effort in the history of unwaged work. Education is not, then, wasted, as it appears at first sight. Rather, it is being unsystematically converted into un- or undercompensated labor in ways that remain to be adequately charted (just as the hidden costs of unwaged domestic labor of women have sustained the economy for so much longer).

Insofar as we participate in the knowledge economy as scholars, writers, and artists, there now exists an explicit responsibility to recognize the cost of our traditionally cherished beliefs in aesthetic or educational ideals. These ideals come at a price, and managers of the new economy are taking full advantage of our disregard of that price. When the outcome is discounted labor on an industrial scale, our traditions of studied indifference to the world of trade and waged labor can no longer only be savored as expressions of faith in some purer life of the mind, or as charming eccentricities to be deemed objects of tourist interest in bohemia or the ivory tower. Those days are over.

Historically, we have found it too challenging, and professionally limiting, to see ourselves as workers. Academics have often viewed their daily teaching and service obligations as an obligatory, even menial, chore that permits them to pursue the true life of the mind in their research—their "real" work—on sabbatical or in summer breaks. Artists contracted by federal or local government programs such as the Comprehensive Employment and Training Act (CETA—in the 1970s, the biggest public commitment to arts-employment subsidies since the WPA) routinely have made a distinction between what they do for a living in the realm of public and community arts, and their own after-hours work as expressive individuals.[49] Even in the WPA years, many artists who qualified for poor relief refused federal assistance through the artists programs because they were averse to being classed as laborers (while others saw the program as a conspiracy to shut them up by offering full-time work). Writers of all stripes continue to regard part-time commercial work as a vile meal ticket that expedites their true calling.

There are, of course, sound reasons for abiding by such distinctions. Unpopular forms of intellectual, artistic, and political expression cannot and will not thrive unless they are independent of commercial or bureaucratic dictates. But these conditions of independence can no longer be defended stubbornly and solely as a matter of humanistic principle, or as a freestanding right within a civilized society. When capital-intensive industry is concentrated around vast culture trading sectors (copyright is now the U.S.'s single largest export), when media Goliaths feed off their control of intellectual property, and when the new Vested Interests routinely barter discount wages for creative satisfaction on the job, the expressive traditions of mental labor are no longer "ours" simply to claim, not when informal versions of them are daily being bought off and refined into high-octane fuel for the next generation of knowledge factories.

The new labor landscape is now hosting efforts to organize sectors where professional identity has been based, in part, on a sharp indifference to being organized. Campaigns can and should build on the recognition that both artists and educators draw on an intimate and shared experience of the traditions of sacrificial labor.[50] The outcome will help to modernize labor politics in the age of the mental labor (the age of the Yale Corporation, the Microserf, and the consolidated push of Time Warner-Bertelsmann-Disney-CNN-Hachette-Paramount-NewsCorp), and it will depend on recognizing the special conditions that apply to pricing wages for thought. We have always known that aesthetics comes at a price, especially for those who do not benefit from the prestige it confers. Now we must learn to recognize that aesthetics is part of a price system, to use a pet phrase of Thorstein Veblen's. No one has really thought this out properly. If we don't, then others, with less to lose and a world of lucrative copyrights to gain, will do it for us.

Notes

Introduction

1. This estimate is drawn from Edna Bonacich and Richard Appelbaum, *Behind the Label: Inequality in the Los Angeles Apparel Industry* (Berkeley: University of California Press, 2000).

2. The Supreme Court decided not to make a judgment, and sent the case back to the California court. But "discovery" was granted to Kasky's lawyers to subpoena Nike's files, a move that promised some interesting revelations. In September 2003, the company decided to settle rather than submit to more rounds of bad publicity and further legal assault. The settlement involved a $1.5 million payment to the Fair Labor Association, of which Nike is a founding member.

3. They also provide a response to the perennial question asked of anti-sweatshop activists—So where can I buy ethically produced clothing?—without having to point overseas: for example, to a company like Zara, the mercurially successful Spanish fashion firm that has retained all control over its manufacturing while eschewing advertising of its brand.

4. Timothy Egan, "Nike: The Swoon of the Swoosh,"*New York Times*, September 13, 1998.

5. While its "general intellect" most truly subsists in activists' massive indulgence of Internet information swapping, the anti-globalization movement (or anti-corporate, anti-capitalist, or alternative globalization movement, as it is sometimes termed) has already generated a considerable amount of literature in print. Among the titles are Naomi Klein, *Fences and Windows: Dispatches from the Front Lines of the Globalization Debate* (New York: Picador, 2002); John Cavanagh et al., *Alternatives to Economic Globalization* (New York: Berrett-Koehler, 2002); J. Beck and Kevin Danaher, eds., *Globalize This! The Battle Against the World Trade Organization and Corporate Rule* (Monroe, ME: Common Courage Press, 2000); Jeremy Brecher, Tim Costello, and Brendan Smith, *Globalization from Below* (Boston: South End Press, 2000): Sarah Anderson and John Cavanagh with Thea Lee, *Field Guide to the Global Economy* (New

York: The New Press, 2000); Amory Starr, *Naming the Enemy: Anti-Corporate Movements Confront Globalization* (London: Zed Books, 2000); Richard Falk, *Predatory Globalization: A Critique* (Cambridge: Polity Press, 1999); Lori Wallach and Michelle Sforza, *The WTO: Five Years of Reasons to Resist Corporate Globalization* (New York: Seven Stories Press, 2000); Tom Mertes, ed., *The Movement of Movements: A Reader* (New York: Verso, 2004); Notes From Nowhere, *We Are Everywhere: The Irresistible Rise of Global Anti-Capitalism* (New York: Verso, 2003); Alexander Cockburn, Jeffrey St. Clair, and Allan Sekula, *Five Days That Shook the World: The Battle for Seattle and Beyond* (New York: Verso, 2001); Mike Prokosch and Laura Raymond, eds., *The Global Activist's Manual: Local Ways to Change the World* (New York: Thunder's Mouth Press, 2002); Andy Opel and Donnalyn Pompper, eds., *Representing Resistance: Media, Civil Disobedience, and the Global Justice Movement* (Westport, CT: Praeger Publishers, 2003); B. Gills, ed., *Globalization and the Politics of Resistance* (New York: Palgrave, 2000); and Walden Bello, *Deglobalization: Ideas for a New World Economy* (London: Zed Books, 2002).

Chapter One:
The Making of the Second Anti-Sweatshop Movement

1. Jacob Riis, *How the Other Half Lives: Studies Among the Tenements of New York* (New York: Charles Scribner's Sons, 1890); Henry Mayhew, *London Labour and the London Poor* (London, Griffin, Bohn, 1851). Leon Stein anthologizes the best accounts at the time in *Out of the Sweatshop: The Struggle for Industrial Democracy* (New York: Quadrangle, 1977).

2. Fredrick Abernathy, John Dunlop, Janice Hammond, and David Weil, *A Stitch in Time: Lean Retailing and the Transformation of Manufacturing* (New York: Oxford University Press, 1999).

3. Roger Waldinger and Michael Lapp have argued that legally low wages are the real problem, and that the evidence for a sizeable underground sweatshop economy is inconclusive. The thesis of the "return of the sweatshop," they argue, was a convenient response to the enigma of large-scale immigration to postindustrial cities, but, in fact, these new Asian and Latino immigrants simply moved into entry-level apparel jobs vacated by white ethnics and other native-born workers. By contrast, participation in the "informal economy" is associated with higher status that comes with the ability to evade taxes and conduct off-the-book business. "Back to the Sweatshop or Ahead to the Informal Sector?," *International Journal of Urban and Regional Research* 17: 1 (March 1993), 6–29.

4. Edna Bonacich and Richard Appelbaum, *Behind the Label: Inequality in the Los Angeles Apparel Industry* (Berkeley: University of California Press, 2000), 4.

5. Gus Tyler, *Look for the Union Label: A History of the International Ladies' Garment Workers Union* (Armonk, NY and London: M.E. Sharpe, 1995), 18–30.

6. This juxtaposition dramatizes the split between craft and industrial unionism that would ultimately pit the AFL against the CIO. See Steve Fraser, *Labor Will Rule: Sidney Hillman and the Rise of American Labor* (New York: Free Press, 1991). Fraser shows how labor recruitment and organization in the industry, which employed immigrant Jews, Italians, Poles, Slovaks, Bohemians, and Lithuanians, often followed regional patterns of kinship, religion, and locale established in the Russian Pale (the majority of owners and manufacturers were established German Jews), and the political divisions between socialist, anarchist, syndicalist, and Bundist workers followed suit.

7. Peter Kwong, *Chinatown New York: Labor and Politics 1930–1950* (New York: Monthly Review Press, 1979); Xiaolan Bao, *Holding Up More than Half the Sky: Chinese Garment Workers in New York City 1948–1992* (Urbana: University of Illinois Press, 2001); Edna Bonacich et al., eds., *Global Production: The Apparel Industry in the Pacific Rim* (Philadelphia: Temple University Press, 1994); and Paul Ong, Edna Bonacich, and Lucie Cheng, eds., *The New Asian Immigration in Los Angeles and Global Restructuring* (Philadelphia: Temple University Press, 1994).

8. See Roger Waldinger, *Through the Eye of the Needle: Immigrants and Enterprise in New York's Garment Trades* (New York: New York University Press, 1986); and Nancy Green, *Ready-to-Wear and Ready-to-Work: A Century of Industry and Immigrants in Paris and New York* (Durham, NC: Duke University Press, 1997).

9. For a succinct analysis of the international supply chain in the global garment industry, based on research by Verite's Heather White and Fredi Munger, see the chapter "Dynamics of the Global Assembly Line" in Pamela Varley, ed., *The Sweatshop Quandary: Corporate Responsibility on the Global Frontier* (Washington, DC: Investor Responsibility Research Center, 1998), 83–108.

10. For trade history, see Jose de la Torre, *Clothing-Industry Adjustment in Developed Countries* (New York: St. Martin's Press, 1986); Joseph Grunwald and Kenneth Flamm, *The Global Factory: Foreign Assembly in International Trade* (Washington, DC: Brookings Institution, 1985); Fariborz Ghadar, William Davidson, and Charles Feigenoff, *U.S. Industrial Competitiveness: The Case of the Textile and Apparel Industries* (Lexington, MA: Lexington Books, 1987); Kitty Dickerson, *Textiles and Apparel in the Global Economy* (Englewood Cliffs, NJ: Prentice-Hall, 1995); I.M. Destler, *American Trade Politics* (Washington, DC: Institute for International Politics, 1986).

11. See Ellen Israel Rosen's discussion of these trade policies in Asia in *Making Sweatshops: The Globalization of the U.S. Apparel Industry* (Berkeley: University of California Press, 2002), chapter 3; and Kala Marathe Krishna and Linh Hui Tan, *Rags and Riches: Implementing Apparel Quotas Under the Multi-Fiber Arrangement* (Ann Arbor: University of Michigan Press, 1998).

12. Annie Phizacklea, *Unpacking the Fashion Industry: Gender, Racism, and Class in*

Production (London: Routledge, 1990), 9.

13. Rosen, 118.

14. Cynthia Enloe, *The Morning After: Sexual Politics at the End of the Cold War* (Berkeley: University of California Press, 1993), 102–43.

15. In *The Power to Choose: Bangladeshi Women and Labour Market Decisions in London and Dakha* (London: Verso, 2000), Naila Kabeer studies the participation of Bangladeshi women in the garment industries of Dakha, where women went out to work in the export factories, and London, where they confine themselves to homeworking. The Dakha women were migrants from rural areas where they had endured open-ended hours in farmwork, pervasive parental supervision, little autonomy in personal lives, and low self-worth in general. By comparison, their experience of urban industrial employment, for all its rigors, was preferable. The women in London were subject to the moral strictures of the Bangladeshi community, largely because of racist exclusion from the mainstream economy. As a result, these women were more dependent on their family networks, and so the gender hierarchies of skilled/unskilled labor and inside/outside work were more rigidly enforced.

16. Kathy McAfee, *Storm Signals: Structural Adjustment and Development Alternatives in the Caribbean* (Boston: South End, 1991).

17. See Naomi Klein's analysis of the brand-building economy in *No Logo: Taking Aim at the Brand Bullies* (London: HarperCollins, 2000).

18. Quoted in, Varley, *The Sweatshop Quandary*, 95.

19. Bonacich and Appelbaum, *Behind the Label*, 13.

20. Jeff Ballinger, "The New Free-Trade Heel: Nike's Profits Jump on the Backs of Asia's Workers," *Harper's Magazine*, August 1992, 46–48.

21. B.J. Bullert, "Strategic Public Relations, Sweatshops, and the Making of a Global Movement" (Working Paper, Joan Shorenstein Center on Press, Politics, and Public Policy, Harvard University, 2000).

22. Kitty Krupat, "From War Zone to Free Trade Zone," in Andrew Ross, ed., *No Sweat: Fashion, Free Trade, and the Rights of Garment Workers* (New York: Verso, 1997).

23. National Labor Committee, *Paying to Lose our Jobs: Free Trade's Hidden Secrets* (NLC, 1993). Subsequent NLC reports include *Haiti After the Coup: Sweatshop or Real Development?* (1993); *The U.S. in Haiti: How to Get Rich on 11¢ per Hour* (1996); *Wal-Mart's Shirts of Misery: Bangladesh Factory Conditions* (1999); *Behind the Label: Made in China* (1998); *Made in China: The Role of U.S. Companies in Denying Human Rights* (2000); *Propping up the Dictators in Burma* (2001); *"Made in the USA?": American Samoa and Indentured Servitude* (2001); and *Bangladesh: The Struggle to End the Race to the Bottom* (2001).

24. Surveys conducted for the Center for Ethical Concerns at Marymount University (November 1995) show that two-thirds of those polled would be willing to pay more for sweat-free clothing. A 1999 poll conducted by the Program on International Policy Attitudes at the

University of Maryland showed three-quarters willing to pay up to 25 percent more. The results of an NBER survey in 1999 paralleled the previous two. See Kimberly Ann Elliot and Richard Freeman, "White Hats or Don Quixotes? Human Rights Vigilantes in the Global Economy," (NBER Conference on Emerging Labor Markets, August 2000). A counter-poll commissioned by the International Mass Retail Association showed that most consumers (46 percent) blame the government's lack of regulation for exploitative labor practices, 29 percent blame the manufacturers, while only 19 percent blame the retailers.

25. Miriam Ching Yoon Louie, *Sweatshop Warriors: Immigrant Women Workers Take on the Global Factory* (Cambridge, MA: South End, 2001).

26. According to Robert Ross, in 1957, the Wages and Hours Division of Department of Labor had one investigator for every 46,000 workers, a ratio that held up until the mid-1970s, after which it dropped systematically. By 1996, the ratio of enforcers to workers was at a low of less than one per 150,000, with less than 800 inspectors overall. While Congress mandated a slight increase shortly thereafter to 940, inertia has prevailed since then. "Sweatshop Police," *The Nation*, September 3, 2001.

27. Press Release, May 20, 1996, National Retail Federation.

28. In 1998, Nike's CEO and founder Phillip Knight announced in a speech at the National Press Club that his company would undertake a series of reforms. Noting that the controversy over sweatshop conditions had made his company's products "synonymous with slave wages, forced overtime and arbitrary abuse," he announced that Nike would adopt new labor policies on health and safety, child labor, and independent monitoring, among other issues. Knight later described the speech as a "watershed event" that signaled a "sea change in the company cuture."

29. "Still Waiting for Nike to Do It" (San Francisco: Global Exchange, 2001).

30. Karl Schoenberger, *Levi's Children: Coming to Terms with Human Rights in the Global Marketplace* (New York: Atlantic Monthly Press, 2000).

31. Kearney's comments are quoted in Harvard Trade Union Program's Report and Summary on a Harvard symposium in October 1998, "Global Labor Standards and the Apparel Industry: Can We Regulate Global Production?," 15.

32. See Liza Featherstone and United Students Against Sweatshops, *Students Against Sweatshops* (New York and London: Verso, 2002).

33. David Gonzalez, "Latin Sweatshops Pressed by U.S. Campus Power," *New York Times*, April 4, 2003, A3.

34. The Council on Economic Priorities introduced a third model code of conduct, SA 8000, which includes provisions for a living wage, and has its own accreditation agency (CPEAA).

35. Daniel Bender, *From Sweatshop to Model Shop: Anti-Sweatshop Campaigns and Languages of Labor and Organizing, 1880–1934* (Ph.D. History Department, New York University, 2001).

36. The Saipan sweatshops have been the target of a class-action dollar lawsuit, brought by the Asian Law Caucus, Global Exchange, Sweatshop Watch of Oakland, and UNITE, and alleging far-reaching abuses of Saipan garment workers. A $20 million settlement for the workers was reached in September 2002. It involves twenty-seven garment manufacturers and twenty-seven retailers, among them the Gap, Sears, Roebuck & Co., Nordstrom, Tommy Hilfiger, Calvin Klein, Target, Abercrombie & Fitch, Talbots Inc., J.C. Penney, and Polo Ralph Lauren. The retailers denied the allegations, and the settlement does not include admission of wrongdoing.

37. See Featherstone's chapter on the politics of race within USAS, 62–68.

38. A recent poll of AFL-CIO unions showed that two-thirds were engaged in international activity "as a necessary extension of their normal organizing and bargaining." The Teamsters drew on an exemplary international campaign to support their successful strike action at UPS in 1997. UPS World Action Day saw over 150 job actions or demonstrations worldwide. Jay Mazur, "Labor's New Internationalism," *Foreign Affairs,* 79:1 (January/February 2000), 86–88.

39. See Kabeer's critique of this tendency in *The Power to Choose*.

40. Heather White, "Educating Workers," in Archon Fung, Dara O'Rourke, and Charles Sabel, *Can We Put an End to Sweatshops?* (Boston: Beacon Press, 2001), 70–72.

41. Pranab Bardhan, "Some Up, Some Down," in *Can We Put an End to Sweatshops?*, 49–53.

42. Paul Krugman, *New York Times,* June 22, 1997.

43. The Academic Consortium on International Trade, founded by Columbia University's Jagdish Bhagwati, is an elite group of free-trade economists, who formed to combat USAS influence over university administrators. Their open letter to college presidents can be found at http://www.spp.umich.edu/rsie/acit/. Their claims were combated by a counter-group, Scholars Against Sweatshop Labor, formed by Robert Pollin and James Galbraith. See /sweat.html.

44. Varley, *The Sweatshop Quandary,* 21.

45. Robert Pollin, Justine Burns, and James Heintz, "Global Apparel Production and Sweatshop Labor: Can Raising Retail Prices Finance Living Wages?" Working Paper, Political Economic Research Institute (University of Massachusetts, Amherst: June 2001). See http://www.umass.edu/peri/sweat.html.

46. Mark Levinson, "Economists and Sweatshops," *Dissent* 44:4 (Fall 1997), 11–13.

47. Richard Freeman, "What Role for Labor Standards in the Global Economy?" Paper, London School of Economics (November 12, 1998).

Chapter Two:
Made in Italy: The Trouble with Craft Capitalism

1. Valerie Steele, in Giannino Malossi, ed., *Volare: L'icona italiana nella cultura globale*

("The Italian Icon in Global Culture") (authored by the Fashion Engineering Unit—a "flexible research structure" of Pitti Immagine) (New York: Monacelli Press and Pitti Immagine, 1999).

2. Mario Boselli, in *Volare*, 21.

3. Nicola White, *Reconstructing Italian Fashion: America and the Development of the Italian Fashion Industry* (New York: Berg, 2001).

4. Rinaldo Gianola, "Design and Fashion: Driving Forces of Italy," in *Made in Italy 1951–2001* (a Project by Luigi Settembrini) (Milan: Skira, 2001), 100.

5. Clean Clothes Campaign, http://www.cleanclothes.org/companies/gucci-arround.htm.

6. "Spotlight on Benetton," *Clean Clothes Campaign Newsletter*, July 11, 1999.

7. The 27 percent estimate is from the IMF. ISTAT, the national statistics institute, puts the figure at 15.4 percent of GDP, though many economists and industrialists believe that the percentage could be twice the official estimate.

8. Gail Edmondson in Prato, Italy (with Kate Carlisle in Rome, Inka Resch in Paris, Karen Nickel Anhalt in Berlin, and Heidi Dawley in London), "Workers in Bondage," *Business Week* (November 27, 2000), 146.

9. "Child Labour Figures Putting Rich Italians to Shame," *The Guardian*, August 1, 1998.

10. Michael Piore and Charles Sabel, *The Second Industrial Divide: Possibilities for Prosperity* (New York: Basic Books, 1984), 213–16.

11. Gail Edmondson and Kate Carlisle, "A Touch of China in Tuscany," *Business Week*, October 22, 2001, 55.

12. M.J. Hogan, *The Marshall Plan: America, Britain, and the Reconstruction of Western Europe* (Cambridge: Cambridge University Press, 1987); C. Esposito, *America's Feeble Weapon: Funding the Marshall Plan in France and Italy* (Westport, CT: Greenwood Press, 1994); David Ellwood, *Rebuilding Europe: Western Europe, America, and Postwar Reconstruction* (London: Longman, 1992).

13. See Nicola White's account in *Reconstructing Italian Fashion*.

14. Sebastiano Brusco, "The Emilian Model: Productive Decentralization and Social Integration," *Cambridge Journal of Economics* 6 (1987) 167–84; Edward Goodman and Julia Bamford with Peter Saynor, eds., *Small Firms and Industrial Districts in Italy* (London, New York: Routledge, 1989); Arnold Bagnasco and Charles Sabel, eds., *Small and Medium-Sized Enterprises* (London: Pinter, 1995); F. Pyke, G. Becattini, and W. Sengenberger, eds., *Industrial Districts and Inter-Firm Cooperation in Italy* (Geneva: International Labour Office, 1990).

15. In this respect, the debate about the Emilian model superseded, in large part, the earlier choices that Antonio Gramsci laid out in "Americanism and Fordism," between a Taylorist organization of labor that was progressive and socialist and one that was passive and Fascist.

16. There is a triumphalist version of the end of the Cold War that assumes the command economies of the socialist bloc were not flexible enough to adapt to the new demands of the global economy. Even though it was touted most by PCI officials, in cities like Bologna, the

Third Italy's model of "flexibility" played an important, early role in this narrative about out-competing the Marxist-Leninist varieties of state communism.

17. Charles Sabel, *Work and Politics: The Division of Labor in Industry* (Cambridge: Cambridge University Press, 1982), 220.

18. More recently, Sabel argues for a revisionist view of industrialization that gives a more central place to craft production, in the essays collected in Charles Sabel and Jonathan Zeitlin, eds., *World of Possibilities: Flexibility and Mass Production in Western Industrialization* (Cambridge: Cambridge University Press, 1997) .

19. Charles Sabel, "Conclusion" in Bagnasco and Sabel, *Small and Medium-Sized Enterprises*, 145.

20. Piore and Sabel note that Arnaldo Bagnasco and Sebastiano Brusco, Italian critics of labor abuse in the early runaway shops, had come to acknowledge "that much of the sweatshop sector had become innovative." *The Second Industrial Divide*, 229.

21. Ian Taplin, "Segmentation and the Organization of Work in the Italian Apparel Industry," *Social Science Quarterly* 70:2 (June 1989), 408–24. See Andrea Wigfield, *Post-Fordism, Gender and Work* (Aldershot: Ashgate, 2001).

22. Fiorenza Belussi, "Benetton Italy: Beyond Fordism and Flexible Specialization" in Swasti Mitter, ed., *Computer-Aided Manufacturing and Women's Employment : The Clothing Industry in Four EC Countries* (for the Directorate-General Employment, Social Affairs, and Education of the European Communities, June 1990 [with assistance from Anneke van Luijken] (London, New York: Springer-Verlag, 1992), 88–90.

23. Mario Mignone, *Italy Today: A Country in Transition* (New York: Peter Lang, 1995), 115.

24. Pauline Conroy Jackson, "Homeworking in Italy in the Age of Computer Technology," in Mitter, 94–101.

25. Michael L. Blim, *Made in Italy: Small-Scale Industrialization and its Consequences* (New York: Praeger, 1990), 151–52.

26. Blim, 125.

27. Josh Whitford, "The Decline of a Model? Challenge and Response in the Italian Industrial Districts," *Economy and Society* 30:1 (2001), 38–65.

28. For example, Gabi Dei Ottati notes that 17 percent of production in the Empoli clothing system is manufactured abroad, and in the Prato district, 25 percent of the final firms had subcontractors overseas. "The Remarkable Resilience of the Industrial Districts of Tuscany," in Francesco Cossentino, Frank Pyke, and Werner Sengenberger, *Local and Regional Response to Global Pressure: The Case of Italy and Its Industrial Districts* (Geneva: International Institute for Labor Studies, 1996), 50.

29. Ted Polhemus, *Diesel: World Wide Wear* (New York: Watson-Guptill, 1998).

30. The origin of the campaign to rebrand Britain lay in a pamphlet produced by the Demos think tank: Mark Leonard, "Britain TM: Renewing Our Identity" (London: Demos, 1997).

31. Angela McRobbie, "Fashion Culture: Creative Work, Female Individualization," *Feminist Review* 71 (2002), 52–56; and *British Fashion Design: Rag Trade or Image Industry?* (London: Routledge, 1998).

32. Thuy Linh Tu, *Outside In: Immigration and Popular Culture in Asian New York* (Ph.D. dissertation, American Studies, New York University, 2003), 79–152.

33. Catalogs from these shows include: Bonizza Giordani Aragno, ed., *Moda Italia: Creativa, Impresa, Tecnologia nel Sistema Italiano della Moda* / Creativity and Technology in the Italian Fashion System (Milan: Domus, 1988); *Italian Furniture 1961–91*; *Volare* (1999, Firenze); *Made in Italy 1951–2001* (Milan, 2001). Other shows and books included Giannino Malossi, ed., *The Style Engine: Spectacle, Identity, Design, and Business* (New York: Monacelli, 1998), and *The Sala Bianca: The Birth of Italian Fashion* (a Palazzo Strozzi exhibition in Firenze in 1992, also at the Guggenheim and Louvre); Giannino Malossi, ed., *La Regola Estrosa: Cent'anni di eleganza maschile italiana* (Firenze, Stazione Leopoldi, 1993); *Latin Lover: A Sud della Passione* (Firenze, Stazione Leopoldi, 1996); and Valerie Steele, *Fashion, Italian Style* (New Haven: Yale University Press, 2003).

34. Raffalleo Napoleone, in *Volare*, 23.

35. Mario Boselli, in *Volare*, 21.

36. Michael Blim, "Italian Women After Development: Employment, Entrepreneurship, and Domestic Work in the Third Italy," *The History of the Family* 6 (2001), 257–70.

37. Piore and Sabel, *The Second Industrial Divide*, 228–29.

Chapter Three:
Friedrich Engels Visits the Old Trafford Megastore

1. For a broad analysis of the impact of the TV/PPV revolution, see Richard Guilianotti, *Football: A Sociology of the Global Game* (Cambridge: Polity Press, 1999), 86–106.

2. Alex Fynn and Lynton Guest, *Out of Time: Why English Football Isn't Working* (London: Simon & Schuster, 1999), 122. In the U.K. the commercial precursor to televised soccer were the pools companies like Littlewoods, which made a fortune out of gambling on match scores. The industry was much reviled by soccer purists, and so none of the revenue found its way into the clubs' coffers.

3. Asa Briggs, "The Media and Sport in the Global Village" in Ralph Wilcox, *Sport in the Global Village* (Morgantown, WV: Fitness Information Technology, 1994), 12.

4. Matthew Beard, "Nike v. Adidas: The Big Match With a Prize Worth Billions," *The Independent*, June 1, 2002.

5. Dan Rookwood, " Beckham and Keane: United They Stand," *The Guardian*, April 30, 2003.

6. The England national team turned down a similar offer from Nike in favor of Umbro's

less intrusive contract.

7. Alex Fynn and Lynton Guest, *For Love or Money: Manchester United and England—The Business of Winning* (London: Andre Deutsch, 1999), 41–42.

8. John Williams, Stephen Hopkins, and Catherine Long, eds., *Passing Rhythms: Liverpool FC and the Transformation of Football* (Oxford: Berg, 2000).

9. A similar kind of image boosterism has been applied to the city's own identity as a crucible of pop culture. See David Haslam's *Manchester, England: The Story of the Pop Cult City* (London: Fourth Estate, 1999).

10. United had almost been sold to Robert Maxwell, another media tycoon, in the mid-1980s, at the time he had acquired Derby, Oxford, and Reading. But the media, at that time, only covered the game. By 1998, Murdoch represented a media complex that funded the game.

11. See the articles by Peter Crowther, Nicholas Finney, and Adam Brown on the MMC's decision to block the bid and in S. Hamil et al., eds., *Football in the Digital Age: Whose Game Is It Anyway?* (Edinburgh: Mainstream, 2000).

12. Mihir Bose, *Manchester Unlimited: The Rise and Rise of the World's Premier Football Club* (London: Orion, 1999), 291. Bose's book presents the most detailed account of the takeover bid. Spearheading the anti-Murdoch campaign were Michael Crick and David Smith, who had authored the first book to capture the disgust of fans with the brash commercialism of the club's directors. *Manchester United: The Betrayal of a Legend* (London: Pelham Books, 1989).

13. Toby Miller, Geoffrey Lawrence, Jim MacKay, and David Rowe, *Globalization and Sport: Playing the World* (London: Sage, 2001); John Sugden and Alan Tomlinson, *FIFA and the Contest for World Football: Who Rules the Peoples' Game?* (Cambridge: Polity Press, 1998).

14. Stanley Holmes and Christine Tierney, "How Nike Got Its Game Back," *Business Week*, November 4, 2002, 120.

15. "Scum Airways," *The Observer*, November 17, 2002.

16. With its stock price in the doldrums, or underpriced, fears of another takeover were rife at the end of 2002. Senior city bankers floated a financial plan to turn Manchester United into a mutual organization owned solely for the benefit of its fans. Ownership would be in the hands of a mutual trust, whose director would be elected partly by supporters. By the spring of 2003, two Irish turf magnates, J.P. McManus and John Magnier, had steadily increased their holdings through their offshore company, Cubic Expressions, to 10.37 percent, making them the largest shareholders in the club, and triggering a fresh round of takeover rumors.

17. Jeff Ballinger has been the veteran Nike watchdog, producing invaluable research on the plight of the company's Indonesian workforce. Only under intense public pressure did Nike issue a "Code of Conduct," and take steps to justify its refusal to take responsibility for the brutal labor practices of its subcontractors. See Jeff Ballinger and Claes Olsson, eds., *Behind the Swoosh: The Struggle of Indonesians Making Nike Shoes* (Uppsala: Global

Publications, 1997). In other Asian countries, Vietnam Labor Watch, Hong Kong Christian Industrial Committee, Asia Monitor Resource Center, China Labor Watch, and Global Exchange have all applied monitoring pressure through their exposés of the company. With the help of No Sweat, the U.K anti-sweatshop organization, SU was able to host one of the best selections of Nike watchdog resources on its website, at http://www.shareholdersunited.org. For other web resources, see Academics Studying Nike at http://cbae.nmsu.edu/~dboje/nike/nike-main.html

18. Sydney Schanberg, "Six Cents an Hour," *Life* 19:7 (June 1996), 38–46.

19. Hong Kong Christian Industrial Committee, "Report on the Working Conditions of Soccer and Football Workers in Mainland China" (Hong Kong; revised version, May 2002). Over the years, the Clean Clothes Campaign has brought pressure to bear on sportswear giants like Adidas, and, along with Global March Against Child Labour, took on FIFA, through their Euro 2000 and World Cup 2002 campaigns (http://www.cleanclothes.org).

20. The World Cup 2002 campaign is summarized at http://www.globalmarch.org/world-cup-campaign/.

21. Edward Baines, *History of the Cotton Manufacture in Great Britain* (London: Fisher, Fisher, and Jackson, 1835), especially Chapter VI.

22. Lajpat Rai, *England's Debt to India: A Historical Narrative of Britain's Fiscal Policy in India* (New York: Huebsch, 1917), 135. Horace Wilson points out in his notes to James Mill's *The History of British India*: "Had not such prohibitory duties and decrees existed, the mills of Paisley and Manchester would have been stopped in their outset and could scarcely have been set in motion even by the power of steam. They were created by the sacrifice of Indian manufacture." Quoted in Noam Chomsky, *Year 501: The Conquest Continues* (Boston: South End Press, 1993), 14.

23. The story of the campaign for an Indian cotton supply is told in detail in Arthur Silver, *Manchester Men and Indian Cotton, 1847–1872* (Manchester: Manchester University Press, 1966). Also see Arthur Redford, *Manchester Merchants and Foreign Trade 1794–1939* (Manchester: Manchester University Press, 1934–1956), two vols.

24. Friedrich Engels, "The Great Towns," in *The Condition of the Working Class in England* (1845), translated and edited by W.O. Henderson and W.H. Chaloner (Oxford: Basil Blackwell, 1958); 75.

25. Ibid., 56.

26. Ibid., 158.

27. National Labor Committee, *Bangladesh: The Struggle to End the Race to the Bottom* (NLC, New York, 2001), iii.

28. Robert Goldman and Stephen Papson, *Nike Culture: The Sign of the Swoosh* (London: Sage, 1998), 5.

29. Andrew Ross, *No-Collar: The Humane Workplace and its Hidden Costs* (New York:

Basic Books, 2003).

30. Tom Vanderbilt, *The Sneaker Book: Anatomy of an Industry and an Icon* (New York: The New Press, 1998), 32–41.

31. Malcolm Gladwell, *The Tipping Point: How Little Things Can Make a Big Difference* (New York: Little, Brown, 2000).

32. In a celebrated article for *The Face* (July 1983), called "The Ins And Outs Of High Street Fashion," Kevin Sampson wrote a much contested account of casuals, locating their origins in Liverpool's Scotland Road neighborhood. Naturally, claims were made on behalf of Manchester and London as the ground zero of casual culture. Also see John Williams, "Kopites, 'Scallies,' and Liverpool Fan Cultures," in Williams, et al., *Passing Rhythms*, 99–128.

33. More analytic literature on the casuals includes Richard Guilanotti, "Soccer Casuals as Cultural Intermediaries," and other essays in Steve Redhead, ed., *The Passion and the Fashion: Football Fandom in the New Europe* (Aldershot: Avebury, 1993), and Steve Redhead, *Sing When You're Winning* (London: Pluto, 1986).

34. Seth Stevenson, "How to Beat Nike," *New York Times Magazine*, January 5, 2003, 28–34.

35. Steve Redhead, *Post-Fandom and the Millenial Blues: The Transformation of Soccer Culture* (London: Routledge, 1997), 30.

Chapter Four: Are the Chinese Losing China?

1. Ching Kwan Lee's analysis of the organization of the Guangdong labor market shows the importance of localism—place-based, or kinship ties—in reproducing the female workforce in a Shenzhen factory. By contrast, a Hong Kong factory owned by the same company relied on familialism as a mode of labor control in a "sunset" labor market. *Gender and the South China Miracle: Two Worlds of Factory Women* (Berkeley: University of California Press, 1998). For other studies of Asian women factory workers in capitalist environments, see Aihwa Ong, *Spirits of Resistance and Capitalist Discipline: Factory Women in Malaysia* (Albany: SUNY Press, 1987); Ping-Chun Hsiung, *Living Rooms as Factories: Class, Gender and the Satellite Factory System in Taiwan* (Philadelphia: Temple University Press, 1996); Diane Lauren Wolf, *Factory Daughters: Gender, Household Dynamics, and Rural Industrialization in Java* (Berkeley: University of California Press, 1992); Janet Salaff, *Working Daughters of Hong Kong: Filial Piety or Power in the Family* (Cambridge: Cambridge University Press, 1981).

2. Lisa Rofel's ethnography of Hangzhou silk factory workers revealed striking generational differences among the women employees; between those who started out as "model workers" in the 1950s, those who challenged all forms of authority during the Cultural Revolution, and those who had been weaned on market risks. *Other Modernities: Gendered Yearnings in China*

After Socialism (Berkeley: University of California Press, 1999).

3. National Labor Committee, *Made in China: Behind the Label* (New York, 1998); Asia Monitor Resource Center, *We in the Zone: Women Workers in Asia's Export Processing Zones* (Hong Kong, 1998); *Asia Pacific Labour Law Review: Workers' Rights for the New Century* (Hong Kong, 2003); Asia Monitor Resource Center, *Smashing the Iron Pot: Workers and Unions Under China's Market Socialism* (Hong Kong, 1988); Hong Kong Christian Industrial Committee, *How Hasbro, Mattel, McDonald's and Disney Manufacture Their Toys* (Hong Kong, 2001); and (with Asia Monitor Resource Center) "Working Conditions in Sports Shoe Factories in China Making Shoes for Nike and Reebok" (Hong Kong, 1997); Chan, *Chinese Workers Under Assault*.

4. Joseph Stiglitz, *Globalization and its Discontents* (New York: W.W. Norton, 2002). Stiglitz's primary analysis of China is in the chapter entitled "Better Roads to the Market."

5. He Qinglian's best-selling book, *China's Pitfall* (Hong Kong, Mingjing Publishing House, 1998), is the most trenchant account of corruption and graft among party cadres. Also see her "China's Listing Social Structure," *New Left Review*, September–October 2002, 69–100.

6. According to the official labor federation's 2002 *Blue Book on Chinese Trade Unions' Safeguarding of the Legitimate Rights and Interests of Workers and Staff*.

7. Bruce Cumings, *Parallax Visions: Making Sense of American-East Asian Relations at the End of the Century* (Durham, NC: Duke University Press, 1999), 158.

8. Ibid., 171.

9. See the case for and against the AFL-CIO's PNTR campaign, in Kent Wong and Elaine Bernard, "Labor's Mistaken Anti-China Campaign," and Mark Levinson and Thea Lee, "Why Labor Made the Right Decision," in *New Labor Forum* 7 (Fall/Winter 2000), 19–29.

10. United States Department of Defense, "Special Briefing on Army Headgear" (March 16, 2001), http://www.defenselink.mil/news/Mar2001/t03162001_t316dsda.html.

11. Rowan Scarborough, "Taxpayers Stuck With Berets," *Washington Times*, August 1, 2001.

12. Bill Gertz and Rowan Scarborough, "Beret Battles," *The Gertz File* (http://www.gertz-file.com/gertzfile/ring051801.html).

13. James Miller, "Patriots Bristle at Imported Flags," *Orlando Sentinel*, June 14, 2002, 25.

14. John Pomfret, "Chinese Working Overtime to Sew U.S. Flags," *Washington Post*, September 20, 2001, A14.

15. Quoted on the website of Flagsource, a "Made in the U.S.A." flag and banner company, "American Flag Manufacturers Speak with One Voice, 'Just Say, I'll Wait,'" http://flag-source.com/supportamerica.htm.

16. The Chentex campaign was a model of international solidarity. It involved not only USAS and the NLC, but also the U.S. steelworkers union, a Taipei group of students and trade

unionists called Taiwan Solidarity with Nicaraguan Workers, trade unionists in Lesotho (where Nien Hsing also had a factory), and media columnists in the *New York Times*, whose high-profile publicity helped pressure the U.S. embassy in Managua to take the side of the workers.

17. Arthur Kroeber, "The Hot Zone," *Wired* 10:11 (November 2002), 200–17.

18. In her study of factory conditions in South China, *China's Workers Under Assault: The Exploitation of Labor in a Globalizing Economy* (Armonk, NY: M.E. Sharpe, 2001), Anita Chan confirms that the Taiwanese had the most militaristic management style. In their joint-venture companies, physical assaults by Taiwanese managers on PRC workers are quite common (46), and are justified by appeals to the effort to dispel the lingering legacy of the "big rice bowl."

19. According to the *Economic Information Daily* (Xinhua, August 24, 2001).

20. Clay Chandler, "A Factory to the World: China's Vast Labor Pool, Low Wages Lure Manufacturers," *Washington Post*, November 25, 2001, A01

21. Tsai Ting-I, "Taipei Sees Biggest Demo Ever," *Taipei Times*, November 24, 2002.

22. Quoted in "Engineers and Scientists, Not Just Factory Workers, Now Come Cheap in China." http://biz.yahoo.com/fo/020820/brawn_and_brains_3.html.

23. Spearheading the anti-China faction of the neoconservative establishment is the group the Project for the New American Century (PNAC), which has advocated a policy of confrontation with Beijing since it was created in 1997.

24. Beijing took the protests so seriously that, in May 2003, extra-stiff sentences (seven-year and four-year prison terms) were handed down to two leaders for acts of "subversion" in the course of organizing the Liaoyang protests.

25. Gordon Chang, *The Coming Collapse of China* (New York: Random House, 2001).

26. Dorothy Solinger, *Contesting Citizenship in Urban China: Peasant Migrants, the State, and the Logic of the Market* (Berkeley: University of California Press, 1999); Li Zhang, *Strangers in the City: Reconfigurations of Space, Power, and Social Networks Within China's Floating Population* (Stanford: Stanford University Press, 2001).

27. James Kynge "Creaking Economy Needs Stronger Foundations," *Financial Times*, October 30, 2002.

28. Aihwa Ong, *Flexible Citizenship: The Cultural Logics of Transnationality* (Durham, NC: Duke University Press, 1999).

29. Ibid., 55–83.

30. China produced the highest number of the world's forty wealthiest people under the age of forty outside the United States, according to *Fortune*'s September 2002 listing. Even the government's statistics, which tend toward boosterism, support a rapid intensification of the Gini coefficient—the formula that measures the gap between a country's rich and its poor—which had soared from 0.15 in 1978, one of the lowest in the world, to 0.48 in 2003, putting China within reach of the most unequal nations.

31. For example, the following statement was issued by the HKCTU:

> We are shocked and deeply disappointed by the election of the All China Federation of Trade Unions (ACFTU) to the ILO Governing Body as a Worker Deputy Member on June 10. This not only marks a major defeat for workers in China who are struggling to achieve the right to freedom of association (a struggle which only recently led to the imprisonment of workers in Liaoyang and Daqing for exercising this right), but also raises serious questions about the current strategy of the international trade union movement vis-à-vis China.

32. See Anita Chan's analysis of pro-labor journalism in *Chinese Workers Under Assault*, and her comments about strategic engagement with the ACFTU in "Labor in Waiting," *New Labor Forum* 11 (Fall/Winter 2002), 54–59.

33. Gregory Mantsios, "Tea for Two: Chinese and U.S. Labor: A Report from China," *New Labor Forum* 11 (Fall/Winter 2002), 61–73.

34. Chan, "Labor in Waiting," 58.

35. Apo Leong and Stephen Frost, "From Security to Uncertainty: Labour and Welfare Reform in China" (Hong Kong: Asia Monitor Resources Center), available at http://www.amrc.org.hk-/Arch/3502.htm.

36. Rofel, 10–28.

37. See Xudong Zhang's Introduction and Wang Hui's analysis of "modernization with Chinese characteristics," in Xudong Zhang, ed., *Whither China: Intellectual Politics in Contemporary China* (Durham, NC: Duke University Press, 2001).

Chapter Five: The Flight of the Silicon Wafers

1. Juan Gonzalez, *Fallout: The Environmental Consequences of the World Trade Center Collapse* (New York: The New Press, 2002).

2. Ibid., 22.

3. Ulrich Beck, *Risk Society: Towards a New Modernity*, trans. by Mark Ritter (London: Sage, 1992).

4. Jack Newfield, "How the Other Half Lives," *The Nation* 276:10 (February 26, 2003).

5. Gonzalez, 128.

6. The full report, entitled "Exporting Harm: The High-Tech Trashing of Asia," was produced by BAN and the SVTC with support from Toxics Link India, Greenpeace China and SCOPE (Pakistan). It can be found online at the SVTC Web site, the single best Web resource on all issues relating to microchip production: http://www.svtc.org/cleancc/pubs/tt2.htm.

7. Rachel Shabi "The E-waste Land," *The Guardian*, November 30, 2002. Also see John

Markoff, "Technology's Toxic Trash Is Sent to Poor Nations," *New York Times*, February 25, 2002.

8. "Chinese Customs Seizes 'Electronic Garbage,'" *People's Daily*, September 18, 2002.

9. Henry Norr, "Drowning in e-waste," *San Francisco Chronicle*, May 27, 2001.

10. In a report undertaken by the Silicon Valley Toxics Campaign and the Computer Take Back Campaign, Sheila Davis and Ted Smith compare the atrocious conditions at the Atwater, California, facility of UNICOR, a prison industrial operator contracted by Dell, with the environmentally responsible conditions at a Micro Metallics facility contracted by Hewlett Packard, in "Corporate Strategies for Electronic Recycling: A Tale of Two Systems" (June 2003), http://www.svtc.org. Within two weeks of the report's publication, Dell had canceled its contracts, and selected two private companies to handle its electronic recycling operations. Laurie Flynn, "Dell to Stop Using Prison Workers," *New York Times*, July 4, 2003.

11. An international network made links, through the Campaign for Responsible Technology, with local labor, environmental, and human rights groups around the world. Much of the groundwork was laid at a European Work Hazards convention in the Netherlands in March 1998.

12. Longtime watchdog Joseph LaDou, a UC professor of occupational medicine, produced the first well-documented study in *Technology Review*, May–June, 1984. In response to the study, manufacturers concluded that glycol ether, a solvent, was to blame for the miscarriages. The chemical has since been phased out, but other internal surveys conducted by Digital Equipment Corporation, IBM, and the SIA suggest that the rates of miscarriage remain very high. In 1992, Myron Harrison, a former IBM industrial physician, published a detailed analysis of the toxicological risks associated with every step of chip-making: "Semiconductor Manufacturing Hazards," in J.B. Sullivan and G.R. Krieger, eds., *Clinical Principles of Environmental Health* (Baltimore: Williams and Wilkins, 1992), chapter 43. Also see J. Weber and M. Parrish, "Implications of IBM Study on Miscarriages," *Los Angeles Times*, October 13, 1992; and the more recent study by LaDou, "The International Electronics Industry," *International Journal of Occupational and Environmental Health* 4:1 (January–March, 1998).

13. Among the books that describe the toxic underbelly of microchip manufacture are Lisa Sun-Hee Park and David Naguib Pellow, *The Silicon Valley of Dreams: Environmental Justice, Immigrant Workers and the High-Tech Global Economy*, (New York: NYU Press, 2003); Dennis Hayes, *Behind the Silicon Curtain: The Seductions of Work in a Lonely Era* (Boston: South End Press, 1989); Chris Carlsson and Mark Leger, eds., *Bad Attitude: The Processed World Anthology* (New York: Verso, 1990); Robert Howard, *Brave New Workplaces* (New York: Viking, 1985); Lenny Seigel and John Markoff, *The High Cost of High Tech: The Dark Side of the Chip* (New York: Harper & Row, 1985); Leslie Byster, "The Toxic Chip," *Environmental Action* 27:3 (Fall 1995), 19–23. Also see Sandra Steingraber, *Living Downstream: An Ecologist Looks at Cancer and the Environment* (New York: Addison-Wesley, 1997).

14. Stephanie Armour, "Workers Take Employers to Court Over Birth Defects," *USA Today*, February 26, 2002.

15. For details of the Santa Clara lawsuit, see Jim Fisher, "Poison Valley," *Salon*, July 30, 2001, http://dir.salon.com/tech/feature/2001/07/30/almaden1/index.html. Also see Susan Q. Stranahan, "The Clean Room's Dirty Secret," *Mother Jones*, April 2002, and Karina Ioffee, "The Clean Room Paradox," *E Andar* (Fall/Winter 2001) (http://www.elander.com/-toxics/stories/cleanroom.html).

16. See part two of Jim Fisher's excellent investigative report, "Poison Valley," http://archive.salon.com/tech/feature/2001/07/31/almaden2/.

17. The press release was ridiculed in an editorial in the *San Jose Mercury News*, March 21, 2002: "Chip Makers Must Do Toxic Chemical Studies, Not Just Consider Them." It called on the SIA "to release the full text of its unpublished report from the independent scientific advisory panel, and the names of the members."

18. The full report, by British Health and Safety Executive, can be retrieved at http://www.hse.gov.uk/statistics/nsukrupt.pdf.

19. These figures are available at the SVTC website. Also see the recent study of data from a microchip plant; Eric Williams, Miriam Heller, Robert Ayres, "The 1.7 Kilogram Microchip: Energy and Material Use in the Production of Semiconductor Devices," *Environmental Science and Technology* 36:24 (December 2002), 5504–5510.

20. Sahra Girshick, Rajesh Shah, and Sissel Waage, "Information Technology and Sustainability: Enabling the Future" (San Francisco: The Natural Step, 2002), 22.

21. Orna Izakson, "The High-Tech Industry Is Poisonous to Low-Wage Immigrant Workers," *E/The Environmental Magazine*, May 24, 2002. Karen Hossfield, "'Their Logic Against Them: Contradictions in Sex, Race and Class in Silicon Valley" in Alondra Nelson and Thuy Linh Tu (with Alicia Headlam Hines), eds., *TechniColor: Race, Technology and Everyday Life* (New York: NYU Press, 2001), 34–63. Offshore, the work hazards in manufacturing were presaged by the earlier outsourcing of information processing to women workers in developing countries. See Ruth Pearson and Swasti Mitter, "Employment and Working Conditions of Low-Skilled Information-Processing Workers in Less Developed Countries," *International Labour Review* 132:1 (1993), 49–79. Karina Ioffee reports that the average salary for a Latina employed in electronics manufacturing is only $23,000. ("The Clean Room Paradox").

22. David Bacon, "Silicon Valley Sweatshops: High-Tech's Dirty Little Secret," *The Nation* 256:15 (April 19, 1993), 517.

23. See the report by the Natural Step (Girshick et al.), suggesting an industry-wide framework for developing sustainability.

24. California Global Corporate Accountability Project, *Dodging Dilemmas: Environmental and Social Accountability in High-Tech Firms* (May 2002), 25–26.

25. Cited by Ted Smith, director of SVTC, in William Van Winkle, "War On High-Tech

Waste," *Smart Computing* 12:10 (October 2001), at http://www.smartcomputing.com/-email.asp?emid=45937.

26. *Dodging Dilemmas*, 54–55.

27. Potential consumers are able to consult the SVTC report card to compare the environmental record of manufacturers, at http://www.svtc.org/cleancc/pubs/2000report.htm.

Chapter Six: Strike a Pose for Justice: The Barneys Union Campaign of 1996

1. Joshua Levine, *The Rise and Fall of the House of Barneys: A Family Tale of Chutzpah, Glory, and Greed* (New York: William Morrow, 1999).

2. Simon Doonan, *Confessions of a Window Dresser: Tales from a Life in Fashion* (New York: Penguin Studio, 1998).

3. In addition, Doonan had done a series of Red Windows, enlisting designers and artists like Jasper Johns, Robert Rauschenberg, and Ross Bleckner to create works of art using red. Proceeds from the auction of the artwork went to the Little Red Schoolhouse in Greenwich Village and the Storefront School in Harlem. A "bad taste" nativity scene, which featured Madonna and Bart Simpson among others, ignited the tabloid and religious press, all of which helped to brand the company, and the color, as notorious in the public eye. Levine, *The Rise and Fall*, 135.

Chapter Seven: The Mental Labor Problem

1. The faculty also includes jazz luminaries such as bassist Reggie Workman, saxophonist Billy Harper, pianist Joanne Brackeen, drummer Joe Chambers, trumpeter Cecil Bridgewater, and pianist Junior Mance.

2. Under the presidency of Bob Kerrey, the New School has vigorously opposed further attempts by the UAW to organize faculty—both part-time and full-time.

3. Indeed, Dewey's vision for the American Association of University Professors, which he founded with Arthur Lovejoy in 1915, was explicitly that it not function as a union, but as a professional organization like the Bar or the American Medical Association. His distaste for Butler's violations of academic freedom at Columbia stemmed from a conviction that universities would be no different from a "factory" if employees could be fired at will. Louis Menand, *The Metaphysical Club* (New York: Farrar, Straus and Giroux, 2001), 413–20.

4. See Thomas Bender's account in *New York Intellect: A History of Intellectual Life in New York City, from 1750 to the Beginnings of Our Own Time* (Baltimore: Johns Hopkins University Press, 1987), 296–300.

5. James McKeen Cattell, *University Control* (New York: Science Press, 1913), 17.

6. Thorstein Veblen, *The Higher Learning in America: A Memorandum on the Conduct of Universities by Business Men* (New York: B.W. Huebsch, 1918).

7. David Riesman, preface to *The Higher Learning*, xv.

8. Western universities, church-affiliated and other special-interest colleges, and land-grant institutions, created under the Morrill Act of 1862, with an emphasis on the "practical" or "mechanic arts," were more inclined to honor a community service ethos that ran counter to the genteel, self-marginalizing spirit of Idle Curiosity. Schools of agriculture, engineering, home economics, and business administration were a particular innovation of the land-grant movement.

9. Thorstein Veblen, *The Engineers and the Price System* (New York: B.W. Huebsch, 1921).

10. William Gaddis, "Stop Player. Joke No. 4," in *The Rush for Second Place*, ed. Joseph Tabbi (New York: Penguin, 2002).

11. James Kraft estimates that, by 1934, 20,000 theater musicians—"perhaps a quarter of the nation's professional instrumentalists and half of those who were fully employed"—lost their jobs as a result of the talkies. Exhibitors "saved as much as $3,000 a week by displacing musicians and vaudeville actors." *Stage to Studio, Musicians and the Sound Revolution, 1890–1950* (Baltimore; Johns Hopkins Univ. Press, 1996), 33, 49.

12. Kraft tells the story in detail in *Stage to Studio*.

13. Some titles, predominantly relating to the for-profit sector, include: Lois Gray and Ronald Seeber, eds., *Under the Stars: Essays on Labor Relations in Arts and Entertainment* (Ithaca, NY: ILR/Cornell University Press, 1996); Michael Storper, "The Transition to Flexible Specialization in the U.S. Film Industry," *Cambridge Journal of Economics* 13 (1989), 273–305; Toby Miller, *Technologies of Truth: Cultural Citizenship and the Popular Media* (Minneapolis: University of Minnesota Press, 1998) and "Television and Citizenship: A New International Division of Cultural Labor," in Andrew Calabrese and Jean-Claude Burgelman, eds., *Communication, Citizenship, and Social Policy: Rethinking the Limits of the Welfare State* (Lanham, MA: Rowman and Littlefield, 1999), 279–92.

14. John Kreidler, "Leverage Lost: The Nonprofit Arts in the Post-Ford Era," *In Motion Magazine* (http://www.inmotionmagazine.com/lost.html).

15. Lawrence Levine, *Highbrow/Lowbrow: The Emergence of Cultural Hierarchy in America* (Cambridge, MA: Harvard University Press, 1988).

16. William Baumol and William Bowen, *Performing Arts—The Economic Dilemma: A Study of Problems Common to Theatre, Opera, Music, and Dance* (New York: Twentieth-Century Fund, 1966), 162.

17. William Bowen and Julie Ann Sosa, *Prospects for Faculty in the Arts and Sciences: A Study of Factors Affecting Supply and Demand, 1987 to 2012* (Princeton: Princeton University Press, 1989); and the later study, William Bowen and Neil Rudenstine, *In Pursuit of the Ph.D.* (Princeton: Princeton University Press, 1992). It has been argued that Bowen's forecast of

abundant jobs would have been realized if universities had not embarked, in the 1990s, on a full-scale program of casualizing its faculty workforce. If colleges were still hiring full-time tenure-track professors, instead of part-timers and adjuncts, today's labor supply would more closely approximate employer demand.

18. Ruth Towse, ed., *Baumol's Cost Disease: The Arts and Other Victims* (Northampton, MA: Edward Elgar, 1997).

19. George Yudice, "The Privatization of Culture," *Social Text* 59 (Spring 1999), 17–34.

20. Gary Larson, *American Canvas: An Arts Legacy for Our Communities* (Washington, DC: National Endowment for the Arts, 1997), 127–28; cited in Yudice, 25.

21. American Assembly, *The Arts and the Public Purpose* (New York: Columbia University, 1997).

22. Peer, a small, independent arts charity in East London, collected and curated a useful dossier of responses to the new policies. Mary Warnock and Mark Wallinger, eds., *Art For All? Their Policies and Our Culture* (London: Peer, 2000).

23. See the NEA Research Division Notes on "Artist Employment in America," www.arts.endow.gov.pub. By 1999, the trends in job growth had reversed, with professional speciality employment now growing at 5 percent, as New Economy companies absorbed many of those trained in the arts, while the growth for artists had dropped to 3.9 percent.

24. NEA Research Division Note #73, April 1999.

25. Randy Martin, "Beyond Privatization: The Art and Society of Labor, Citizenship, and Consumerism," *Social Text* 59 (Spring 1999), 38–39.

26. Gary and Seeber, *Under the Stars*, 6.

27. Charles Landry, *The Creative City: A Toolkit for Urban Innovators* (London: Comedia, 2000); Richard Florida, *The Rise of the Creative Class: and How It's Transforming Work, Leisure, Community, and Everyday Life* (New York: Basic Books, 2002).

28. Andrew Ross, *No-Collar: The Humane Workplace and Its Hidden Costs* (New York: Basic Books, 2003).

29. Building on her studies of petty entrepreneurs in the British fashion industry, Angela McRobbie offers an analysis of the creative work as the new entrepreneurial model in "Clubs to Companies: Notes on the Decline of Political Culture in Speeded Up Creative Worlds," *Cultural Studies* 16:4 (2002), 516–531; and "Everyone is Creative: Artists as Pioneers of the New Economy," (August 30, 2001), www.opendemocracy.net/themes/article-7-652.jsp.

30. Baumol and Bowen, 99.

31. Ibid., 371.

32. Linda Marie Fritschner, "Literary Agents and Literary Traditions: The Role of the Philistine," in Judith Huggins Balfe, ed., *Paying the Piper: Causes and Consequences of Art Patronage* (Urbana: University of Illinois Press, 1993), 54–72. Also James Hepburn, *The Author's Empty Purse and the Rise of the Literary Agent* (London: Oxford University Press, 1968).

33. Partly in response to the disastrous consequences of the 1996 Telecommunications Act, which opened the way for rapid concentration of media interests in a range of industries, the Future of Music Coalition was formed to petition for musicians' rights on a broad front. Composed of "musicians, lawyers, academics, policymakers and music industry executives," the coalition, according to its Web site (www.futureofmusic.org), aims to debate and lobby on "some of the most contentious issues surrounding digital technology, artists' rights and the current state of the music industry."

34. Harold Rosenberg, "The Profession of Art: The WPA Art Project," *Art on the Edge: Creators and Situations* (New York: MacMillan, 1975), 195–205.

35. Michael Denning, *The Cultural Front: The Laboring of American Culture in the American Century* (New York: Verso, 1996).

36. C. Wright Mills, "The Cultural Apparatus," in *Power, Politics, and People,* ed. Irving Horowitz (New York: Ballantine, 1963), 405–22.

37. C.L.R. James, *American Civilization*, edited and introduced by Anna Grimshaw and Keith Hart, with an afterword by Robert A. Hill (Oxford: Blackwell, 1993), 123.

38. Frances Stonor Saunders, *The Cultural Cold War: The CIA and the World of Arts and Letters* (New York: The New Press, 1999).

39. For analysis in general of these developments see Cary Nelson, ed., *Will Teach for Food: Academic Labor in Crisis* (Minneapolis: University of Minnesota Press, 1997); Randy Martin, ed., *Chalk Lines: The Politics of Work in the Managed University* (Durham, NC: Duke University Press, 1998) and Cary Nelson and Stephen Watt, *Academic Keywords: A Devil's Dictionary for Higher Education* (New York: Routledge, 1999); Stanley Aronowitz, *The Knowledge Factory: Dismantling the Corporate University and Creating True Higher Learning* (Boston: Beacon, 2000); Benjamin Johnson, Patrick Kavanagh (translator), and Kevin Mattson, eds., *Steal This University: The Rise of the Corporate University and the Academic Labor Movement* (New York: Routledge, 2003); Sheila Slaughter and Larry Leslie: *Academic Capitalism: Politics, Policies, and the Entrepreneurial University* (Baltimore: Johns Hopkins University Press, 1997); Gary Rhoades, *Managed Professionals: Unionized Faculty and Restructuring Academic Labor* (Albany: SUNY Press, 1998); all of the issues of *Workplace: A Journal for Academic Labor,* and the special issue of *Social Text* 20:1 (Spring 2002).

40. Marc Bousquet, "The Waste Product of Graduate Education: Toward a Dictatorship of the Flexible," *Social Text* 20:1 (Spring 2002), 81–104.

41. Mickie McGee, "Hooked on Higher Education and Other Tales from Adjunct Faculty Organizing," *Social Text* 20:1 (Spring 2002), 61–80.

42. A recent study of full-time faculty at sixteen midsized colleges and universities found faculty members worked an average of 53.6 hours per week. "Nota Bene," *Academe*, July-August 1999, 11.

43. Alex Molnar, *Giving Kids the Business: The Commercialization of America's Schools*

(Boulder, CO: Westview Press, 1996), 3.

44. Ibid., Chapter two.

45. See Richard Lewontin's persuasive survey of the growth of the Cold War university in tandem with the defense needs of the national security state, "The Cold War and the Transformation of the Academy," in Noam Chomsky, Richard Lewontin, et al., *The Cold War and the University* (New York: The New Press, 1997), 1–34.

46. David F. Noble, *Digital Diploma Mills: The Automation of Higher Education* (New York: Monthly Review Press, 2001).

47. Henry C. Lucas Jr., *Information Technology and the Productivity Paradox: Assessing the Value of the Investment in IT* (New York: Oxford University Press, 1999); John Thorp, *The Information Paradox: Realizing the Business Benefits of Information Technology* (New York: McGraw-Hill, 1999); Leslie Willcocks and Stephanie Lester, eds., *Beyond the IT Productivity Paradox: Assessment Issues* (New York: John Wiley, 1999); Jessica Keyes, *Solving the Productivity Paradox: TQM for Computer Professionals* (New York: McGraw-Hill, 1994).

48. Tiziana Terranova, "Free Labor: Producing Culture for the Digital Economy," *Social Text* 63 (Spring 2000), 33–58.

49. See Steven Dubin's study of Chicago's artists-in-residence programs funded by the Comprehensive Employment and Training Act (CETA) in the late 1970s, *Bureaucratizing the Muse: Public Funds and the Cultural Worker* (Chicago: University of Chicago Press, 1987).

50. NVAG, the National Visual Artists Guild, has set up an organizing committee to liaise with the National Writers Guild, the Graphic Artists Guild, UNITE, the UAW, and the steel workers union.

Acknowledgments

Over the course of the eight years in which this book evolved, dozens of colleagues and comrades have shaped its contents either through advice, example, facilitation, or through our work together. The incomplete list of those whom I can remember, and thus am able to thank, includes: Kitty Krupat, Jeff Ballinger, Charles Kernaghan, Barbara Briggs, Alan Howard, Ginny Coughlin, Susan Cowell, Jo-Ann Mort, Medea Benjamin, Robert Ross, Elaine Bernard, Jack Trumpbour, Naomi Klein, Roberto Galtieri, David Ellwood, Marilyn Young, Anders Stephanson, Federico Romero, Michael Blim, Angela McRobbie, Walter Johnson, Steve Fagin, Adrienne Ferrari, Oliver Houston, Jonathan Michie, Apo Leong, Alice Kwon, Stephen Frost, Perry Leung, Fred Chiu, John Erni, Xudong Zhang, Aihwa Ong, Tani Barlow, Hyun Ok Park, Ching Kwan Lee, Toby Miller, Michael Denning, George Yudice, Stanley Aronowitz, Steve Fraser, Danny Walkowitz, Bruce Robbins, Ellen Willis, Randy Martin, Faye Ginsburg, Molly Nolan, Christine Harrington, Jeff Goodwin, Lisa Duggan, Phil Harper, Robin Kelley, Cary Nelson, Arlene Davila, Kristin Ross, and members of the No Sweat coalition and GSOC support group at NYU.

Alison Redick was a meticulous research assistant. Maggie Gray, whom I first met at a labor rally (how many can say that of a spouse?), was an exacting commentator on my prose and an accomplice of the highest sort.

I am thankful to Colin Robinson at the New Press for renewing our habit of publishing together, and to Abby Aguirre and Sarah Fan for ushering the manuscript safely through.

Some portions of "The Rise of the Second Anti-Sweatshop Movement" were originally published in *No Sweat: Fashion, Free Trade and the Rights of Garment Workers* (New York: Verso, 1997). "Strike a Pose for Justice" was originally published in K. Krupat and P. McCreery, eds., *Out at Work: Building a Gay Labor Alliance* (University of Minnesota Press, 2001). An earlier version of "The Mental Labor Problem" was published in *Social Text* (Summer 2000).

Index

Note: Page numbers in italics indicate photographs.